AF341981

UNEASY
COMMUNION

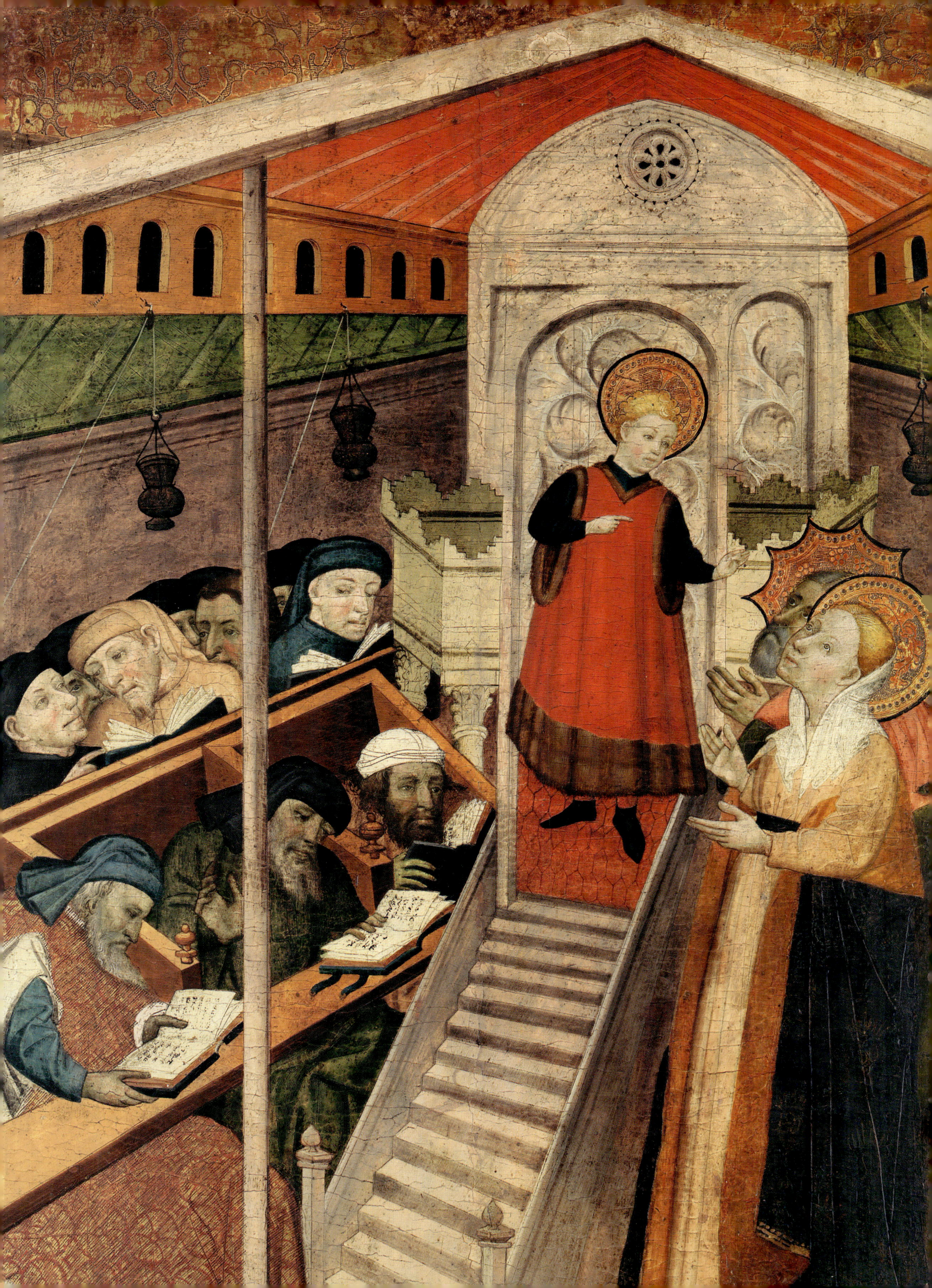

UNEASY COMMUNION

Jews, Christians, and the Altarpieces of Medieval Spain

EDITED BY VIVIAN B. MANN

Contributions by Thomas F. Glick, Carmen Lacarra Ducay, Vivian B. Mann, and Marcus B. Burke

MUSEUM OF BIBLICAL ART
MOBIA

g

Museum of Biblical Art, New York in association with D Giles Limited, London

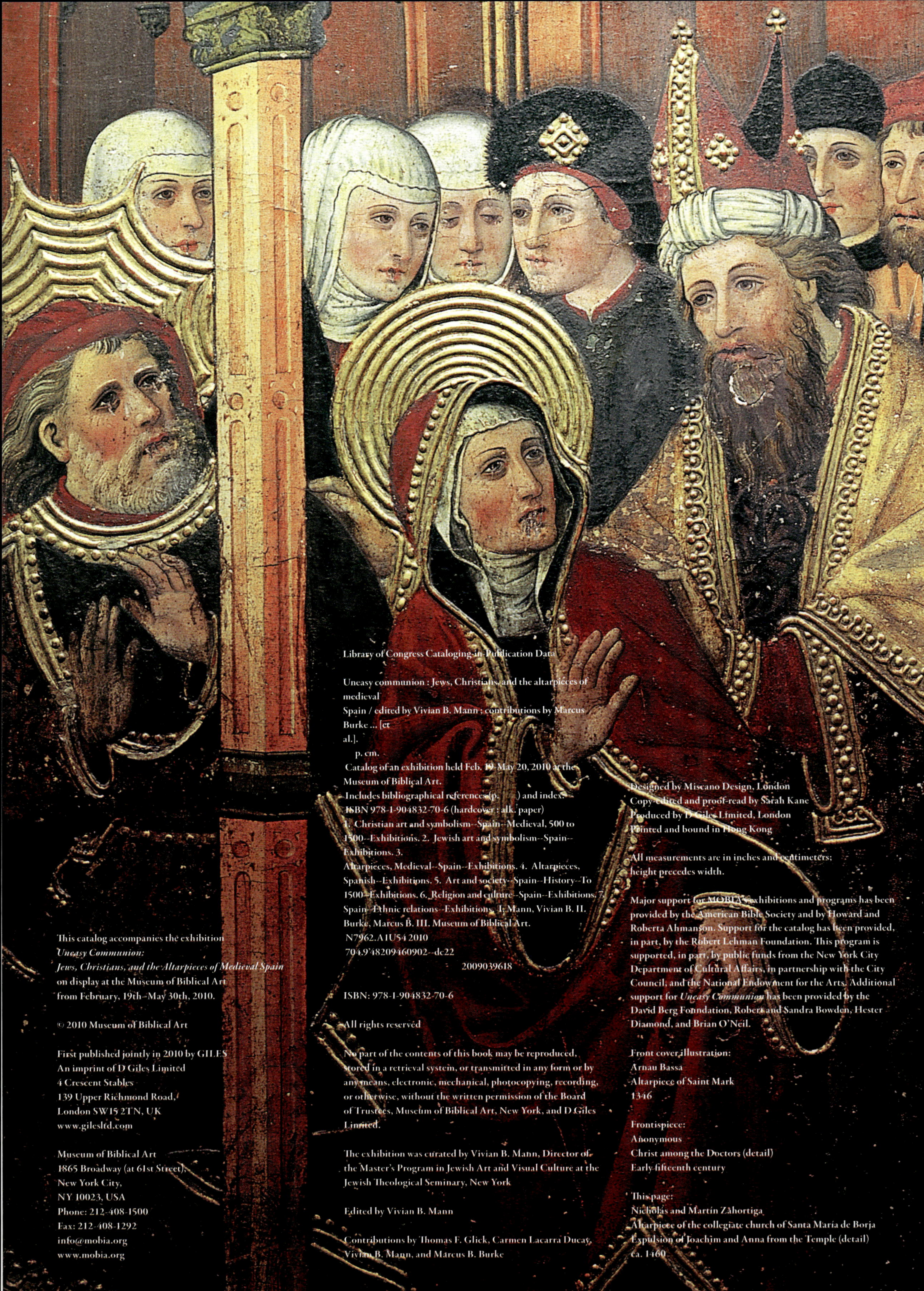

Library of Congress Cataloging-in-Publication Data

Uneasy communion : Jews, Christians, and the altarpieces of medieval
Spain / edited by Vivian B. Mann ; contributions by Marcus
Burke ... [et
al.].
    p. cm.
 Catalog of an exhibition held Feb. 19-May 20, 2010 at the
Museum of Biblical Art.
 Includes bibliographical references (p.   ) and index.
 ISBN 978-1-904832-70-6 (hardcover : alk. paper)
1. Christian art and symbolism--Spain--Medieval, 500 to
1500--Exhibitions. 2. Jewish art and symbolism--Spain--
Exhibitions. 3.
Altarpieces, Medieval--Spain--Exhibitions. 4. Altarpieces,
Spanish--Exhibitions. 5. Art and society--Spain--History--To
1500--Exhibitions. 6. Religion and culture--Spain--Exhibitions. 7.
Spain--Ethnic relations--Exhibitions. I. Mann, Vivian B. II.
Burke, Marcus B. III. Museum of Biblical Art.
N7962.A1U54 2010
704.9'48209460902--dc22

                    2009039618

This catalog accompanies the exhibition
Uneasy Communion:
Jews, Christians, and the Altarpieces of Medieval Spain
on display at the Museum of Biblical Art
from February, 19th–May 30th, 2010.

© 2010 Museum of Biblical Art

First published jointly in 2010 by GILES
An imprint of D Giles Limited
4 Crescent Stables
139 Upper Richmond Road,
London SW15 2TN, UK
www.gilesltd.com

Museum of Biblical Art
1865 Broadway (at 61st Street),
New York City,
NY 10023, USA
Phone: 212-408-1500
Fax: 212-408-1292
info@mobia.org
www.mobia.org

ISBN: 978-1-904832-70-6

All rights reserved

No part of the contents of this book may be reproduced,
stored in a retrieval system, or transmitted in any form or by
any means, electronic, mechanical, photocopying, recording,
or otherwise, without the written permission of the Board
of Trustees, Museum of Biblical Art, New York, and D Giles
Limited.

The exhibition was curated by Vivian B. Mann, Director of
the Master's Program in Jewish Art and Visual Culture at the
Jewish Theological Seminary, New York

Edited by Vivian B. Mann

Contributions by Thomas F. Glick, Carmen Lacarra Ducay,
Vivian B. Mann, and Marcus B. Burke

Designed by Miscano Design, London
Copy edited and proof-read by Sarah Kane
Produced by D Giles Limited, London
Printed and bound in Hong Kong

All measurements are in inches and centimeters;
height precedes width.

Major support for MOBIA's exhibitions and programs has been
provided by the American Bible Society and by Howard and
Roberta Ahmanson. Support for the catalog has been provided,
in part, by the Robert Lehman Foundation. This program is
supported, in part, by public funds from the New York City
Department of Cultural Affairs, in partnership with the City
Council, and the National Endowment for the Arts. Additional
support for *Uneasy Communion* has been provided by the
David Berg Foundation, Robert and Sandra Bowden, Hester
Diamond, and Brian O'Neil.

Front cover illustration:
Arnau Bassa
Altarpiece of Saint Mark
1346

Frontispiece:
Anonymous
Christ among the Doctors (detail)
Early fifteenth century

This page:
Nicholas and Martin Zahortiga
Altarpiece of the collegiate church of Santa Maria de Borja
Expulsion of Joachim and Anna from the Temple (detail)
ca. 1460

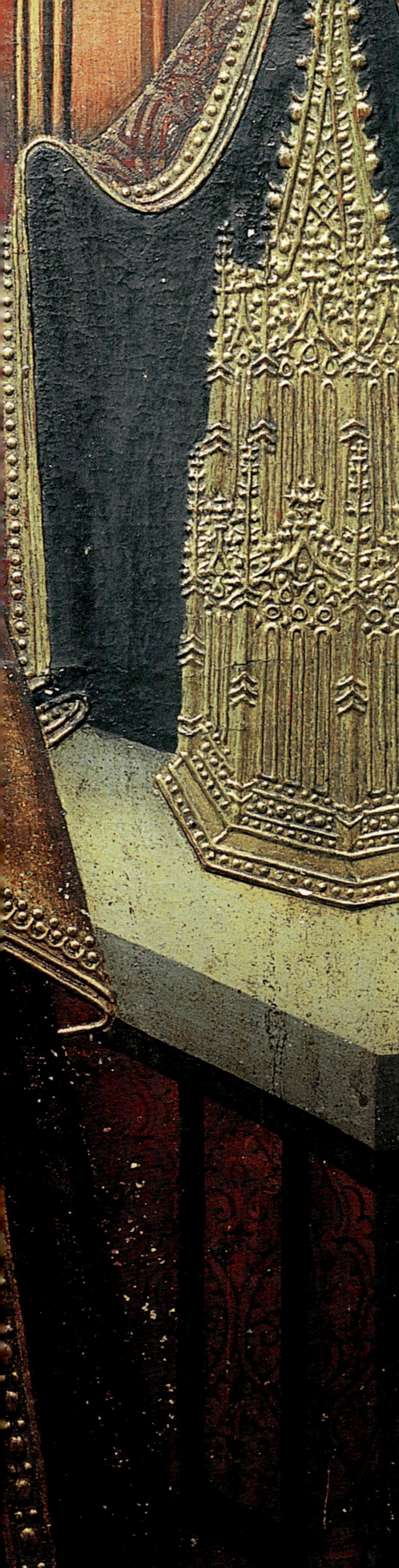

CONTENTS

FOREWORD AND ACKNOWLEDGMENTS

— *Ena Heller*

MOBIA's mission is to celebrate and interpret art related to the Bible and its cultural legacy in Jewish and Christian traditions. It follows that a special interest of the museum is to find points of connection between these traditions, be they cultural exchanges based on the common heritage or, at the opposite pole, conflicts brought about by historical and religious prejudice.

The exhibition which occasioned the publication of this volume is a perfect fit for MOBIA, as it illustrates both ends of that spectrum well. *Uneasy Communion,* the result of Vivian Mann's outstanding research, reveals an unusual example of *convivencia* in the practice of the arts in the Crown of Aragon, while at the same time uncovering signs (sometimes faint, often menacing) of the ongoing conflicts which would culminate in the Expulsion of 1492. In other words, artistic practice both confirms and nuances our previous understanding of *convivencia,* aptly defined by Thomas Glick as a coexistence that includes both "mutual inter-penetration and creative influence" and "mutual friction, rivalry and suspicion." The ways in which these contradictory notions are illustrated side by side in the fourteenth- and fifteenth-century altarpieces from Aragon constitute the innovation and surprise of this exhibition.

I am grateful to Dr. Mann (Jewish Theological Seminary, New York) for leading us on this fascinating journey of discovery, for conceptualizing the exhibition and assembling an incredible team of scholars for this volume: Marcus Burke (The Hispanic Society of America), Thomas F. Glick (Boston University), and Carmen Lacarra Ducay (Universidad de Zaragoza). Together, their essays offer a thoughtful and thorough presentation of the history, art history, and historiography of the relationships between Jews and Christians in medieval Spain; new research and an often overlooked vantage point will make this volume an important research tool. I thank them all for their knowledge and passion for the field.

An exhibition is never a solitary accomplishment and *Uneasy Communion* is no exception. Many institutions and their talented staffs have come together to make it happen, on both sides of the Atlantic. In the United States, The Hispanic Society of America was an early and steadfast institutional partner, essential to the success of the exhibition. We are grateful to them for their generosity in lending from their remarkable collection, and the commitment and expertise of their staff, led by curator Marcus Burke. At the same time, *Uneasy Communion* would have stayed in research stages had it not been for the generosity

Pere Espalargues
Altarpiece with Scenes from the Life of the
Virgin from the Church of Enviny
Presentation of Jesus in the Temple
Catalonia, 1490
Tempera on panel
The Hispanic Society of America (A5/5)

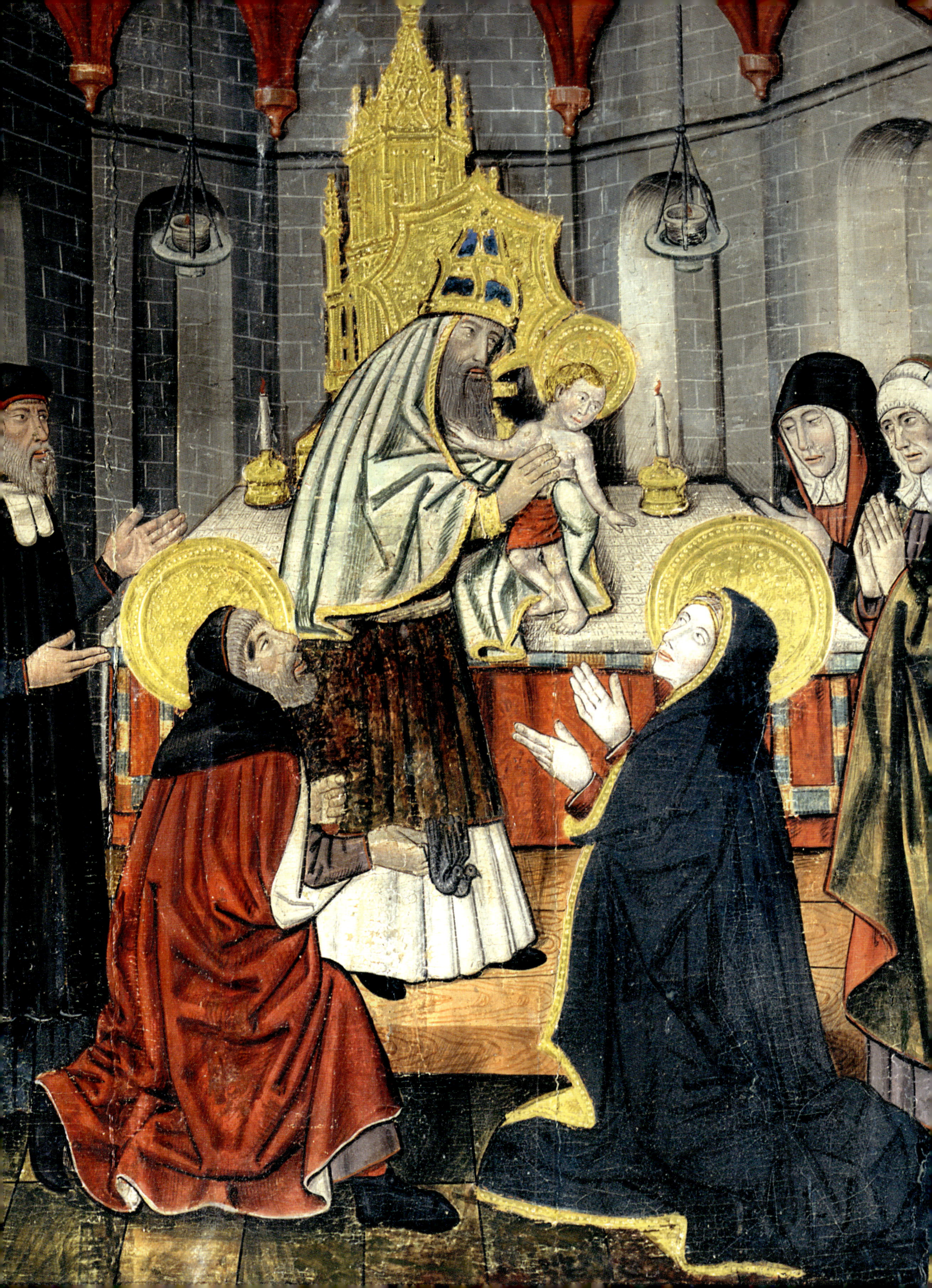

of the many institutions here and abroad who have entrusted us with loans from their collections. I am grateful to all of them: The British Library, London; J. Paul Getty Museum, Los Angeles; The Metropolitan Museum of Art, New York; Museu de Ceràmica, Barcelona; Museo Lázaro Galdiano, Madrid; Museu Nacional d'Art de Catalunya, Barcelona; Museo de Teruel; Museo de Zaragoza; and The Royal Library, Copenhagen.

I would also like to thank Claudia Nahson, who translated Lacarra Ducay's essay, and our associates in Spain, Javier Bona and Daniel Muñoz, who helped obtain vital loans and secure important images for the publication. This beautiful volume owes much to Ute Keyes, whose knowledge of publications and perfectionism have made a difference every step of the way as well as to Michelle Oing and Kate Williamson on the MOBIA staff, and to Dan Giles and Sarah McLaughlin at our publishing partners D Giles Limited in London. I thank them all, for without their expertise and dedication this volume would not be such a perfect match between a scholarly text and a beautifully accessible work.

The exhibition itself was the product of the knowledge, creativity, and hard work of many other MOBIA staff, led brilliantly by Paul Tabor, Director of Exhibitions. I thank him and the curatorial staff, as well as the entire MOBIA staff, who contributed in ways large and small to the success of this project. Last but certainly not least, I am immensely grateful to the funders who helped us transform an idea into a groundbreaking exhibition: the National Endowment for the Arts, the David Berg Foundation, Howard and Roberta Ahmanson, American Bible Society, and an anonymous Jewish foundation. This volume was also partly funded by a grant from the Robert Lehman Foundation. We thank them all for their vote of confidence in a young museum with large ambitions. A special thank you to MOBIA staff members Lisa Dierbeck and Megan Whitman for helping prepare successful grant proposals that secured funding and made this exhibit possible.

The highlight of my job is the opportunity to learn something new with every exhibit. Sometimes it is about a period, a style or an artist I knew little about; at other times it is about making new, unexpected connections; other times still, it is about correcting historical prejudices or shedding new light on familiar notions. With *Uneasy Communion*, it was all of these things and more. This catalog will surely do the same for its readers, while the exhibition is on view at MOBIA as well as long after it comes down from its walls.

A NOTE ABOUT THE VOLUME

The essays featured in this volume, conceived as a companion to the exhibition *Uneasy Communion,* take us on a journey from the general to the particular, from a study of Jewish communities within Spanish society of the fourteenth and fifteenth centuries to a survey of painting; to specific artworks that address the issue of Jewish–Christian relationships; and finally to a historiography of scholarly dealings with these relationships over time.

The first essay, by Prof. Thomas F. Glick, explores the complex landscape of the relationships between Christians and Jews in medieval Aragon, which included many instances of relatively peaceful coexistence and collaborations in various fields (particularly science and scholarship), shadowed by as many times of friction and conflict. Thus on the one hand there is documented scholarly interaction within which Jews played a key role in translating and transmitting Greek science, medicine, and philosophy. On the other hand, however, the period in question witnesses an increasing number of polemical treatises and public debates voicing anti-Jewish sentiment, culminating in anti-Jewish riots and pogroms.

The historical reality of the period in Aragon reveals a duality also present in art, as the following two essays illustrate: there is a constant tension between acceptance and prejudice, between cooperation and conflict. The essay by Carmen Lacarra Ducay is a comprehensive survey of fourteenth- and fifteenth-century painting in Aragon. The most notable extant examples of mural painting (which influenced the iconography and style of the *retablos*) and panel painting are analyzed. This overview points to stylistic similarities between different pictorial media, while at the same time suggesting that painting provides historians of medieval Aragon with highly valuable information about contemporary society and everyday life. As the following essay by Vivian Mann demonstrates, this information concerns not only Christian, but also Jewish, life.

Mann's essay articulates the thesis of the exhibition that occasioned the publication of this volume: a new look at the art of fourteenth- and fifteenth-century Aragon can illuminate the relationships between Christians and Jews at the time, and nuance our understanding of *convivencia* as it continued after the Christian Reconquest, through the pogroms of the fourteenth century and up until the Expulsion of 1492. This study, and the present volume more generally, intends to fill a gap in the scholarship of Jewish–Christian coexistence in medieval Spain, which to date has not used the art of the period as a source of valuable information. Art created by both Christian and Jewish artists, though, offers valuable glimpses into both the understanding of the Other (Christian artists portrayed Jewish life with unusual accuracy while Jewish artists worked alongside Christians in ateliers employed by the Church) and the ever-present conflict (illustrated in scenes of disputations, forced baptisms, desecration of the host and so on).

This duality that both history and art illustrate so well has also had, as the last essay in the volume by Marcus Burke demonstrates, an unusual history in post-medieval Spain. Burke provides a much-needed historiography of Jewish studies in Spanish art history, documenting (and contextualizing) the surprising absence of the study of Jewish contributions to medieval Spanish society until very recently. This historical absence—best illustrated by the fact that as late as the 1980s works on *retablos* analyzing at length an artist like Juan de Leví make no mention of the role that his ethnic origin and religion may have played in his artistic expression—validates once again the thesis of this exhibition and volume.

Ena Heller, Ph.D.
Executive Director

JEWS AND CHRISTIANS IN THE MEDIEVAL CROWN OF ARAGON

— Thomas F. Glick

The history of the Jews in what became the medieval Crown of Aragon can most likely be dated to the Carolingian Hispanic March (ninth century AD), encompassing roughly the present-day Spanish provinces of Girona and Barcelona. The Carolingians employed Jewish administrators there in the late eighth century, and Vic was reputed to have been a completely Jewish town at the end of the eighth and beginning of the ninth century. The "Ispamia," to which the Gaons of Babylonia directed letters, was the Spanish March, not (as is frequently presumed) Muslim Spain.[1] The Jewish communities of western Europe developed symbiotically through negotiation between themselves and the Carolingian authorities, perhaps based partly on elements of an exilarchy model advanced by the Jews themselves.[2] By the late fourteenth century there were a maximum of 60,000 Jews in the Crown of Aragon (six to seven per cent of the population), dispersed among many population centers and settlements (figure 2).

COMMUNAL AUTONOMY

The standard approach to the history and structure of autonomous Jewish communities is to assume that the Jewish community "drew its power from Jewish sovereignty in antiquity and from its members' readiness to accept its jurisdiction...the only heir of ancient Jewish sovereignty..."[3] This kind of interpretation rests on foundation myths perpetuated by medieval Jewish communities to the effect that they were continuers of geonic authority, established at the time of the Babylonian exile. What actually happened was quite different. European Jewish

1. Hispano-Moresque haggadah
    The Egyptians Overtake the Israelites in Baal-Zephon (Ex. 14:9)
    Castile, ca. 1300
    Ink and gouache on vellum
    6 × 4 in., 97 fols.
    British Library, London, Ms. 2737

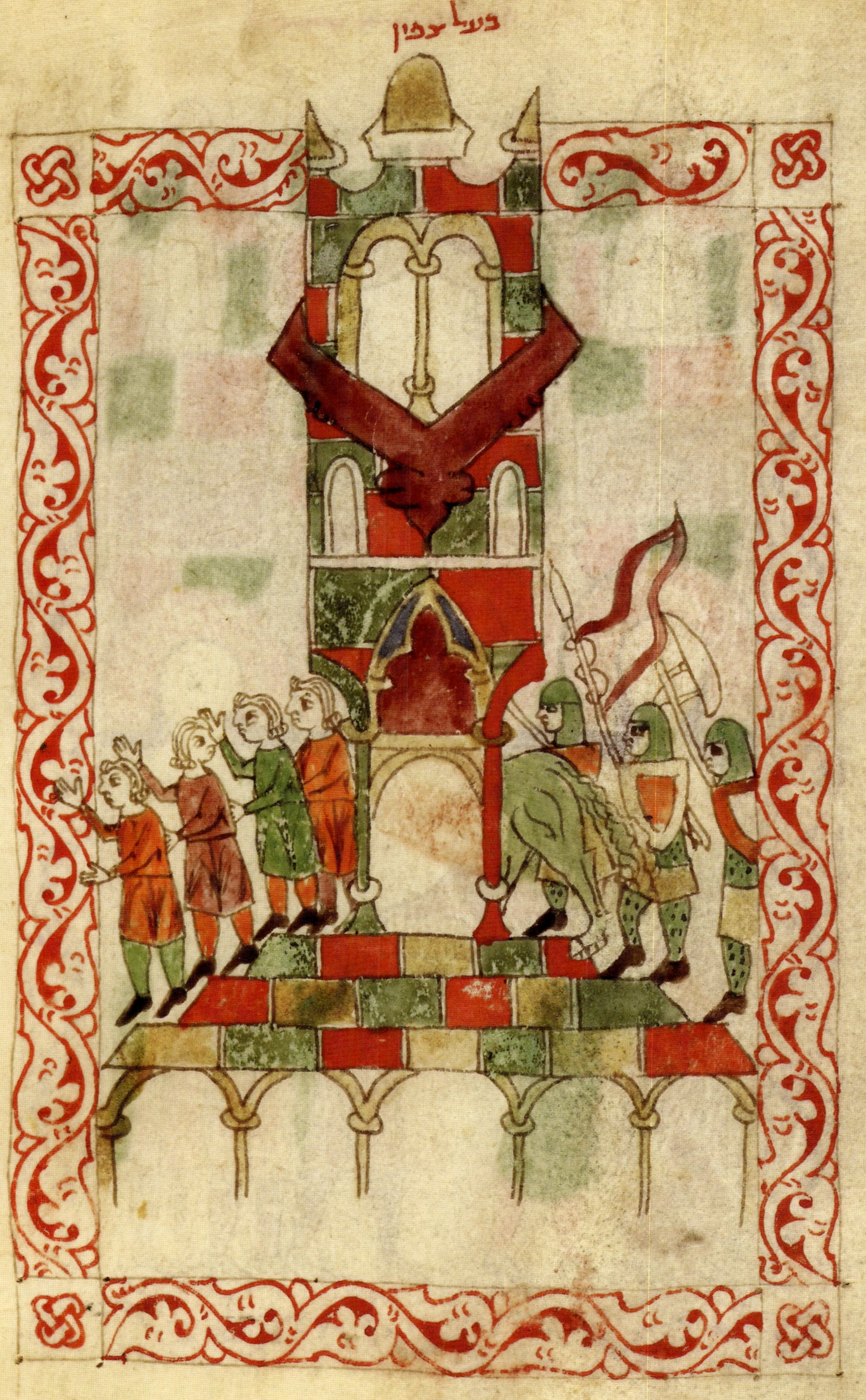
בניו עבדיו

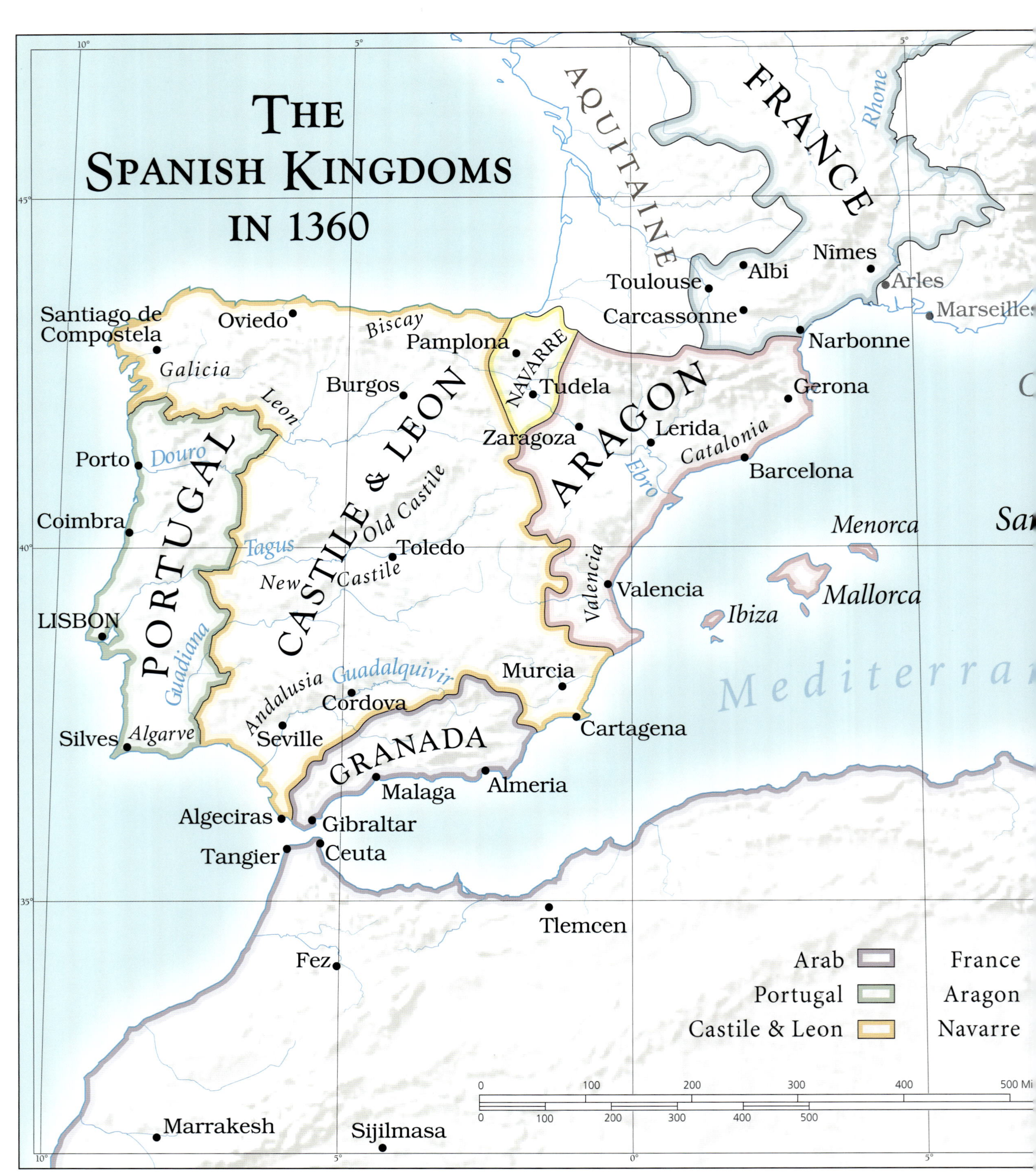
THE
SPANISH KINGDOMS
IN 1360

AQUITAINE
FRANCE
Rhone
Nîmes
Albi
Toulouse
Arles
Carcassonne
Marseilles
Narbonne
Santiago de Compostela
Oviedo
Biscay
Pamplona
NAVARRE
Galicia
Burgos
Tudela
Gerona
Leon
CASTILE & LEON
Zaragoza
Lerida
Catalonia
ARAGON
Porto
Douro
Ebro
Barcelona
Coimbra
Old Castile
Menorca
Tagus
Toledo
San
New Castile
Valencia
LISBON
Valencia
Mallorca
PORTUGAL
Guadiana
Ibiza
Andalusia
Guadalquivir
Murcia
Mediterran
Cordova
Silves
Algarve
Cartagena
Seville
GRANADA
Malaga
Almeria
Algeciras
Gibraltar
Tangier
Ceuta
Tlemcen
Fez
Arab   France
Portugal   Aragon
Castile & Leon   Navarre
0   100   200   300   400   500 Mi
0   100   200   300   400   500
Marrakesh
Sijilmasa

2. Map of Spanish Kingdoms in 1360
Allan Cartography

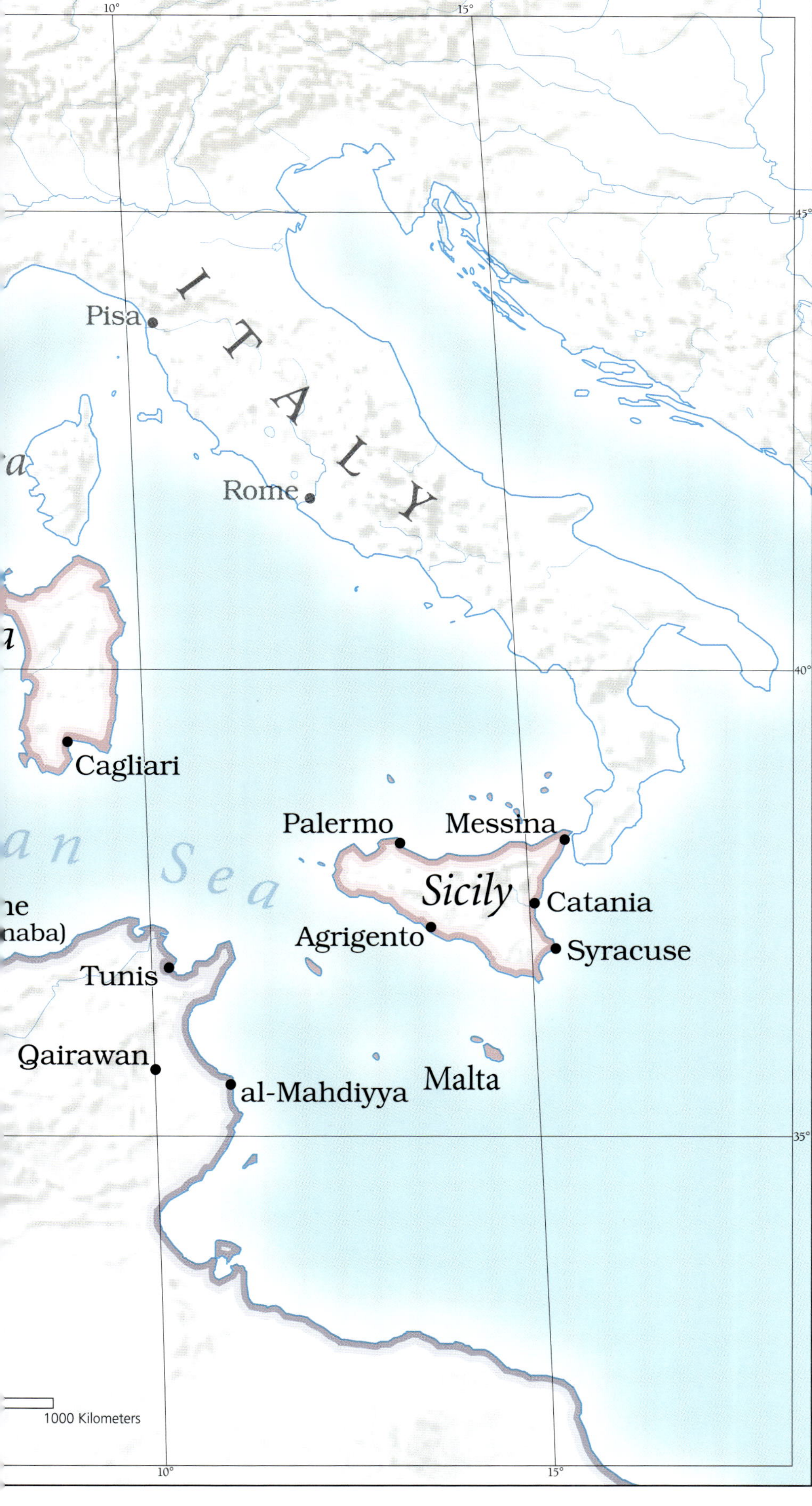

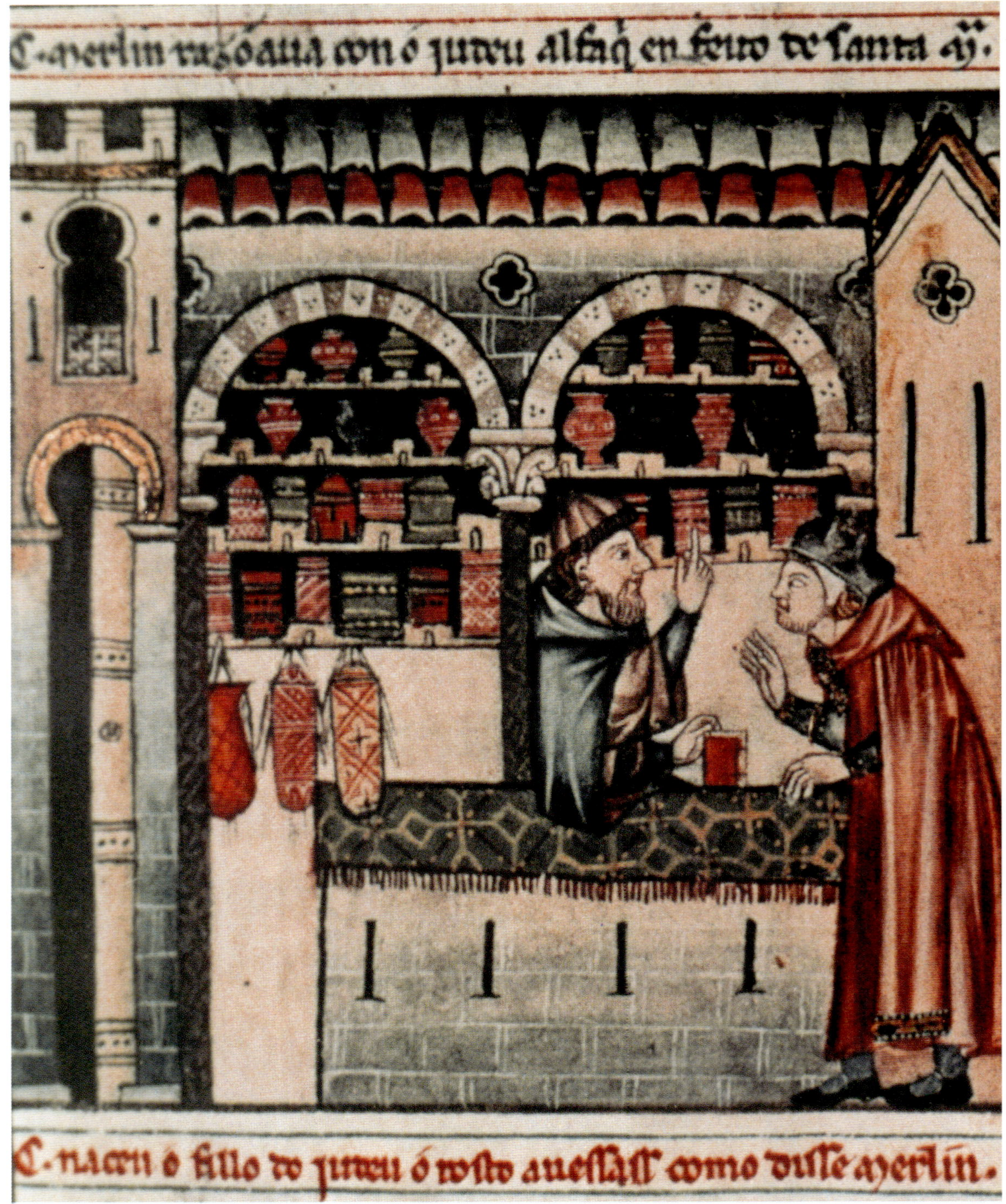

3. *Cantigas de Santa Maria*
   Commisioned for Alfonso X the Wise
   ca. 1280
   Ink on vellum
   Biblioteca de El Escorial, Madrid
   Ms. T-I-1

communities in fact owed their structure to prescriptions developed in the Carolingian period whereby institutional machinery for the control of various subject minorities by the central power was elaborated. This was a civil, not a religious, issue. Once these institutions were in place, however, over a period of time they were Judaized, that is, naturalized into Jewish society by being given a patent of authenticity, by having a geonic context constructed for them. As Elka Klein noted, Jews organized themselves into communities not because of Talmudic precedent, but because they lived in a society in which such collective activity was normal: in "Talmudic times, ordinances (*taqqanot*) were made by the rabbis. The authority of an individual community to make ordinances was in itself an innovation in the middle ages…"[4]

Leaving aside for the time being the interaction of Jewish and Christian elites, we can say that the interaction of Jews with all other levels of Christian society—whether formal interaction, via institutions of governance such as the judicial or tax systems, or non-formal, namely day-to-day interaction between Jewish and Christian townspeople—was regulated via the statutes of autonomy conceded to Jewish communities (figures 3, 4). The prevailing view of Jewish self-governance, however, has tended to presume a standard set of rights, privileges, and duties that establishes in its perfect form a complete framework in which Jewish life can be lived out in peace with the broader society, according to halakhic norms within the community, and in conformity with a model of self-governance that Jews had brought with them from the East. In this construction, broken agreements of whatever kind, popular aggression against Jews, proselytization, unlawful taxation, and so forth, can then all be portrayed as violation by Christians of this formal model. Thus Assis notes that the king constantly *interfered* in the economic life of the community, where the notion of interference connotes the expectation that autonomy would be breached. But there was no autonomy in any pristine sense. The king ruled a set of *aljamas*[5] as if they were little cities; he intervened in their affairs just as he did in those of Valencia, Barcelona, and other towns via his local officials, and sometimes personally as the situation required. Communal governance was subject to and conditioned on royal assent; it therefore always had an *ad hoc* dimension to it, and it *required* constant negotiation. The problem with the autonomy model is that reality always falls short of the model, or the king breaches it, for example. The current model has much less explanatory power than it is given credit for, particularly when it is romanticized. For Assis the "*qehilah* became the Jews' miniature homeland in which they were able to conduct their religious, cultural, social, and national life with an intensity that enabled them to preserve their separate identity." Whatever the *aljamas* were, they were not miniature homelands. They were, at best, places of partial security, partial protection from the constant menace of the ambient society. Negotiation over communal status had fundamentally to do with money. In simple terms, Jews were recognized as a source of cash (because of the wealth of the Jewish urban elites). What that cash purchased was freedom from day-to-day surveillance, which permitted them to worship according to their tradition and organize a variety of community services, none of which had much to do with

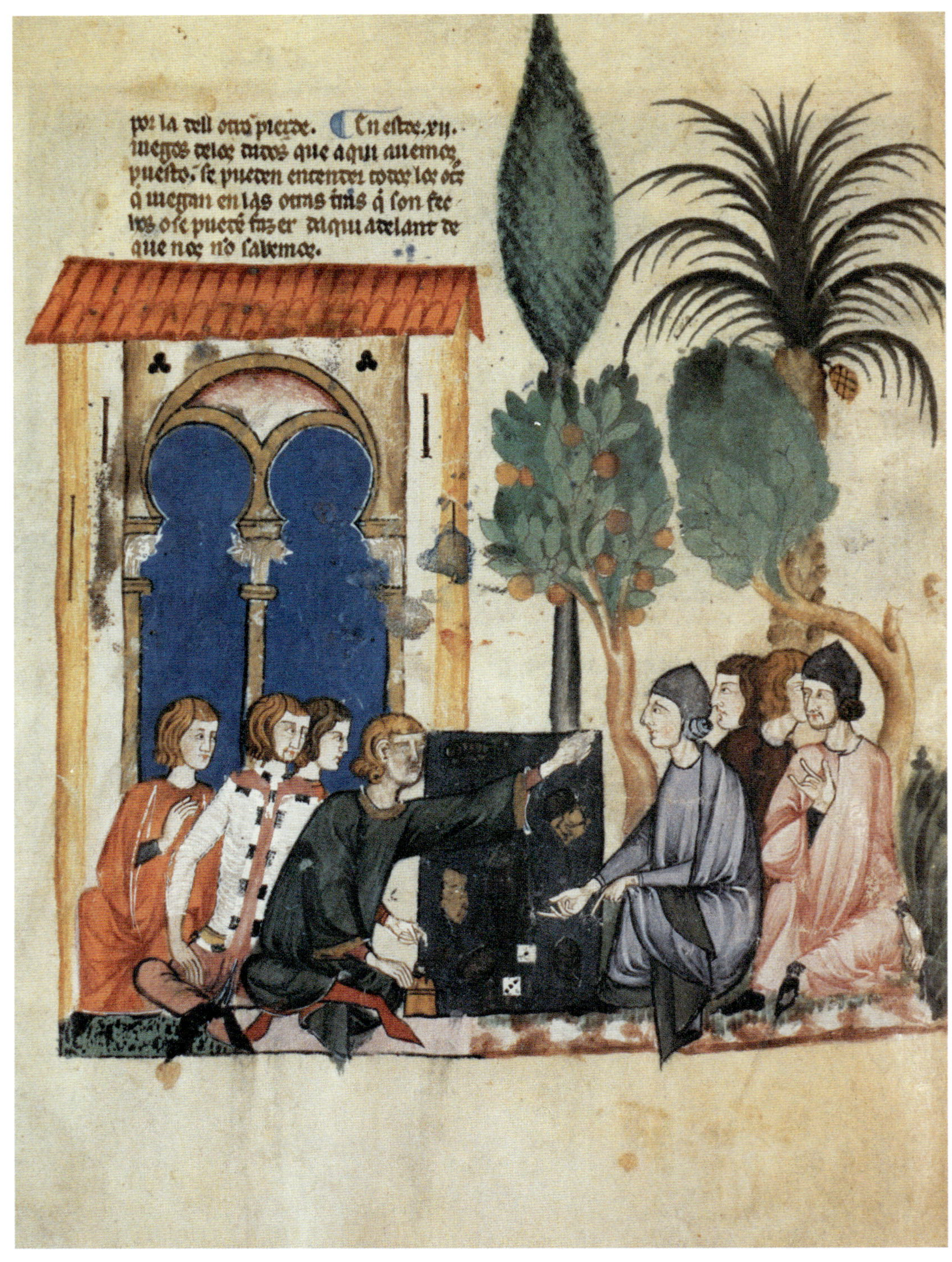

4. *Libro del ajedrez, dados y tablas (Book of Chess, Dice and Tables)*
   Commissioned by Alfonso X the Wise
   1283
   Manuscript
   16 ½ × 12 in.
   Biblioteca de El Escorial, Madrid
   Ms. T-I-6

geonic principles per se. An added cost of this freedom from surveillance was to oblige the community to monitor itself with whatever monies were left over after the burden of taxation was relieved. Self-monitoring is a structural feature of all such autonomous institutions, whether cities themselves, craft guilds, irrigation communities, or other such.[6] Solomon ibn Adret, the great scholar and communal leader of Barcelona, understood this better than most modern historians do; in a discussion of craft guilds, he noted that "any guild whose members are of the same craft is like an autonomous city."[7]

Although each culture had ingrained views of models of autonomy, with more or less remote antecedents, such antecedents had no effect whatever on daily interaction, in regard to which "autonomy" must be understood as a *process*, not a juridical *state*. By process, I mean to indicate that all rules, of whatever provenance and whether formal or non-formal, governing interaction with the surrounding society are constantly under negotiation. So any appeal to a standard model bears the risk of overgeneralization or, at the extreme, of a hyper-literalist approach to institutions, a systematic misconception.

Since the status of taxes specifically and financial obligations generally were always changing subject to the dynamics of market conditions, or the needs of the public fisc, or the play of political interests, etc., existing charters of autonomy had to be renewed or new ones written and granted. Among the issues that came up constantly and that consistently required renegotiation were measures governing the non-payment of taxes, or those specifying when it was or was not permitted for Christians to be allowed late payment of debts to Jews, or Jews to Christians.[8] The reason for this is obvious: debts and their repayment were fraught with contestation, the obligation of the debtor to the lender always being in part dependent on the tripartite division of powers between the king, the community, and the Christian debtors who were always testing the waters to see how much the king would let them get away with.

Here is a kind of revelatory dynamic: on occasion, James I promised most Jewish communities not to grant deferment of loan payments owed by Christians to Jews. Sometimes his stated will was indefinite; sometimes for one or a few years. But some individual Jewish communities were denied the right to have payment of their loans (to Christians or to other Jews) deferred. Sometimes the king gave such a pledge to all communities of a specific region. All such arrangements affected the flow of money and therefore the entire Jewish community, because money lending was such an important part of its economy.[9] The king was involved not only because of his interest in keeping the economy functioning smoothly, but also because in cases of infringements, the royal treasury always received a portion of whatever fines were paid. The pursuit of self-interest by the various players was one of the principal dynamics of the negotiation of "autonomy."

The king was self-interested in the profit of his Jewish servants: he had a stake in Jewish gains. James II helped Jewish lenders to recover their money, placing his bureaucracy at the disposal of Jewish lenders. Only royal officials could force Christian debtors to pay

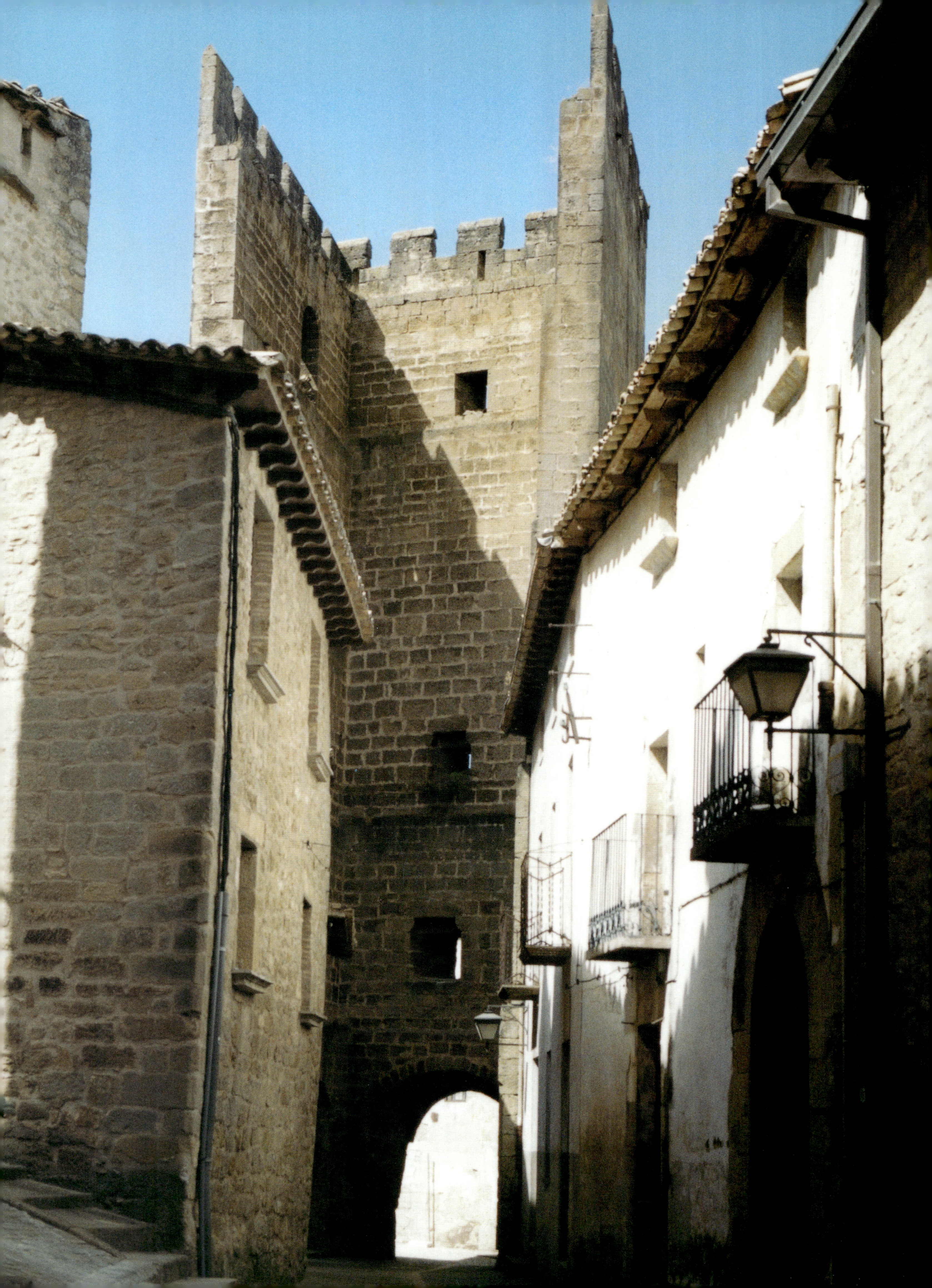

their loans back. Many such debtors were in small towns and villages, so the royal officials involved were local: bailiff, *veguer*, *sobrejuntero*.[10] Then, too, from the end of the thirteenth century, the incidence of Jews borrowing from Christians rises.[11] A similar issue was whether Christian clients of Jews had or did not have to pay taxes internal to the *aljama* (e.g., a sales tax); thus, the *aljama* of Orihuela raised a tax (*sisa*) in 1322 within the community, but the king insisted that no Christian pay.[12]

Christians recognized halakhah as (using the Arabic term) the *sunna* (*çuna*), that is, the customary law code of the Jews. And Jews, reciprocally, understood that in specific circumstances their "sunna" had to be brought into line with that of the Christians. A point of halakhah, therefore, might have to be abandoned if it contravened a local law.

INSTITUTIONAL ACCULTURATION

Jewish communities came quite naturally over time to resemble the Christian communities in which they were embedded (figure 5). Were that not the case, the recreation of culturally Spanish communities in places like Constantinople and Salonica in the sixteenth century would make no sense. (Those communities were "Spanish" in various ways, including their language, folklore, craft technologies, medical standards and practice).

The development of parallel institutions provides a glimpse into the dynamic of Jewish–Christian relationships, which to an extent were structured on institutions that required a high degree of parallelism and mutual conformity in order for anything to happen. As Assis explains, "Since the structure of Jewish society was almost an exact duplicate of Christian urban society, some similar developments in municipal governments and communal administration were only natural. Certain similarities...were the result of analogous circumstances pertaining in both societies. Social classes and class struggle in city and *qehilah*, class representation in the local governing bodies...and the subsequent constitutional and institutional reforms in both municipal and communal administration."[13]

Ibn Adret understood that the *qehilah* acted with "governmental permission" as dictated by the needs of the times, "not so much by the laws of the Torah. Its jurisdiction... came from the power of the kingdom."[14] The *aljama*, in other words, had to bring itself into conformity with the statutes and standards of mainstream society, in the same way as the laws of an American state have to be in conformity with those of the federal government. Such adjustments could be substantive or merely convenient. Various charters defined whether and under what circumstances Jews were permitted to use lawyers in civil suits, receive copies of the charges against them, etc.[15] Determination of which court procedures were available for Jews involved a particular kind of negotiation; moreover, such charters demonstrate the ways in which Jews used royal courts. The policy of Jewish communities generally was to discourage Jewish participation in the Christian court system (which was almost always royal justice, because

5. Porto de la Reina
    Jewish Quarter, Sos del Rey Católico

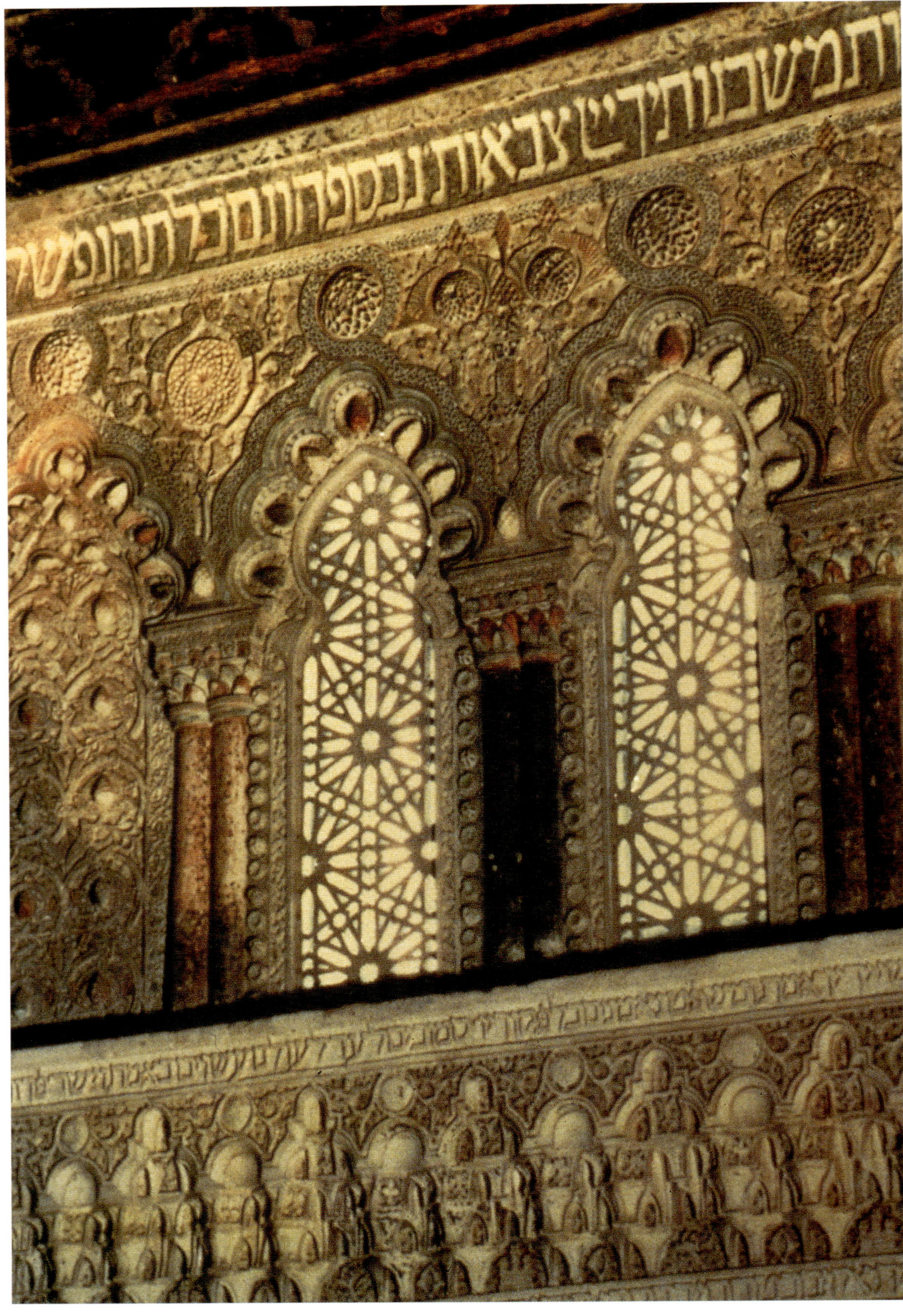

Jews were royal property), since it was perceived as a threat both to the power of *aljama* officials and to group cohesion. The *taqqanot*, or ordinances by which the *aljama* ruled itself, specified clearly which legal procedures and law codes were proper and which were not, for members of the community. Thus they would typically specify the jurisdictional authority of halakhah and Jewish custom, the regulations governing the appointment of *aljama* judges (*dayyanim*), and the obligation of Jewish litigants to appear in their courts—a directive in part aimed at preventing Jews from appealing to royal justice.[16] An example of an adjustment of convenience: in 1320, the *aljama* of Barcelona reduced its wine measure to the volume of the Christian one used in the city.[17] Ordinances typically are an expression of optimality: how relationships, rights, and duties should be construed under optimal conditions.

What is happening socially within Jewish communities in this period is the transformation of Jewish society from a socially undifferentiated population, led by a small prepotent elite, into a society stratified into three classes—called in Latin documents *maiores*, *mediocres*, and *minores*, engendering what Myerson terms "aggressive status competition" within *aljama* populations.[18] Put plainly, Jewish society came to reflect the standard class divisions of the Christian world, for the same reasons: the revival of commerce, both long-distance and local, which generated a class of well-to-do burghers in the Christian world, stimulated the same social differentiation in the *aljama*. The revival of trade fomented, in turn, the flourishing of artisan crafts and the emergence of craft guilds within the Jewish community (figures 7, 8). The creation of guilds and confraternities among craftsmen also reflected the same social tensions as those that swept through Christian artisan communities in the course of the fourteenth century.

What happens in the *aljamas* from the late thirteenth century, and lasting throughout the fourteenth century, was agitation by the middle and lower classes for constitutional reform (the issuance of new *taqqanot*) that would give them an equal say with the elite in the *aljama*'s governance. So, "agitation and dissent that accompanied the elections in the *aljamas* of Valencia and Murviedro [Morvedre] in 1327 led to royal intervention and changes in the election system in both communities."[19] The reform movement reflected the wealth of the *aljamas* and resentment of control by self-serving elites. Similarly in 1386, lower-class Christian artisans and middle class merchants in Barcelona demanded equal representation on the town council along with the *maiores*, or *ciutadans honrats* (honored citizens).[20] The class-based model of resistance, therefore, was common to Christian and Jewish society and triggered very similar social movements aimed at a greater share in the town governance, especially when it came to taxation. This pattern of social antagonism and reform of *taqqanot* (communal ordinances) became a standard one: it succeeded in some cases (e.g., Morvedre after the electoral reform of 1403) and failed in others (Barcelona, first quarter of the fourteenth century).[21]

Burns's analysis of the Latinate wills of Jews in the Crown of Aragon provides insight into the interpenetration of the Jewish and Christian legal worlds.[22] All Jews made Hebrew wills; but some also drew up last testaments in Latin as well. The latter, however, were not

7. Michael Lupi de Çandiu (illuminator)
Vidal Mayor of James I, Initial N: Two Men Speaking before the King
and Another Man Exchanging a Goblet for a Purse of Money with a Jew
Aragon, second half of the thirteenth century
Tempera colors, gold leaf, and ink on parchment
14 × 9 in.
J. Paul Getty Museum, Los Angeles (83.MQ.165.175v)

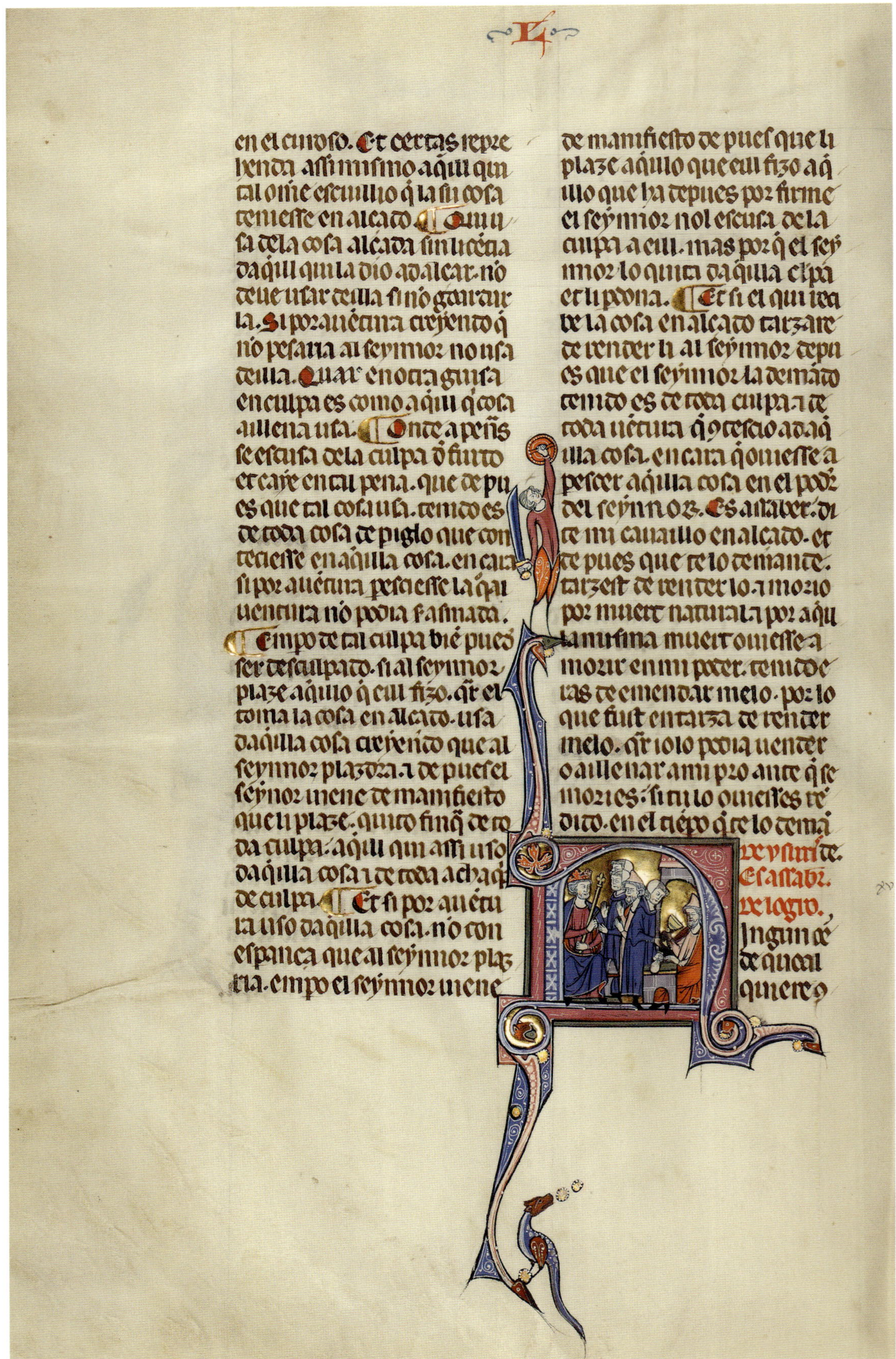

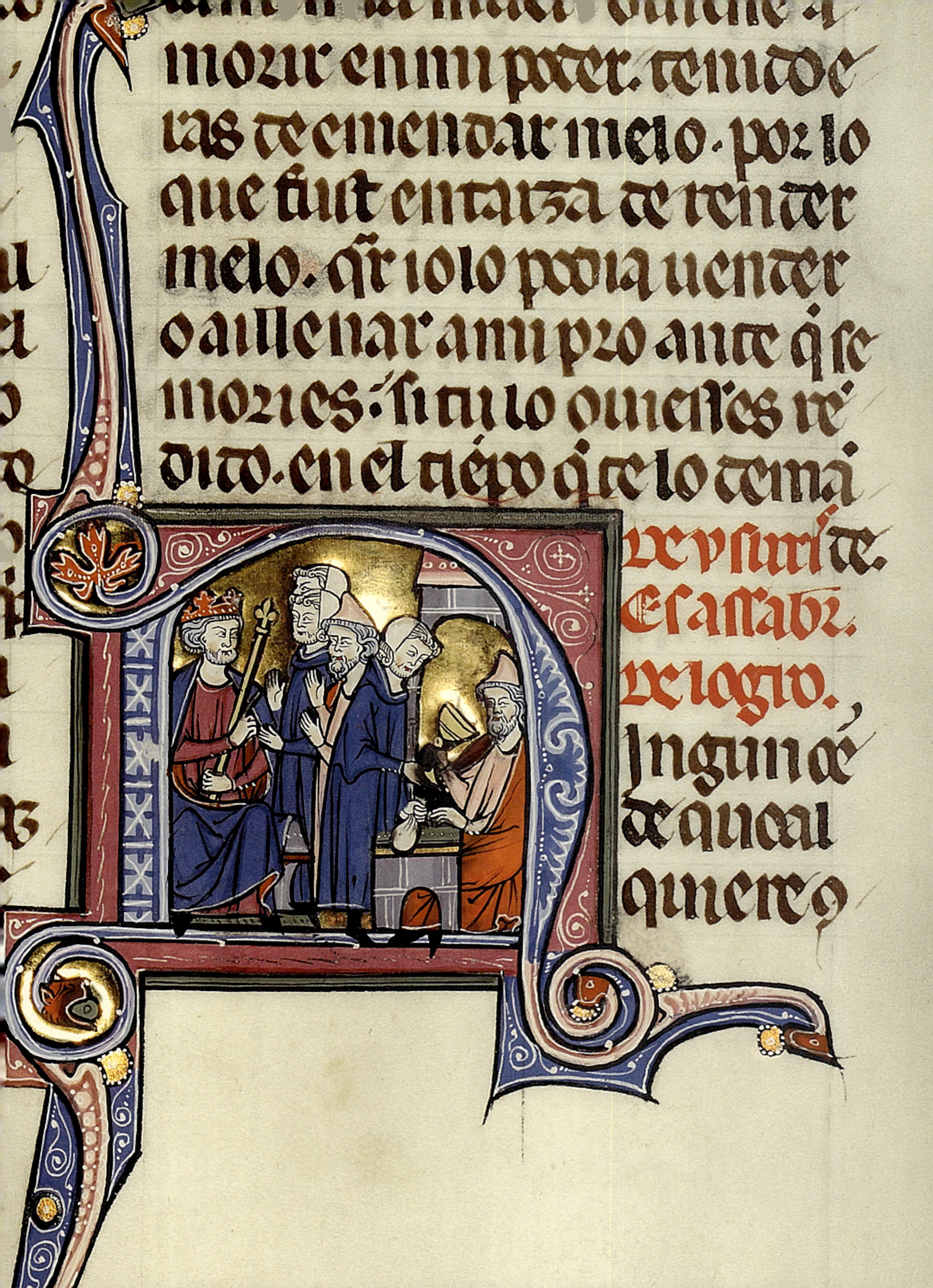

morir en mi poder. tenude-
ras de emendar melo. por lo
que fust en tarda de render
melo. Mas iolo podria uender
o aillenar ami pro ante que se
mozies. Si tu lo ouieses uen-
dido. en el tiempo que te lo tenia

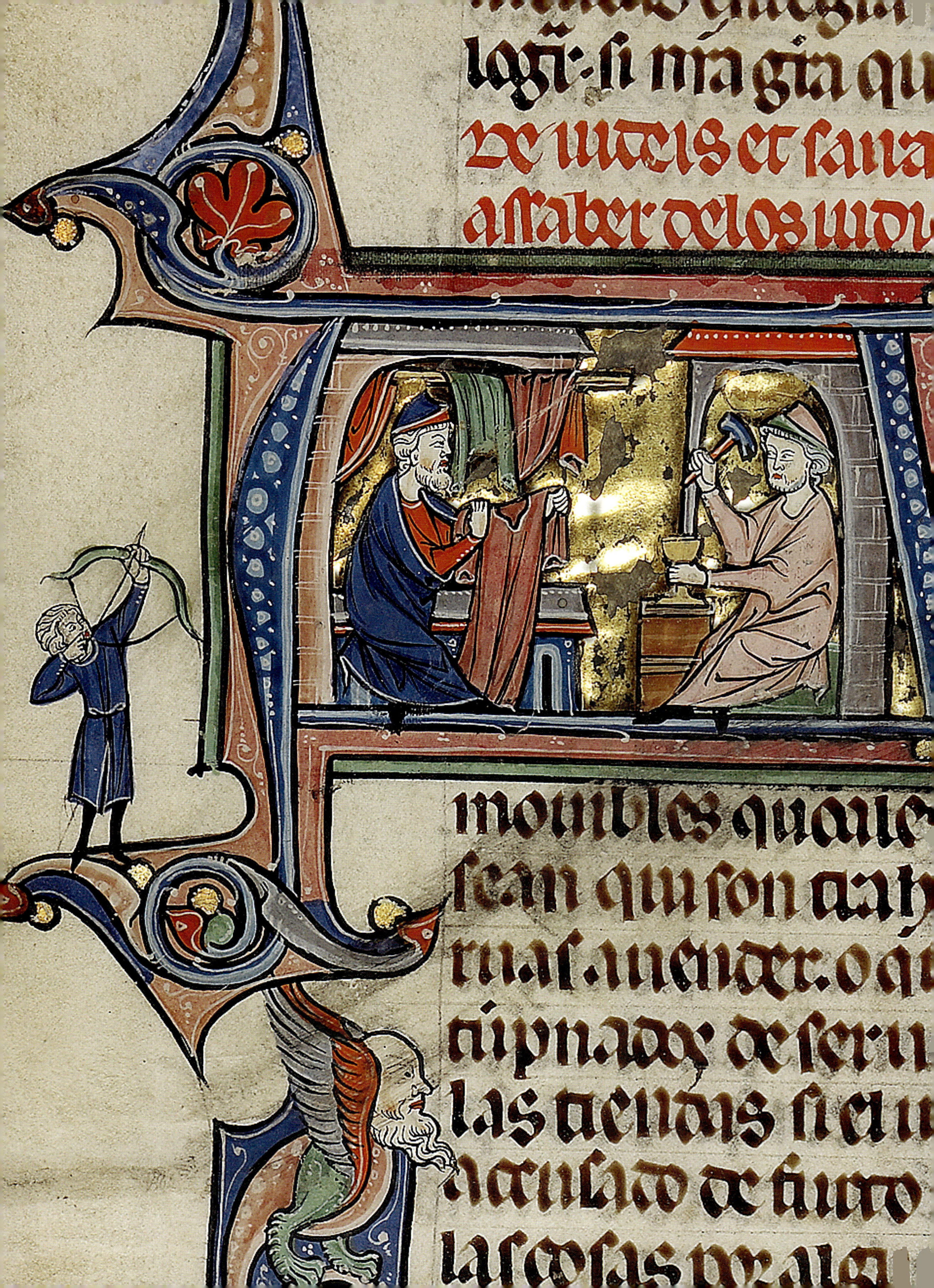

lagñ: si ñra gña qu
de iudeis et sana
a saber delos iudi

moubles que aue
sean qui son a a..
ruas. auendr o d..
aipnados descriu
las tiendas si a u
atuisad de tutto
las cosas prala

8. Michael Lupi de Çandiu (illuminator)
    Vidal Mayor of James I, Initial A: Two Jews in Conversation
    Aragon, second half of the thirteenth century
    Tempera colors, gold leaf, and ink on parchment
    14 × 9 in.
    J. Paul Getty Museum, Los Angeles (83.MQ.165.243v)

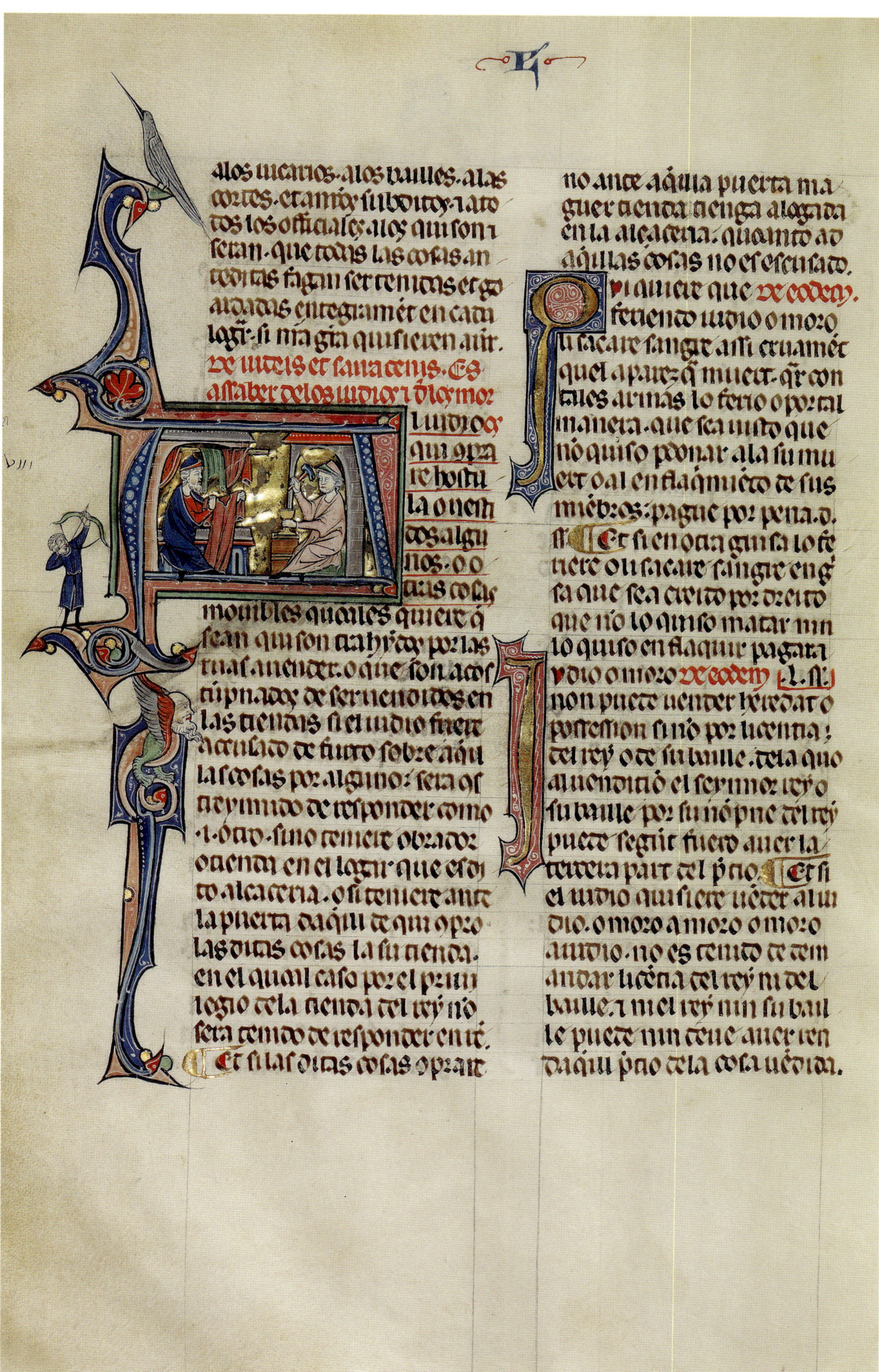

simply translations of the former, because the romanizing law code of the Crown of Aragon had different prescriptions for testamentary dispositions. There were two reasons why a Jew would go to the trouble of drawing up a Latin will paralleling another in Hebrew. First, a Latin will was enforceable under the normal legal procedures available to all citizens of the realm, thus assuring the testator that if either the Jewish community or his own family did not carry out the terms of his will faithfully, royal justice would do so. This precaution acquires particular significance when one considers the social unrest that traumatized the Jewish communities of Aragon and Catalonia from the mid-thirteenth through mid-fourteenth century, when social strife was common within the *aljamas* of the region.

A second motive was that by making a Latin will a Jewish testator could realize, or cause to be enforced, personal objectives that were incompatible with Jewish law. For example, Jewish law did not recognize a "universal heir;"[23] thus a man could make his wife his sole heir under the principles of Roman law, but not in Jewish law. In fact, Jews interacted normally and easily with the ambient Christian world, particularly in the legal realm. Jews normally recorded their business contracts with Christian notaries, for example. So in this context the Latin will was an outgrowth of both the commercial world of medieval Europe in which Jews were active participants, and of the revival of Roman law in thirteenth-century Spain.

Mudejars, the Muslim minority in the Crown of Aragon, had a penchant for blood feuds and, inasmuch as most of their scholarly class had left the country, they were much more aggressive in their appeal to royal justice.[24] Jewish interaction with Christian law was more passive: adjusting halakhah, where possible, to bring it into accord with the law of the country at large—in effect, broadening the compass of halakhah—made appeals based on distinctions between the two law codes less necessary.

VIRTUAL DISPUTATIONS

A genre of literature common to the three Abrahamic religions of medieval times was a polemical treatise, in the form of a dialogue between scholars of different religions. These were typically structured in such a way as to make the interlocutor of the writer's own religion win against more or less inept challengers. In all such disputes, Gilbert Dahan concludes,

> ...because each party assumes its true identity, the dialogue is honest. Sometimes it is a familiar conversation among neighbors; more often it is strained confrontation between adversaries with a serious purpose, because it is a matter of showing which faith is superior, less to convince the questioner than to reassure all those who are listening and are on the same side...It is an austere game for the most part, in which the participants are totally engaged. In that respect, the medieval dispute seems exemplary to us. Compromise is not possible. There is no cheating, no tempering of ideas. One can only arrive at whatever syncretism there is; that is the only alternative."[25]

9. Levi ben Isaac ben Caro (scribe)
Moreh Nevukhim (*Guide to the Perplexed*) by Maimonides
Barcelona, 1348
Ink and gouache on vellum
8 × 5 in.
Det Kongelige Bibliotek, Copenhagen (Cod. Heb. 37, fol. 114a)

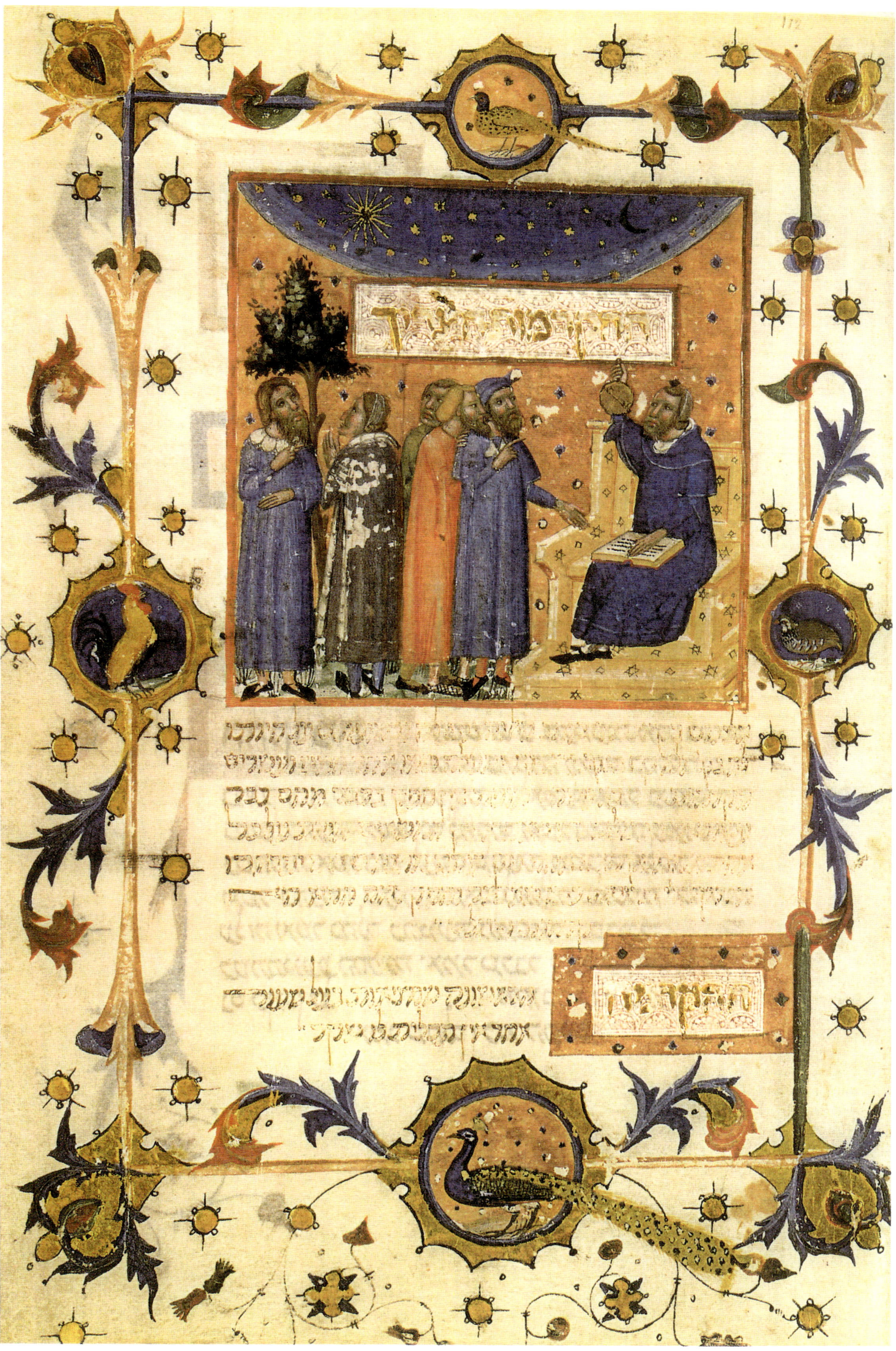

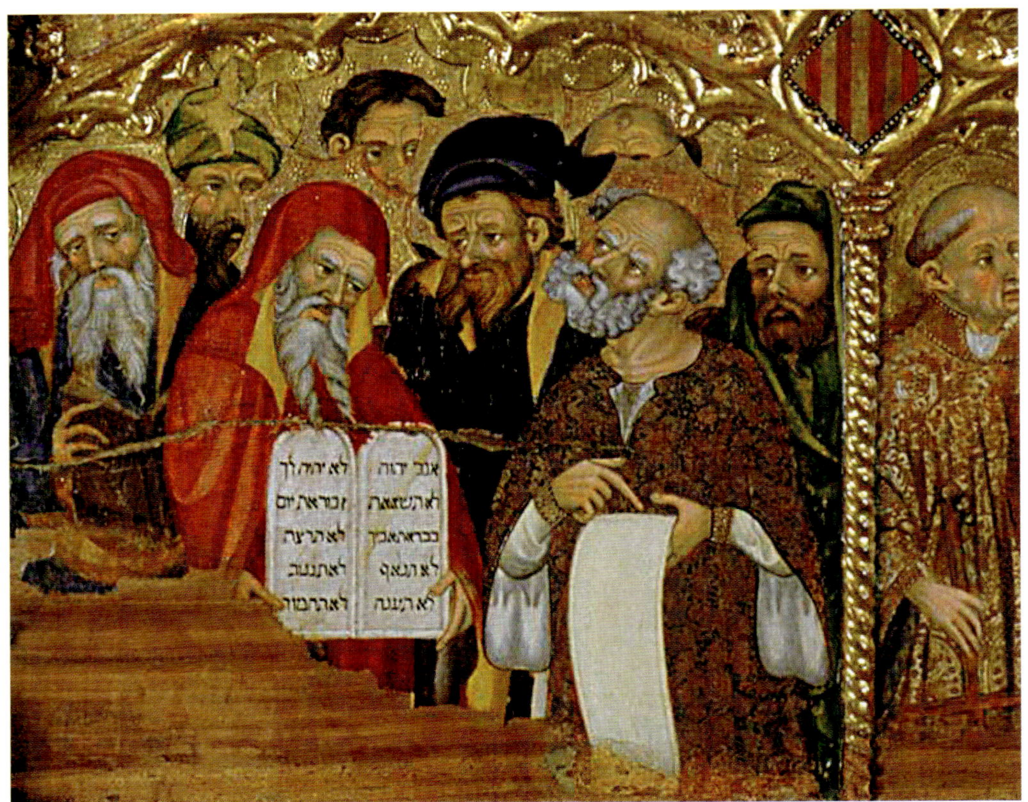

An exception to the common format is *The Book of the Gentile and the Three Wise Men* (*Llibre del Gentil i els Tres Savis*) by the Mallorcan friar Ramon Llull, whose view was that Jews and Muslims must only be won over by reason (figure 10). Exhibiting some epistemological modesty, he put honest arguments in the mouths of each. Llull devised a method, which he called the "great art" (*ars magna*), for converting Jews and Muslims by reason alone. In order to do this he had to attain some mastery of those cultures. He dedicated one of his works to three Jewish scholars of Barcelona, one of whom, Master Abram Denanet, is most likely Solomon ben Abraham ibn Adret. Another was Judah Salmon, who had once mediated between Ibn Adret and the Kabbalist Abraham Albulafia, and may therefore have been a conduit through which Llull could have accessed Kabbalah. An anonymous Kabbalistic treatise called *Sefer ha-Yashar*, probably written by someone in the circle of Naḥmanides, seems also to have been a source of Llull's knowledge of Kabbalah, including such rhetorical devices as the tree of knowledge (Latin, *arbor scientiae*), which was one of Llull's favorites metaphors.[26]

The *Book of the Gentile*, written in the mid-1270s, was "Llull's first attempt at the implementation of the general principles of the Art in the context of a religious disputation."[27] In it, a pagan ("Gentile") comes upon three scholars—a Muslim, a Christian, and a Jew—who

10. Pere Serra, Guerau Gener, and Lluís Borrassà
Altarpiece of the Virgin of Santes Creus
A Disputation between Moses and Saint Peter (detail)
1403–11
Tempera and gilding on wood
215 × 135 in.
Monastery of Santes Creus, Tarragona

were enjoying each other's company on their way to a forest outside of a city, "talking about their respective beliefs and about the things they taught their students." They come upon the Gentile who inquires about their beliefs, "for I have never heard anyone speak of the God you mention, nor have I ever heard anyone speak of resurrection."[28] The wise men then lecture the Gentile on points of theology, simply laying out the views of each. At the end of the discussion, just when the Gentile is about to announce his preference, the wise men say they would rather not know, explaining that "in order for each to be free to choose his own religion, they preferred not knowing which religion he would choose."[29]

Elsewhere, Llull recounts the case of an Arabic-speaking friar who was expelled from Tunis after instructing the sultan in Christianity. The friar had learned Hebrew and used to dispute frequently in Barcelona "with a certain Jew." Historians suspect the friar to have been the Catalan Dominican Ramon Martí, author of *Pugio Fidei*, an anti-Jewish polemic written around 1280. In that case, the Jew would have been ibn Adret who is said to have debated with Martí and to have discussed the same matters with Llull.[30] In this fashion, it has been possible to determine the probable sources of Llull's knowledge of Jewish theology and Kabbalah, as well as to establish that such contacts were frequent and friendly.

PUBLIC DISPUTATIONS

Two important formal disputations between Jewish and Christian scholars took place in the Crown of Aragon. First was the Disputation of Barcelona, which took place in the palace of James I of Aragon between July 20 and 24, 1263. In this debate the Jews were represented by Moshe b. Naḥman "Naḥmanides," the great Talmudist and Kabbalist from Girona, the Christians by a Dominican friar, Paul Christiani, a converted Jew. Naḥmanides was ordered to appear but insisted that he should be allowed to speak freely, without fear of punishment. The questions disputed were the standard ones that were aired in all such polemics: had the Messiah appeared or not; did the Bible hold that the Messiah was divine or human; and which of the two faiths in dispute was the truer? Paul's method of using rabbinical texts to prove that Christ was the Messiah was an innovation in interfaith polemics; this was a test of his method. At one point Naḥmanides lectured the king on not having guaranteed free speech sufficiently. On the final day of dispute, the king called an end to the proceedings and concluded: "I have never seen a man whose case is wrong argue it as well as you have done."[31] Eventually the king yielded to the demand of the Dominicans that Naḥmanides be exiled; after several years of wandering, Naḥmanides left Europe in 1267, settled in Jerusalem, and never returned.

One of the more scurrilous points raised by Christiani was whether or not it was proper for a Christian to address a Jew as *magister* (*mestre*, in Catalan), a title routinely applied by Christians to Naḥmanides. Christiani argued that no Jew in exile could properly be called "rabbi", for the Torah said that the "scepter shall not depart from Judah." "I replied somewhat mockingly," Naḥmanides reports in the *Vikuaḥ*, his account of the disputation:

> This is not relevant to the Disputation, and even so, what you say is not true. For *mester* is not the equivalent of 'Rabbi' but of 'Rav' and the title 'Rav' is used in the Talmud for teachers who did not have a *semikhah* [diploma of ordination]. But I just confess that I am not really a *mestre* or even a first-rate disciple. I said this in the way of modesty.[32]

What is most striking about Naḥmanides' performance is his ability to demonstrate, in plain language, to the king, that Christiani's arguments were flawed. That Christiani was humiliated is clear enough from his pained reaction to the deference shown to the Jew. Even here, Naḥmanides got the best of him because the fact was that he and others of similar prestige received such passing deference routinely.

ANTI-JEWISH VIOLENCE

In 1320 the so-called Shepherd's or Pastoureaux Crusade crossed the Pyrenees from France in order to fight the Muslims. They began to slaughter Jews, however, more or less systematically in the towns of Aragon they traversed. When this news reached the king, James II, he issued an order to the effect that anyone striking or harming any Jew or Muslim would be hanged. The first massacre of note happened at Montclus, a royal castle near Lérida. This castle, where the Jews sought refuge, was partly financed by the local *aljama*, who paid the salary of the castellan. Three hundred thirty-seven were killed, while others accepted conversion. Some survivors claimed in the royal court that local officials made "no attempt to seize, retain, or capture the said murderers or robbers present there." The *aljama* of Montclus had been the center of a Jewish credit network involving large and small transactions throughout the local countryside. When the Pastoureaux and their local accomplices destroyed or stole credit notes (among other documentation), the king sent royal officials to copy the records of local notaries in an attempt to recreate the network of obligations. The resulting ambiguities and irregularities only increased local hatred of Jews.[33]

Among a stock repertoire of libels directed routinely at Jews was host desecration (figures 11,12). Usually, Jews become ensnared when they purchased wafers, which were stolen by Christian thieves for the value of the metal case, or pyx, in which the host is kept. Three cases were reported in the mid-fourteenth century (in Barcelona 1367, Huesca 1377, and Lérida 1383). Oddly enough, all three were instigated by noblemen (the crown prince John, and a count, the king's nephew), in their capacity as provincial governors. In the first two cases, it seems clear that because the Jews were royal property and the prince was at odds with his father, attacking Jews was a way of getting back at the king. The king put a stop to these frivolous suits, but not before several Jews had been tortured and burned.[34]

11. Guillem Seguer
Altarpiece of the Trinity and the Eucharist from the
monastery of Vallbona de les Monges
Desecration of the Host (detail)
1349–1350
Tempera on wood
43 × 87 in.
Museu Nacional d'Art de Catalunya, Barcelona
(MNAC 9920)

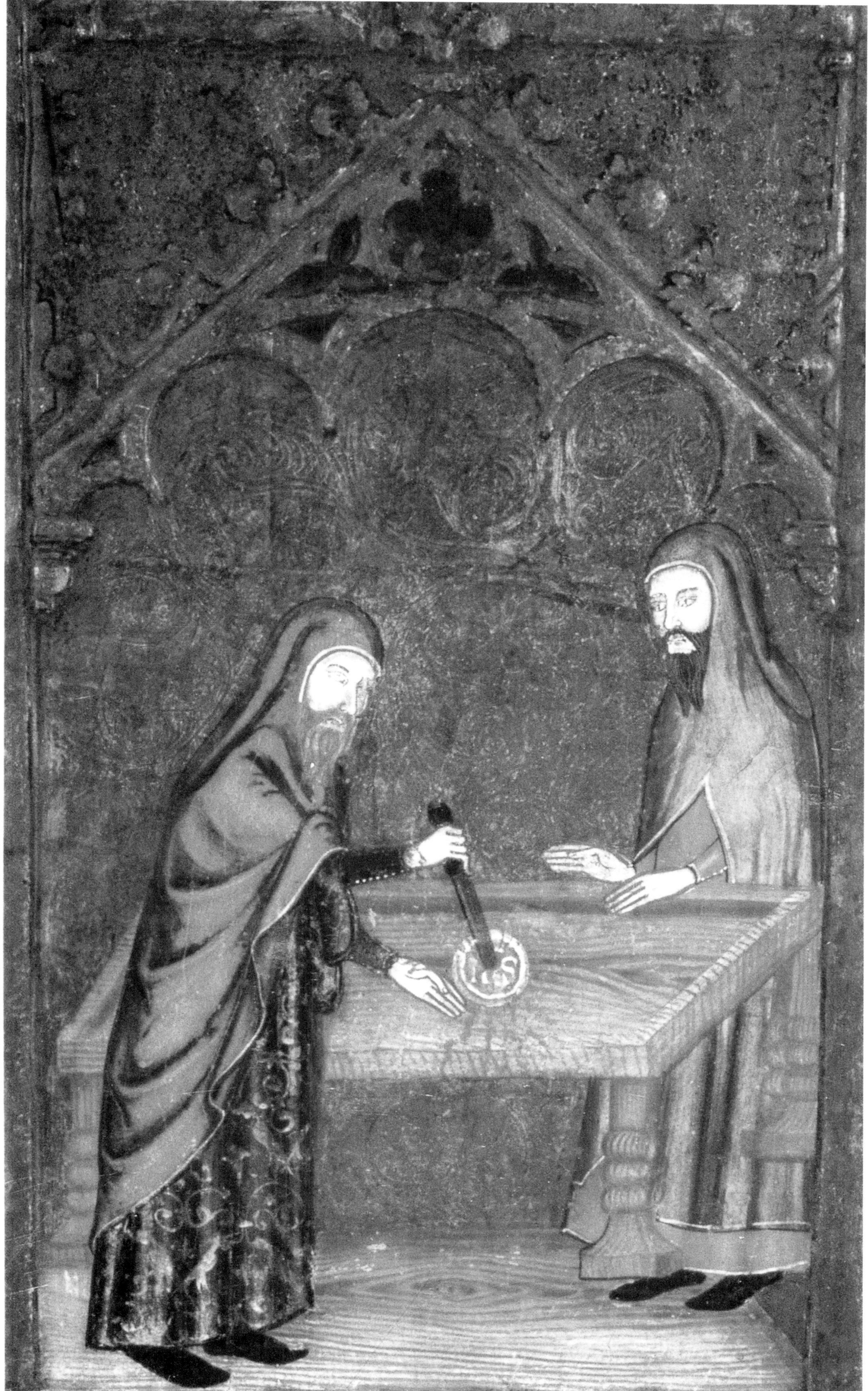

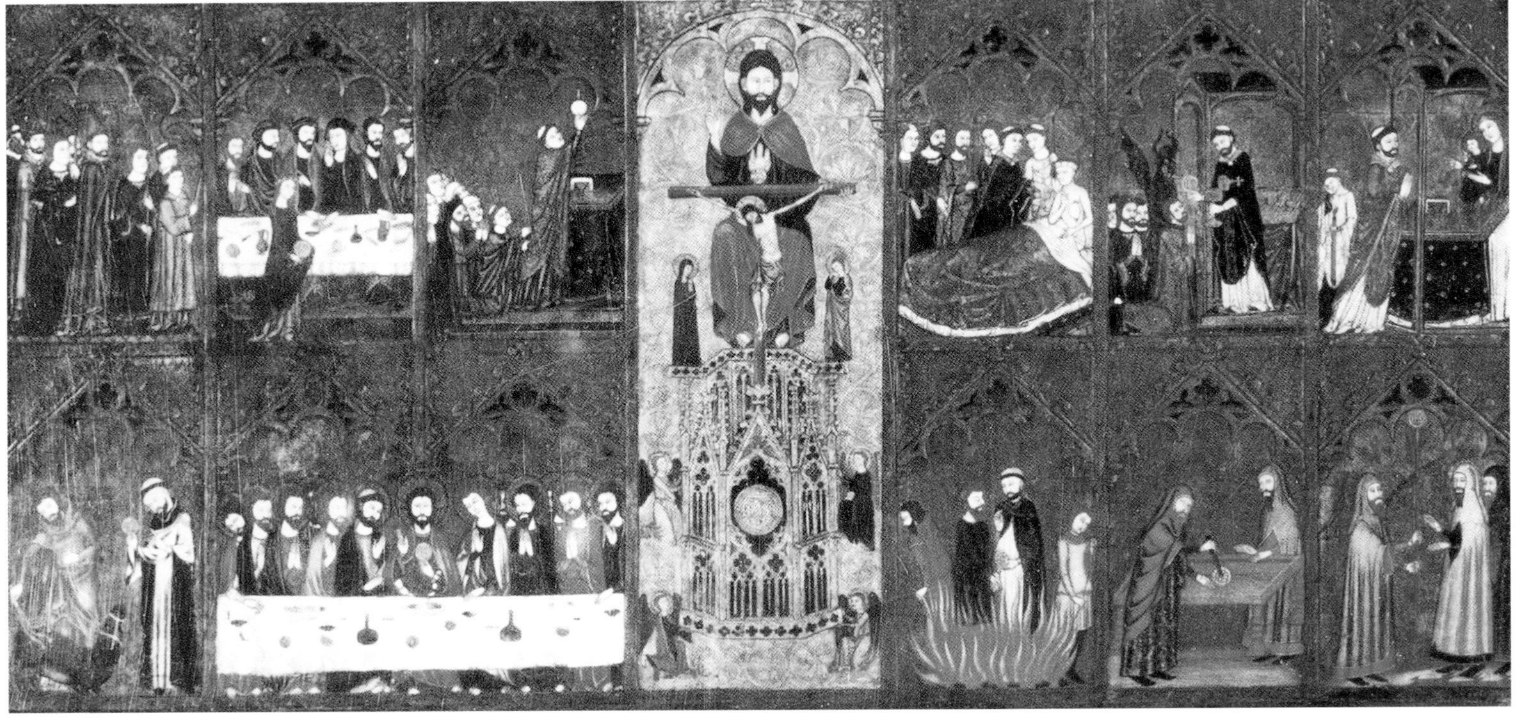

Localized anti-Jewish riots were common during Holy Week as the result of a type of ritualized or sacred violence that had grown up over centuries as a kind of replaying of the Jews' supposed role in the Crucifixion. This ritualized violence was so notorious that news of it even turned up in the writings of a Muslim intellectual named al-Qarafi (ca. 1285). The Franks, he reports,

> have three days in the year that are well known, when the bishops say to the commonfolk: "The Jews have stolen your religion and yet the Jews live with you in your own land." Whereupon the commmonfolk and the people of the town rush out together in search of Jews, and when they find one they kill him. Then they pillage any house that they can.[35]

The pattern was that on Maundy Thursday or Good Friday young clergy—"tonsured students or clerics," no more than adolescent boys—would throw rocks at the walls of the Jewish quarter, accompanied by a lot of noise. In general, these were not face-to-face battles, but an annual ritual which did, of course, always have the capacity for getting out of hand, ending up in invasions of the Jewish quarter. Sometimes these activities were even described as *jocs*, games. There was a serious fracas in Girona in 1331. A royal bailiff sent to intervene reported: "You see what a game the clerics are making for us, that they do not wish to be prevented by us from stoning the Jews." The ritualized throwing of stones at the ghetto wall was all about "vengeance, difference, and boundaries."[36]

12. Guillem Seguer
Altarpiece of the Trinity and the Eucharist from
the monastery of Vallbona de les Monges
1349–1350
Tempera on panel
43 × 87 in.
Museu Nacional d'Art de Catalunya, Barcelona
(MNAC 9920)

THE POGROMS OF 1391 AND THEIR AFTERMATH

Antonio Ubieto has demonstrated the correlation between anti-Jewish violence and economic depression. Indeed, anti-Jewish measures provide a rough index of epochs and regions of economic depression. (The opposite is also true: Jews were found in high positions in government in times of economic expansion.[37]) The depression of the early twelfth century was a factor contributing to the sack of the Jewish quarter of Saragossa in 1138. A century later there was another period of extended depression, which Ubieto associates with persecutions in 1275 and 1278, an extraordinary tax on Jews in 1282, the anti-Jewish strictures of the Cortes (parliament) of 1300–1, and the anti-Jewish strictures of the 1308 synods of Tarragona. Towards the end of the thirteenth century, the papal prohibition against trading with Muslims led to the collapse of the economy of Barcelona. A revival in the early fourteenth century was cut short by the Black Death in 1348, initiating a precipitous economic decline with major economic repercussions (failure of the bank of Barcelona, 1381–83) and the pogrom and ruin of the Jewish quarter in 1391.[38] The pogroms of 1391 display the features of typical "status panic," whereby middle- and lower-class Christians feel both threatened and displaced by middle-class Jews, whom they view as rivals. The class differentiation that we have noted within Jewish communities no doubt emerged at a time when similar structures were developing in Christian society, whereby a resurgence first in overseas, then in local trade emboldened the artisan class to seek a share of power.

Anti-Jewish violence, incited by the inflammatory preaching of the fanatical priest Ferrán Martínez, began in Seville on June 6, 1391. However, the dangers presented by the heightened climate of antisemitism had not been lost on the municipal authorities. In March 1390, a year in advance of the mass murders, the town council of Valencia, in an attempt to protect its Jewish citizens, ordered the Jewish quarter circled round with a wall, for the Jewish quarter had previously consisted of just a network of streets inhabited by Jews. The work began on March 1390 and must have proceeded fitfully, because on July 7, 1391, just two days before the outburst of anti-Jewish violence in Valencia, the works department was still strengthening the wall, which was actually a disjointed network of small walls, blocking off streets.[39]

In the Crown of Aragon, violence was pretty much restricted to the Kingdom of Valencia and Catalonia (figure 2). News of violence in Orihuela and Alicante incited a mob led mainly by artisans to attack the Jewish quarter of Valencia city on July 9, 1391. A "pseudo-religious" atmosphere of exaltation (according to Wolff) attended by rumors of miracles made it impossible for officials to rein in, and 100–150 Jews were killed. News of the Valencia uprising reached Xàtiva the next day at the same time as notice of similar killings in nearby Alcira. On July 17, the city council of Barcelona deployed 1,000 soldiers, who successfully protected the Jewish quarter until the slaughter of one hundred Jews on August 5 initiated four days of terror. By August 7, the movement had become a full-fledged lower class uprising, aimed at wealthy clerics and merchants, as well as Jews. The remaining Jews surrendered the next day and many were baptized. In all 150–400 Jews died, and the Crown's attempts to intervene all failed.[40]

The Jews of Saragossa had been spared a pogrom, but the other large communities, with the exception of Morvedre, were irreparably destroyed. The royal government under John I attempted to re-establish some of these devastated *aljamas*. To this end he ordered the Barcelona community dissolved on September 10, 1392, and three weeks later ordered it re-established in a new quarter. Only a few returned, however, and in 1395 the remaining Jews left the city.[41] In the wake of the destruction of the Valencia *judería*, the only viable community was that of Morvedre just to its north. Meyerson makes clear that the success of this *aljama* up to the Expulsion of 1492 depended to a point on a "bourgeois outlook" shared by the leading Jewish and Christian families of the town

> ...that manifested itself in specific economic strategies. Jewish and Christian elites both invested in tax farms, the leasing of public utilities, and urban and rural real estate. They did not simply proceed along parallel economic paths, however. Their paths frequently crisscrossed to form a dense web of economic interdependence... Some local [Christian] notables leased property to Jews...Indeed, the censal [income in the form of an annuity], more than anything else, structured the economic relationship between Christian elites and the Jewish community, and gave the former a vested interest in the growth and prosperity of the latter...Trust freed Jews and Christians to designate an adherent of the other faith as a procurator, their legal agent for carrying out essential business.[42]

It remained for Saragossa, untouched by the mass murders, to attempt to regroup the Jewish communities of Aragon, under the leadership of the great philosopher Ḥasdai Cresques (Crescas). Crescas drafted, and won community approval for, some new *taqqanot*, designed to reinforce the power of *aljama* officials. But in February 1399, upon complaints from the middle and artisan classes, the queen—Maria de Luna—intervened and reinstated an older procedure whereby officials were elected by representatives of the three classes. The queen wanted not only to tone down Ḥasdai's authoritarian conception of public administration, but also to restrain extreme democratizing elements; and so she prohibited the holding of general assemblies of the *aljama* without an order from her royal steward or the written consent of the (democratically elected) governing council. Thus the same social tensions as had surfaced before 1391 remained in force until the Expulsion, as did the Crown's close oversight of communal administration.[43] Maria de Luna, as regent, was a micro-manager. In Morvedre, she was a resolute protector of Jews, governing the *aljama* closely. She granted her bailiff appellate jurisdiction over any cases involving Jews and gave him a supervisory role in Jews' civil suits. She managed the *aljama* so as to encourage its economic growth. She intervened more than once in the *aljama*'s electoral system, trying to balance the interests of the oligarchs against those of the other two estates. This was a carefully negotiated and closely monitored autonomy.[44]

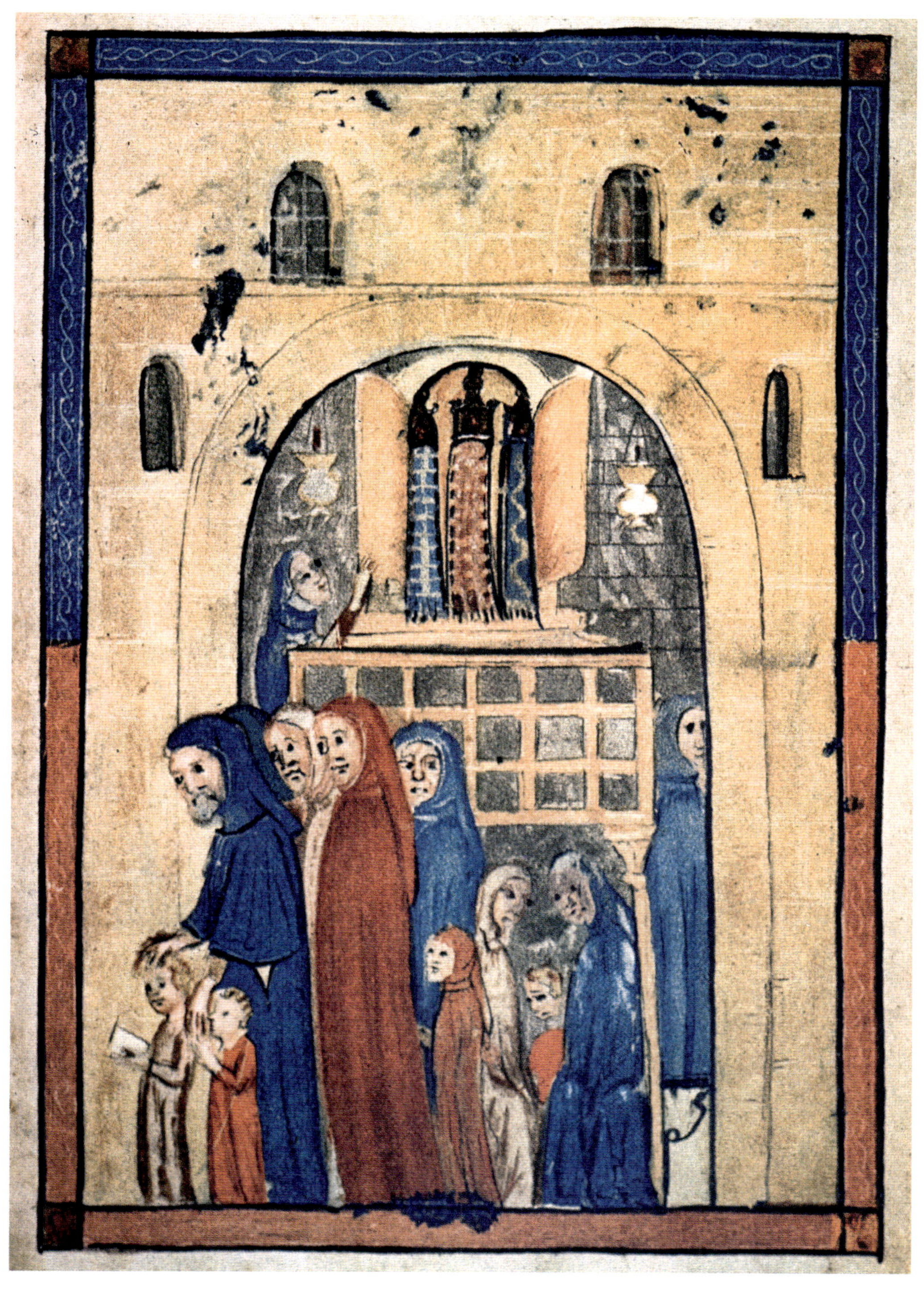

13. The Sarajevo Haggadah
Jews Leaving the Synagogue
Spain, second half of the fourteenth century
Ink and gouache on parchment
8 × 6 in., 165 pages
National Museum, Sarajevo

In October 1391, Ḥasdai Crescas described the misfortunes suffered in the pogroms in a letter to the Jewish community of Avignon. The events in Barcelona were particularly horrific:

> The number of murdered [on the first day] amounted to 250 souls; the rest fled into the castle, where they were saved. The enemies plundered all streets inhabited by Jews and set fire to some of them. The authorities of the province, however, took no part in this; instead, they endeavored to protect the Jews with all their might. They offered food and drink to the Jews, and set about punishing the wrongdoers, when a furious mob rose against the better classes in the country and fought against the Jews who were in the castle, with bows and missiles, and killed them in the castle itself. Among the many who sanctified the name of the Lord was my only son...Amongst [the Jews] were many who slaughtered themselves and others who threw themselves down from the tower and whose limbs were already broken before they had reached half-way down...[45]

SCHOLARLY INTERACTION

Jews had shown minimal interest in science until they were absorbed into the Islamic world where, from the eighth century, a vast movement of translation and transmission of Arabized Greek science, medicine, and philosophy was underway. Jews played a key role in this movement, both as authors and as translators (figure 14). Because Jewish scholars were fluent in Arabic and also the Romance tongues of the places where they lived, their role as cultural intermediates was a natural one. At the same time, the twelfth century witnessed the creation of Hebrew science, that is, science written in Hebrew, by virtue of the translation of the classical corpus, as reworked and modernized by writers of Arabic. These two movements wherein the same texts, by and large, were made available in Latin and Hebrew originated simultaneously in Aragon. They were, in effect, two different linguistic and cultural expressions of the same phenomenon. The interests demonstrated by the architects of Hebrew science, Abraham ibn Ezra of Tudela and Abraham bar Ḥiyya of Barcelona (but originally from Huesca), and translators such as Plato of Tivoli and Hugh of Santalla, suggests that they all had access to the library of al-Mu'taman, the scholarly king who ruled Saragossa from 1081 to 1085. Hugh of Santalla reported for example that Bishop Michael of Tarazona (1119–1151) had discovered Ibn al-Muthanna's commentary of the astronomical tables of al-Khwarizmi in a chest in Rueda del Jalón. This important Arabic astronomical treatise was translated into Hebrew by Ibn Ezra, who was likely to have seen the same manuscript.[46] The fact that this group of Jews and Christians formed, without any doubt, "a textual community" is strongly suggestive of personal relationships as well.

The initial interest of the translators and the creators of Hebrew science alike was in astrology and practical science. The combination of Indian celestial tables, a revival of

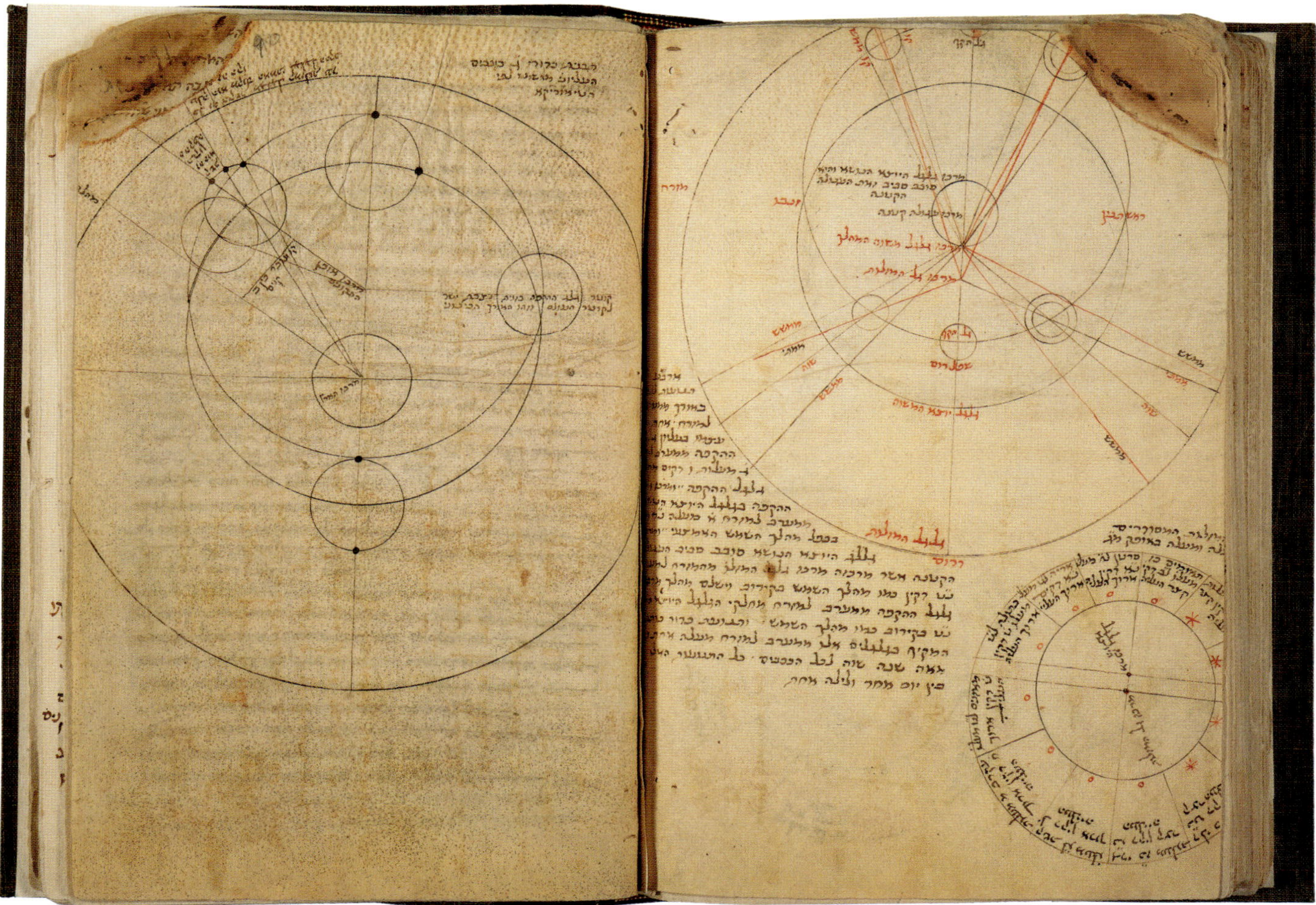

Ptolemy's astronomical theory, and the astrolabe as refined by the Arabs, together with Indian numerals, provided a powerful method for observing and predicting celestial phenomena. Christian and Arab princes of the thirteenth century routinely employed court astrologers, and philosophers of the three religions began to interpret Scripture in the light of astrological theory. Ibn Ezra made his living by traveling around Europe drawing up astronomical tables for the rich and powerful, who showed him the deference owed to the *magister* that he was. He traveled freely from country to country, much as any contracted specialist would today.

Translation from Arabic into Latin or the Romance languages was almost always done by teams of two translators, one a Christian who knew Latin, the other an Arabic-speaker, usually a Jew. Typically, the Arabic speaker would read aloud from the Arabic text, translating it at sight into the local Romance tongue; the Christian would then write the words down in

14. Abraham bar Hiyya
Sefer Tsurat ha-Eretz (Book of the Form of the Earth)
Spain, fifteenth century
Ink on parchment
8 × 5 in., 107 folios
The Library of the Jewish Theological Seminary, New York
Fols. 89v–90r (MS 2550)

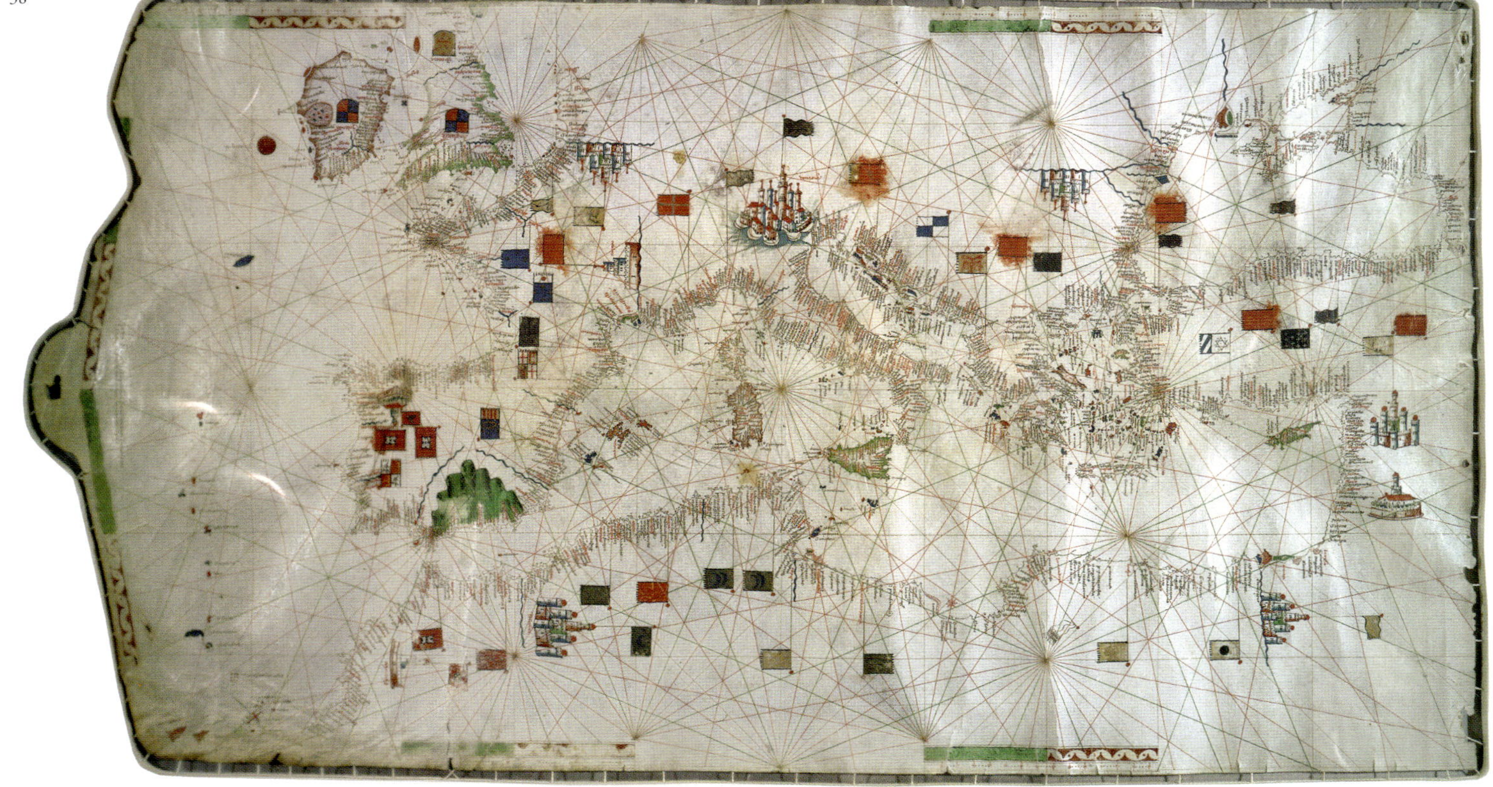

Latin. Thus Abraham bar Ḥiyya partnered with Plato of Tivoli on the Latin translation of Bar Hiyya's great geometry text, the *Sefer ḥibbur ha-meshiḥah ve ha-tishboret* (*Treatise on Measurement and Calculation*), which became the most influential geometry text of the medieval Latin world, circulating in Plato's Latin translation as the *Liber Embadorum* (*Book of Measures*). What is interesting about translation teams is that the Arabic-speaking Jew, addressed as *magister*—master—by his Christian partner, was almost always the senior member of the team. In this situation, the Jew has lower social status than the Gentile but also has intellectual capital that the latter wishes to obtain. To do so, he will defer to the Jew, acknowledging the latter's higher status, in order to gain the information or skills he desires.[47]

The second great moment of Jewish–Christian scientific collaboration in the Crown of Aragon was the mid-fourteenth century, with two foci, Barcelona and Mallorca. Astronomical activity in Barcelona was led by two Christians and a Jew, working under the patronage of Peter IV the Ceremonious. The Christians, Pere Gilbert and Dalmau Ses Planes, redacted a first work called *Tables and Almanac*, begun by Pere Gilbert, and continued after his death in 1362 by his disciple Dalmau Ses Planes, who was accused of having murdered his

15. Petrus Roselli
Portolan chart
1468
Ink and gouache on parchment
7 ½ × 9 in.
The Newberry Library, Chicago

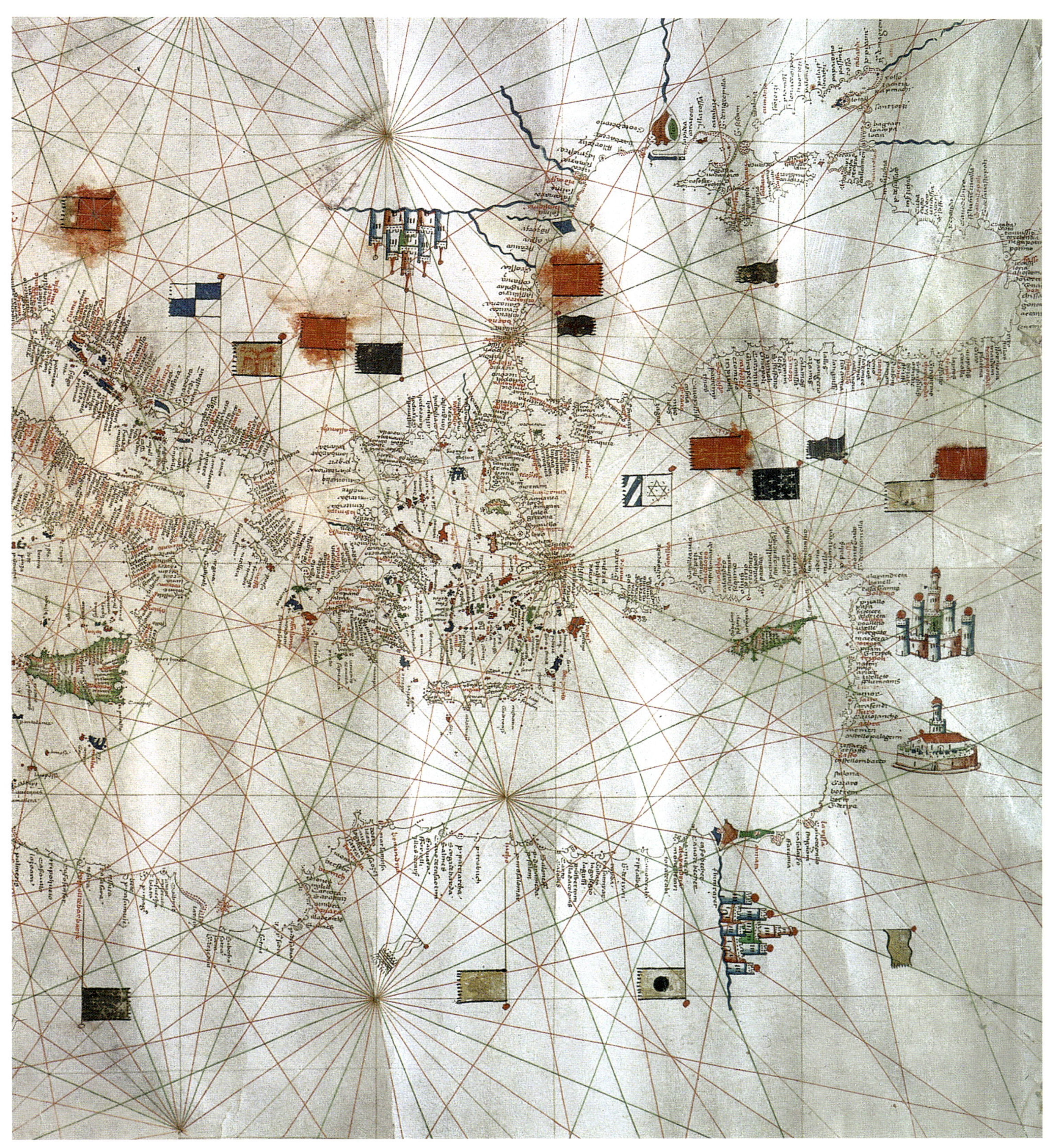

mentor. By the time Ses Planes finished the project the tables were out of date and so the king ordered a new set drawn up by a Jew, Jacob ben Abi Abraham Isaac al-Carsono, known in Catalonia as Jacob Carsuno. Carsuno was a Sevilian Jew who, in 1375–76, had written a treatise on the astrolabe in Arabic. In 1378 he was in Barcelona where he was attached to the royal household as "astrolabist and translator" and translated this work into Hebrew. The *Tables of Barcelona* were redacted in three versions, one each in Catalan, Latin, and Hebrew. These *Tables* were important because Carsuno based them on the Arabic tables of Ibn Kammad, which in turn incorporated material from the classical tables of al-Khwarizmi and al-Battani.

The king's astrolabists, who built the instruments for the king's court, were mainly in Mallorca and Perpignan. In Mallorca were the Jews Isaac Nafucí and Vidal Efraim Girondí. Perpignan was the seat of a family of Jewish instrument makers and astronomers, the Bonjorns. Jacob b. David Bonjorn was employed by the royal household in the same period. In his *Tables*, Bonjorn calculates solar and lunar cycles in which he mentions previous tables, those of Bar Ḥiyya and Levi ben Gerson, as well as the tables of Alfonso X the Wise of Castile.[48]

Mallorca too was the home of the Jewish cartographers Abraham Cresques (1325–1397) and his son Yehuda (b 1410), described as master makers of maps and compasses (*magistri buxolarum et mapamundi*), who made portolan maps for the commercial maritime trade (figure 15). They produced maps not only for ship's captains but also for various noble households. Abraham was the principal author of the famous Catalan Atlas of 1374, preserved in the Bibliothèque Nationale de France. Yehuda was caught up in the violence of 1391 and converted to Christianity with the name Jaume Ribes (ending up in Lisbon where, as James of Mallorca, he was employed by Henry the Navigator).[49]

JEWISH AND CHRISTIAN MEDICAL DOCTORS

There were many more Jewish physicians in Aragonese and Catalan towns than were needed to treat the *aljama* population, so they routinely practiced among Christians as well.[50] Even as secular and church mistrust of Jewish physicians grew in the course of the thirteenth century (as evidenced in legislation prohibiting Jews from prescribing for Christians or from treating them unless accompanied by a licensed Christian doctor), they continued to treat Christian patients routinely.[51] The royal household employed many Jewish physicians and were always on the lookout for new ones: in 1326 the queen was informed by a courtier that the best doctor "in these parts" was a Jew from Barcelona named Benvenist Izmel.[52] Christian physicians also had Jewish patients, one *aljama* going so far as to contract with one to care for its entire population.[53] As for the content of medical practice, Jewish and Christian medicine was identical. Christian medical works were translated into Hebrew, and Jewish doctors were allowed to attend lectures at the medical school in Montpellier when it was part of the Crown of Aragon (1213–1349), although not to receive degrees there. The most important Jewish physician in Montpellier around 1300, Jacob ben Machir ibn Tibbon (ca. 1236–1307) both boasted that "our wisdom and science are known to the Gentiles" and is known to have collaborated with more than one Christian scholar on various translations of Arabic scientific treatises.[54]

THE FINAL BLOW: THE DISPUTATION OF TORTOSA

The second disputation was that of Tortosa, which played out in three phases in 1413 and 1414.[55] The architect of the debate was a convert named Jerónimo de Santa Fé, formerly Joshua Halorki, the pope's physician, who had been converted by the Dominican Vicente Ferrer, an anti-Jewish activist who liked to force his way into synagogues and deliver hostile sermons there. Each Jewish community was ordered by the pope to send two to four scholars to the papal court at Tortosa (the pope was the schismatic Benedict XIII, the Aragonese nobleman, Pedro de Luna). Such leaders that remained in Aragon duly appeared (Joseph Albo, for example, and Profeit Duran). In grueling daily sessions, the Jews spoke first and were then questioned. The atmosphere was hostile and when the Jews complained that the discussion was not free, they were told that they were not there to dispute, but to be instructed. The topics and strategies were the familiar ones. Jerónimo de Santa Fé attempted to demonstrate, on the basis of the Babylonian Talmud, that the Messiah had already come, to which Joseph Albo replied: "Even if it were proved to me that the Messiah had already come, I would not consider myself a worse Jew for all that."[56] The delegates were perceived by their congregants as ineffective. During a long recess in the disputation, between September and October 1413, the Jewish attendees were forcibly detained in Tortosa and forbidden to go home. It was at this juncture that quite a few members of the Jewish elite converted. One of these, Vidal de la Cavallería, turned up the following spring as high treasury official Gonzalo de la Cavallería, a not uncommon pattern, his attitude towards his former correligionists being "a blend of cordiality and malice" (in Baer's words).[57]

The growing incidence of *conversos* in high places in the wake of the pogroms of 1391 and the Disputation of Tortosa was the stimulus that drove the Inquisition in its earliest phase. It was plain to see that, on the whole, *conversos* and Jews still formed a single socio-economic network. Jews were beyond the jurisdiction of the Inquisition, but those who, from the start, were suspected of "Judaizing" (now viewed as apostasy) were not. The description of that phenomenon is beyond the scope of this inquiry.

ENDNOTES

1   Arthur J. Zuckerman, *A Jewish Princedom in Feudal France, 768–900* (New York: Columbia University Press, 1972), 48, 319.

2   André Graböis, "Remarques sur l'influence mutuelle de l'organisation de la communauté juive et de la paroisse urbaine dans les villes entre le Rhin et la Loire à la veille des croisades," in *Le istituzioni ecclesiastiche della "Societas christiana" dei secoli XI–XII. Diocesi, pievi e parrocchie* (Milan: Vita e Pensiero, 1977), 546–58. If Graböis' argument that the autonomy of Jewish communities was the model for European medieval urban autonomy generally is correct, then the model was already a few centuries old by the time he picks up the story in the eleventh century.

3   Yom Tov Assis, *The Golden Age of Aragonese Jewry: Community and Society in the Crown of Aragon, 1213–1327* (London: Littman Library of Jewish Civilization, 1997), 19.

4   http://www.the-orb.net/encyclop/religion/judaism/jewmajor.htm (accessed June 15, 2009). See Elka Klein, *Jews, Christian Society, and Royal Power in Mediaeval Barcelona* (Ann Arbor: University of Michigan Press, 2006), 27.

5   The *aljama* was a corporate body legally recognized by the civil authorities; it was typically conterminous with a Jewish quarter housing the entire community (Assis, *Golden Age*, 70).

6   See my article, "'Thin Hegemony' and Consensual Communities in the Medieval Crown of Aragon," in *El feudalisme comptat i debatut: formació i expansió del feudalisme català*, eds. M. Barceló, *et al.* (Valencia: Universitat de València, 2003), 523–38.

7   Quoted by Assis, *Golden Age*, 252.

8   See Assis, *Golden Age*, 46–47.

9   Yom Tov Assis, *Jewish Economy in the Medieval Crown of Aragon, 1213–1327: Money and Power* (Leiden: E. J. Brill, 1997), 23–24.

10 Assis, *Jewish Economy*, 60–61. The three officers mentioned were all local government officials, with similar duties.

11 Assis, *Jewish Economy*, 71.

12 Assis, *Jewish Economy*, 105.

13 Assis, *Golden Age*, 69–70.

14 Assis, *Golden Age*, 19.

15 Assis, *Golden Age*, 27.

16 See Assis, *Golden Age*, 36; Mark D. Meyerson, *A Jewish Renaissance in Fifteenth-Century Spain* (Princeton: Princeton University Press, 2004), 171.

17 Assis, *Jewish Economy*, 96.

18 Meyerson, *Jewish Renaissance*, 157. In Catalan, the lower and middle classes were denominated *mans menor e mitjana*; ibid., 167.

19 Assis, *Golden Age*, 82–89.

20 Philippe Wolff, "The 1391 Pogrom in Spain: Social Crisis or Not?," *Past & Present*, no. 50 (Feb. 1971), 4–18, on 5.

21 On Morvedre, see Meyerson, *Jewish Renaissance*, 165. On Barcelona, see Assis, *Golden Age*, 93, 95.

22 The following discussion is based on Robert I. Burns, S.J., *Jews in the Notarial Culture: Latinate Wills in Mediterranean Spain, 1250–1350* (Berkeley: University of California Press, 1996), 2–31 *passim*. See also Assis, *Jewish Economy*, 2.

23 In Roman law, any individual could be named principal heir, which was "universal" because that person was heir to both the assets and liabilities of the testator. In Jewish law, "a decedent's daughter is precluded from taking any portion of her father's estate if he is survived by sons or descendants of sons. Second, the mother and the mother's family are not heirs of a decedent. Third, a husband inherits from his wife, but a wife does not inherit from her husband"; Mary F. Radford, "The Inheritance Rights of Women under Jewish and Islamic Law," *Boston College International and Comparative Law Review* 23 (2000), 162–63.

24 See the vivid descriptions of trials involving Mudejares by Mark Meyerson, *The Muslims of Valencia in the Age of Fernando and Isabel: Between Coexistence and Crusade* (Berkeley: University of California Press, 1991), 209–24.

25 Gilbert Dahan, *The Christian Polemic against the Jews in the Middle Ages* (Notre Dame, Ind.: University of Notre Dame Press, 1998), x.

26 Harvey J. Hames, *The Art of Conversion: Christianity and Kabbalah in the Thirteenth Century* (Leiden: Brill, 2000), 146–148 (tree), 178 (circle of Naḥmanides).

27 Hames, *Art of Conversion*, 158.

28 *Book of the Gentile and the Three Wise Men*, in *Selected Works of Ramon Llull (1232–1316)*, ed. Anthony Bonner, 2 vols. (Princeton: Princeton University Press, 1985), I, 93–304, on 113.

29 Ibid., 300. See also Hames, *Art of Conversion*, 158–89, where Hames sets out in great detail the Kabbalistic structure of the exposition of the Jew in the *Book of the Gentile*.

30 Hames, *Art of Conversion*, 111–12.

31 From Naḥmanides' account of the disputation, the *Vikuaḥ* (Argument): http://medspains.stanford.edu/demo/barcelona/disputation.html (accessed June 15, 2009). See also Robert Chazan, *Barcelona and Beyond: The Disputation of 1263 and its Aftermath* (Berkeley: University of California Press, 1992).

32 Quoted by Thomas F. Glick, "'My Master, The Jew': Observations on Interfaith Scholarly Interaction in the Middle Ages," in *Jews, Muslims and Christians In and Around the Crown of Aragon*, ed. Harvey J. Hames (Leiden: E. J. Brill, 2004), 157–82, on 174, from "The *Vikuaḥ* of Naḥmanides: Translation and Commentary," in *Judaism on Trial*, ed. H. Maccoby (Rutherford, N.J.: Farleigh Dickinson University Press, 1982), 102–50, on 106–7.

33 David Nirenberg, *Communities of Violence: Persecution of Minorities in the Middle Ages* (Princeton: Princeton University Press, 1996), 69–92.

34 Miri Rubin, *Gentile Tales: The Narrative Assault on Late Medieval Jews* (Philadelphia: University of Pennsylvania Press, 1999), 109–15.

35 Cited by Nirenberg, *Communities of Violence*, 200. By "Franks," Qarafi meant western European Christians.

36 Nirenberg, *Communities of Violence*, 211 (game), 218 (vengeance).

37 Antonio Ubieto Arteta, *Ciclos económicos en la Edad Media española* (Valencia: Anubar, 1969), 7.

38 Ubieto Arteta, *Ciclos económicos*, 75–85 *passim*; 90, 102.

39 Thomas F. Glick, "Cob Walls Revisited: The Diffusion of Tabby Construction in the Western Mediterranean World," in *On Pre-Modern Technology and Science: Studies in Honor of Lynn White, Jr.*, eds. B. Hall and D. West (Los Angeles: Center for Medieval and Renaissance Studies, UCLA, 1976), 147–59, on 149–50.

40 Wolff, "The 1391 Pogrom in Spain," *passim*.

41 Yitzhak Baer, *A History of the Jews in Christian Spain*, 2 vols. (Philadelphia: Jewish Publication Society, 1961–66), II, 120–21.

42 Meyerson, *Jewish Renaissance*, 90–91, 103.

43 Baer, *Jews in Christian Spain*, II, 126–29.

44 Mark Meyerson, "Defending their Jewish Subjects: Elionor of

Sicily, Maria de Luna, and the Jews of Morvedre," in *Queenship and Political Power in Medieval and Early Modern Spain*, ed. Theresa Eremite (Aldershot, England: Ashgate, 2005), 55–77, on 66–70.

45 *A Treasury of Jewish Letters*, ed. Franz Kobler, 2 vols. (Philadelphia: Jewish Publication Society, 1954), I, 272–75, on 274.

46 Julio Samsó, "Traduccions i obres científiques originals elaborades en medis jueus. El desenvolupament de l'hebreu com a llengua científica," in *La ciència en la història dels paisos catalans. I. Dels àrabs al Renaixement*," eds. Joan Vernet and Ramon Parés (Valencia: Universitat de València, 2004), 297–325, on 314.

47 See, on this score, Glick, "'My Master, The Jew,'" 168.

48   Josep Chabàs, "L'activitat astronòmica a l'época del rei Pere (segle XIV)," in Vernet and Parés, eds., *Ciència*, 483–514 *passim*.

49 Mercè Comes, "La cartografia a Mallorca i a Barcelona", in Vernet and Parés, eds., *Ciència*, 515–73, on 548–49.

50 Michael R. McVaugh, *Medicine before the Plague: Practitioners and their Patients in the Crown of Aragon, 1285–1345* (Cambridge: Cambridge University Press, 1993), 57.

51 McVaugh, *Medicine*, 59–60, 98.

52 McVaugh, *Medicine*, 61.

53 McVaugh, *Medicine*, 63. The *aljama* was that of Castelló d'Empúries, the Christian physician, Ramon de Tesarach.

54 Joseph Shatzmiller, "In Search of the 'Book of Figures': Medicine and Astrology in Montpellier at the Turn of the Fourteenth Century," *AJS Review* 7 (1982), 387–407, on 386.

55 The Latin documentation of the Disputation of Tortosa in Antonio Pacios López, *La Disputa de Tortosa*, 2 vols. (Madrid: C.S.I.C., 1957); English excerpts in Maccoby, ed., *Judaism on Trial*, 187–215. Hebrew account (English excerpt), ibid., 168–86. See also Baer, *Jews in Christian Spain*, II, 170–243; Dahan, *Christian Polemic*, 38–40; Rubin, *Gentile Tales*, 97–98.

56 Quoted by Colette Sirat, *A History of Jewish Philosophy in the Middle Ages* (Cambridge: Cambridge University Press, 1990), 380.

57 Baer, *Jews in Christian Spain*, 214.

OVERVIEW OF THE ALTARPIECES OF ARAGON IN THE FOURTEENTH AND FIFTEENTH CENTURIES

— Carmen Lacarra Ducay
Translated by Claudia Nahson

INTRODUCTION

In the fourteenth century, Gothic painting in Aragon began to absorb stylistic trends characteristic of the most important workshops on the Iberian Peninsula. Due to geographic proximity, its closest relationships were with the art of the remaining states that formed the Crown of Aragon[1] (Catalonia, Valencia, and Mallorca) and with the neighboring Kingdom of Navarre. These regions had incorporated French Gothic formulas into their art which were succeeded by Italian trends, and, afterwards, during the fifteenth century, by Flemish and Germanic ones.

I. MURAL PAINTINGS

Although the names of a number of painters who were active in Aragon during the second half of the thirteenth and first half of the fourteenth centuries are known, the works that can be attributed to them are scarce. Their art is traditionally referred to as "Franco-Gothic," a style that originated in the Pyrenees, and that incorporated French courtly tendencies. This art constitutes the beginning of a "linear" Gothic style known as the *"artes del color."* The centers of Gothic mural painting were in the province of Huesca, in the northern regions

16. Jaume Serra
Altarpiece of the Holy Sepulcher
Descent into Hell
1381
Tempera on panel
Museo de Zaragoza, Saragossa

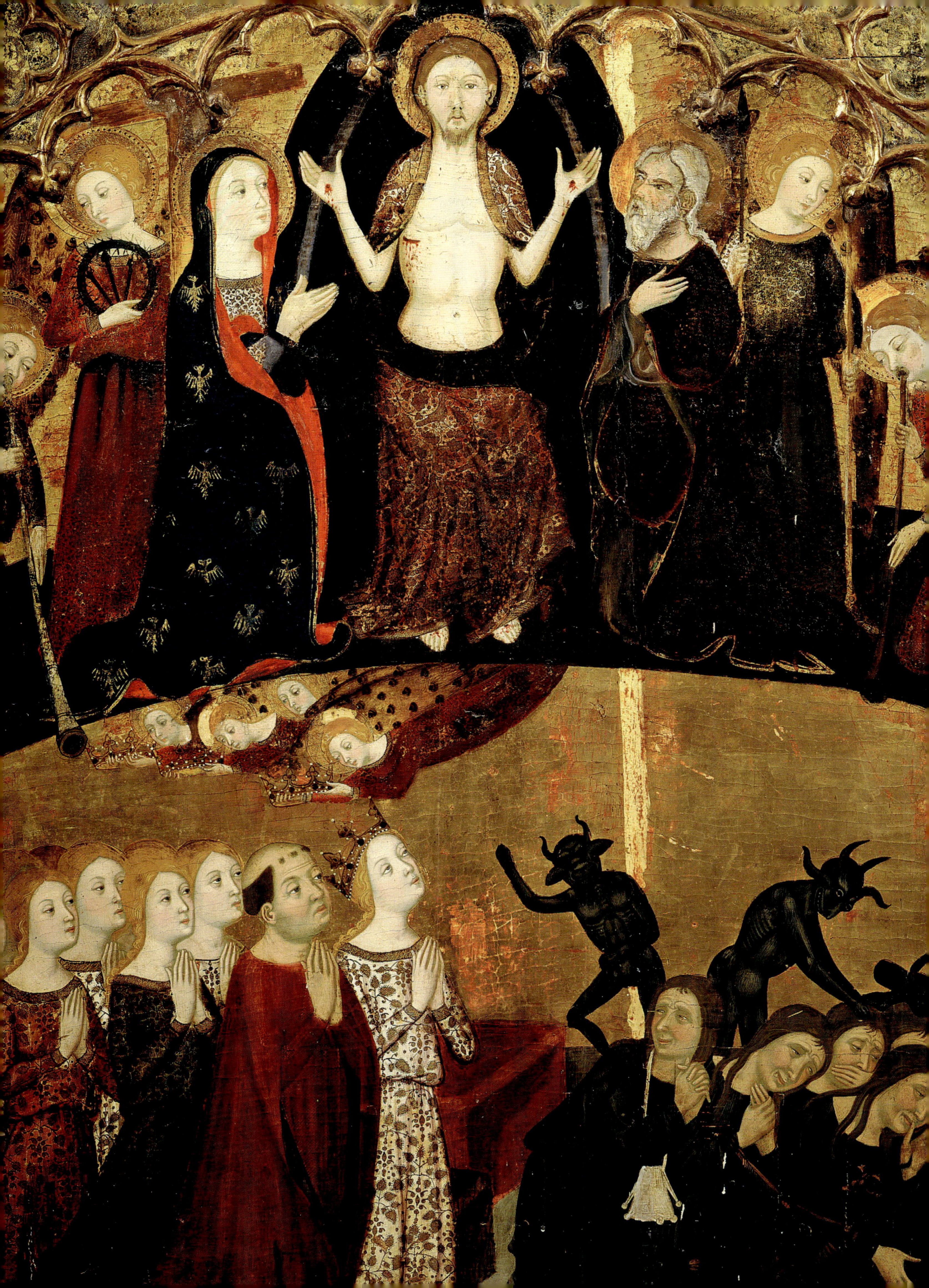

of the province of Saragossa, in the middle section of the Ebro River Valley, in the city of Daroca and its surroundings, in southern Aragon, and in the province of Teruel. The period of major activity, the first half of the fourteenth century, coincides with the linear Gothic tendency or Franco-Gothic style that persisted until the second half of the century in certain regions of southern Aragon. Certain examples of mural painting dating to the second half of the fourteenth century betray an Italianate tendency, such as the paintings discovered in an outbuilding of the sanctuary of Santa María de Salas, near the city of Huesca.

The mural paintings preserved in Aragon belonging to the Franco-Gothic style are primarily religious in nature; however, a few secular examples of notable artistic and historical interest are extant, such as the paintings that decorate the Torre del Homenaje in the Calatravan castle of Alcañiz (Teruel), which was dedicated after the reconquest of Valencia by James I of Aragon (1213–1276). Examples such as this indicate that secular painting also enjoyed a certain degree of popularity in Aragonese society.[2]

At the end of the fourteenth and beginning of the fifteenth centuries, new stylistic trends paved the way for the International Gothic—a style of greater iconographic complexity. Notable for their historic value are the mural paintings that decorate the primitive main chapel of the collegiate church of Santa María in Daroca (Saragossa), created by Enrique de Bruselas (Brussels), a painter residing in Daroca in 1372. Dedicated to the Dormition and Coronation of the Virgin Mary, and also featuring the Apostles, the paintings were later hidden behind a *retablo* made in the first half of the fifteenth century. Enrique de Bruselas (or Enrique Estencop), who had previously worked in the cathedral of Valencia, was known as a painter of altarpieces, with an extensive documented oeuvre in the city of Saragossa from 1387 to 1400, both in mural and panel painting.

During the fifteenth century, mural painting continued to be used, although less frequently, as decoration for the interiors of both religious and secular buildings. Although the number of existing examples is scarce, their presence indicates the continuity of a tradition of ornament with a long history in Aragon.

II. PANEL PAINTING

In Aragon, panel painting reaches its zenith during the fifteenth century. It is in this period that the *retablo* (Latin, *retrotabulum*) triumphs as an art form. A wooden structure composed of a number of architecturally configured elements and created to be placed behind the altar table, the *retablo* both presents Christian narrative programs and embellishes the back wall of church chapels.

In an earlier period, during the second half of the thirteenth and beginning of the fourteenth centuries, the paintings created in Aragonese workshops to decorate church chapels were altar frontals or *frontales*. Following Romanesque tradition, the frontals were painted on panel and placed in front of the altar table. They were built of a single rectangular panel. Given their shape and greater proximity to the faithful as well as their small size, they are stylistically linked to the art of illumination. Occasionally, the same painters created both types of works.

A number of Gothic altar frontals dating to the second half of the fourteenth and beginning of the fifteenth centuries from the province of Huesca have survived, pointing to their popularity as a form of altar furniture that was more economical than the larger *retablos*. For example, a beautiful altar frontal, originally from the chapel of the Santos Apóstoles Felipe y Santiago el Mayor that was situated at the end of the south nave of the cathedral of Huesca, is today in the Museu Nacional d'Art de Catalunya. Painted in distemper on panel, it features the figures of Saints Philip and James the Greater in the central section, and, on the sides, two superimposed scenes depicting passages from the legendary biography of each saint that reflect the influence of Aragonese manuscript illumination of the third quarter of the fourteenth century. As is true of other Aragonese works dated to the fourteenth and fifteenth centuries, major emphasis is placed in this work on the recreation of interior spaces and on secondary figures of a popular character.

From the old parochial church of Castro (Huesca) dedicated to San Román come two paintings on panel with the figures of Saints Peter and Paul (today in the Museo Diocesano in Barbastro), that may have been part of a *retablo* dating to the beginning of the fourteenth century, according to the inscription on the beam on which the panels once rested: "Fo efecto lo present retaulo anno MCCCIII" (This *retablo* was made in the year 1303). The depictions of the two enthroned saints, identified by their iconography and the inscriptions "Santus Petrus" and "Santus Paulus," are elegantly drawn and brilliantly colored, primarily in red and blue, and are related to miniatures and mural paintings from the province of Huesca of the same style and date.

Beginning in the second half of the fourteenth century, there are frequent reports of *retablo* painters from Catalonia who had either relocated to the cities of Saragossa and Huesca and worked there for the high clergy and the nobility, or who sent works created in Barcelona to Aragon, in fulfillment of commissions by Aragonese authorities.

The first documented painters absorbed Italian influence from Florence and Siena, received via Avignon—the residence of the Papal See from 1309 to 1404. While the Italians Simone Martini, his brother Donato, and his brother-in-law Lippo Memmi, were active in the papal city from 1340 to 1344, Giotto di Bondone worked in Naples from 1328 to 1332, invited by King Robert of Anjou, who had married Princess Sancha of Mallorca, his second wife, in 1304. An early proponent of an Italian style in the Kingdom of Aragon was the Barcelonese painter Ferrer Bassa, who, by order of the king of Aragon, Peter IV the Ceremonious (1336–1387), created two *retablos* between the years 1338 and 1342, one dedicated to the Virgin Mary and the other to Saint Martin of Tours, for the chapel in the royal palace in Saragossa, the Alfajería. He was paid a sum of 3,000 Barcelonese sueldos. These works have not survived but their presence in the capital of Aragon may have been a determining factor in the change in style that can be perceived in Aragonese painting during the second half of the fourteenth century. A few years later, Ramón Destorrent, another Catalan painter working for the Aragonese Crown in an Italian style, painted a *retablo* dedicated to the Seven Joys of the Virgin Mary, which was installed in Saragossa on October 8, 1358.

Another painting preserved in the Palacio de los Duques de Villahermosa in Pedrola (Saragossa) comes from the parochial church of Alcalá de Ebro (Saragossa), which benefited from the dukes' patronage for many years. The work, in egg distemper on panel, which can be dated between 1340 and 1350, was created in the Italo-Gothic style derived from Giotto's Neapolitan School. It features a Crucifixion witnessed by the Virgin Mary and John the Evangelist, Longinus, and Stephaton, with a praying female figure at the foot of the Cross who may be the wife of Don Lope de Luna, the third lord of Pedrola (1322–1360) and the first count of Luna (1348–1360).

The presence in Saragossa between 1367 and 1372 of a painter of altarpieces known as Rómulo de Florencia who painted the main *retablo* for the Convento de la Orden de Predicadores of Huesca in 1367 has led some authors to also attribute to him the magnificent altarpiece of Saint Vincent Martyr in Estopiñán (Huesca), today in the Museu Nacional d'Art de Catalunya. This work raises many questions regarding its creator and chronology that are yet to be answered. It is a triptych with a depiction of the deacon Saint Vincent in the central panel and, on each side, six scenes of his life and the martyrdom he suffered in the city of Valencia during the reign of the emperor Diocletian. He is accompanied by his preceptor Valerius, bishop of Saragossa. The miniature gables that crown the panels are devoted to the Entombment and the Noli me Tangere[3] on the sides, and, to the Crucifixion, at center. A couple of figures, depicted in small scale, kneel at the feet of Saint Vincent—they are a Dominican friar and a knight in armor with emblazoned shield, doubtless the donors whose identity is unknown. The work clearly betrays Italian influence and was created either by an Aragonese painter trained in Tuscany or by an Italian artist such as Rómulo de Florencia who resided in Aragon.

The Italo-Gothic style, inspired by models created by Sienese painters active in Avignon during the first half of the fourteenth century, is well represented in Aragon by the *retablo* of the Resurrection, created in the years 1381 and 1382 by the Barcelonese Jaume Serra for the Monasterio de la Resurrección in Saragossa. This *retablo* was commissioned by the Aragonese friar Martín de Alpatir, canon of Jerusalem and holder of treasurer for the archbishop of Saragossa, Don Lope Fernandez de Luna (1352–1382). As stated in Alpatir's will, drawn up in Saragossa on June 24, 1381, the friar requested to be buried in the chapter house of the monastery whose generous patron he had been. Serra received a payment of three hundred Aragonese gold florins for the altarpiece. His *retablo*, however, did not remain in its original location for long. In the middle of the sixteenth century, during restoration work performed at the monastery, the painting was removed from the chapter house and replaced by a more modern altarpiece. Fortunately, almost all of Serra's panels were preserved until the end of the nineteenth century

17. Bonanat Zahortiga
Virgin of Mercy
1430–40
Tempera on wood
87 × 49 in.
Museo Nacional d'Art de Catalunya, Barcelona

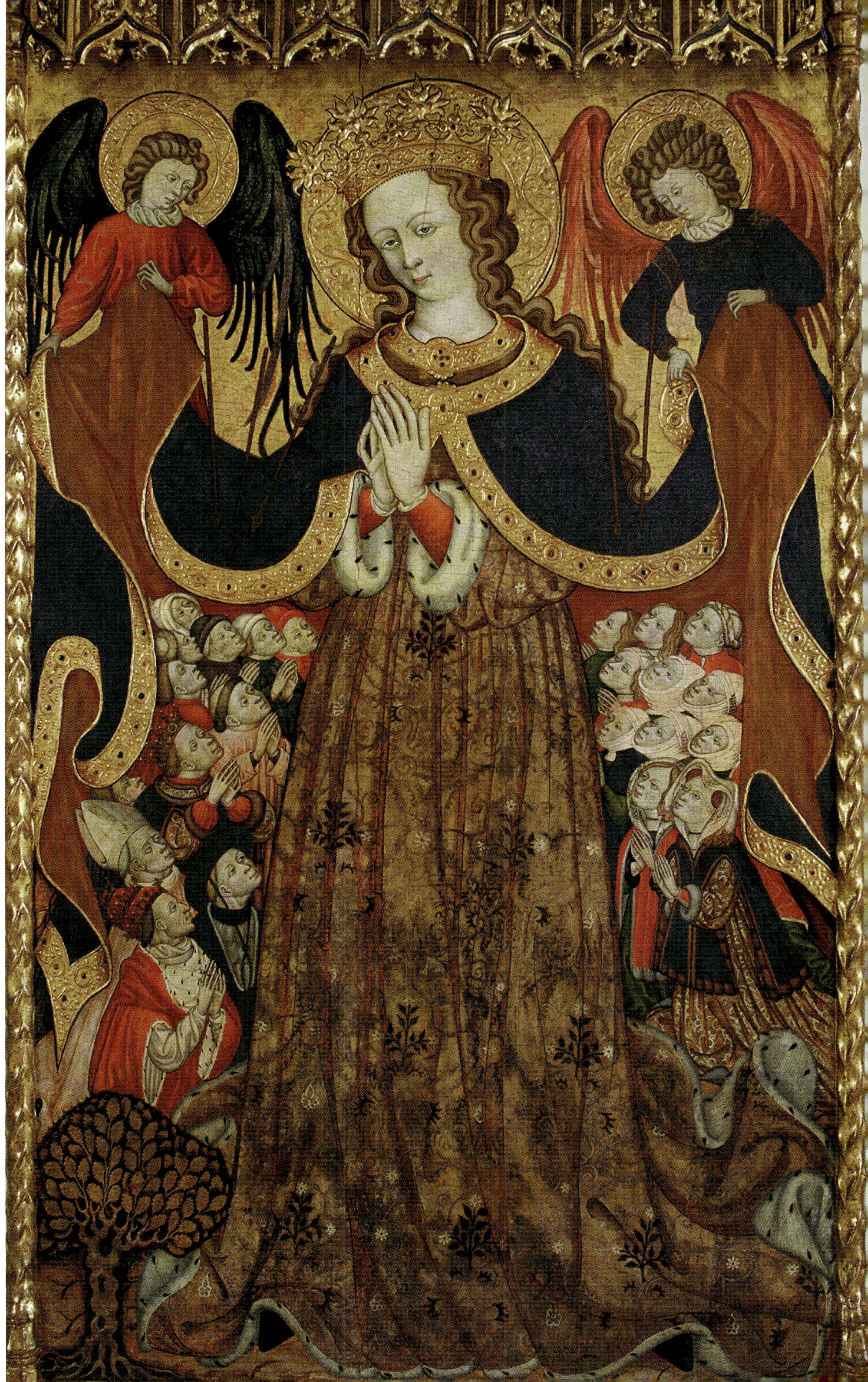

on the monastery's premises. In 1920 the *retablo* was acquired by the Real Academia de Bellas Artes de San Luis of Saragossa for the museum of that city, where it is today. By the time of its acquisition by the museum, the *retablo* was already incomplete.[4] Based on the surviving panels, it has been possible to reconstruct the original structure—a *retablo* of three panels, each three storeys high, devoted to scenes of the life of the Virgin Mary as a collaborating agent in the work of Redemption, above a predella whose iconography may have featured the most important scenes of the Passion. At left, from top to bottom, were the Annunciation, the Nativity, and the Epiphany (now lost); at right were the Coronation of Mary, the Dormition, and the Descent into Limbo. In the center, as an attic or *coronamiento*, was a depiction of the Crucifixion. The Last Judgment was prominently featured at center, and below it was the main scene—the Resurrection—a fitting subject since the *retablo* had been commissioned for the Monasterio de la Resurrección in Saragossa (figure 16). The two principal scenes are of particular interest as they feature a portrait of the donor, Friar Martín de Alpatir, easily identifiable both by his physiognomy, which coincides with the friar's portrait engraved on his tombstone, and by his vestments as canon of the Orden del Santo Sepulcro. In the Last Judgment scene, Alpatir is depicted among the Blessed at the right hand side of Jesus, and in the Resurrection he appears kneeling at right, witnessing the miracle.

The *retablo* at the Monasterio de la Resurrección in Saragossa is the only extant altarpiece by Jaume Serra with a known date (between 1381 and 1382) and city of creation (Barcelona). The work is of particular interest as it reflects the artist's style at the height of his maturity, when he had begun to work collaboratively with his brother Pere Serra, who would survive him and head the family workshop for some time after Jaume's death. The presence of such an important *retablo* in Saragossa inspired other painters who imitated the work. In fact, in 1384, shortly after Serra's work was completed, Sancho la Foz and his sister Oria Sánchez de la Foz, residents of Saragossa, established the chapel of San Julián y Santa Lucía in the same monastery, adjacent to its chapter house, and a *retablo* dedicated to these saints was to be created within a year of signing the commission. Preserved in one of the monastery's buildings to this day, the *retablo* is of medium size, with a predella of five panels featuring scenes of the Passion (the Kiss of Judas, Jesus before Pilate, the Flagellation, the Deposition, and the Lamentation) that communicate a feeling of deep suffering, in the manner of fourteenth-century Tuscan painting. The other panels are devoted to the depiction of episodes from the legend of Saints Julian and Lucy of Syracuse spread over three panels of two storeys each, with the areas in between, the *entrecalles*, occupied by figures of saints and the coat of arms of the La Foz family. This work is important due to its iconography: its scenes are set in richly depicted surroundings, populated by secondary figures dressed according to contemporary fashion.

Another work, Nuestra Señora de los Ángeles (Our Lady of the Angels) by the painter from Brussels, Enrique Estencop, in the church of Nuestra Señora de la Asunción in Longares (Saragossa) is based on the Serra altarpiece. The work was commissioned on September

3, 1391 by Don Francisco de Aguilón, parish priest of Longares, who had been appointed by Martín de Alpatir as overseer of works at the Monasterio de la Resurrección on June 29, 1381. Don Francisco de Aguilón also served as executor of Alpatir's will. The *retablo*, missing its central panel, is today located in a secondary chapel of the church in Longares. The central Enthroned Virgin and Child surrounded by angels is now in the Museu Nacional d'Art de Catalunya.

A gradual transition from a Gothic style under Italian influence to the style known as International Gothic takes place during the last years of the fourteenth century. Once again, it was Catalan painters, such as Lluís Borrassà, who are credited with the introduction of this new stylistic trend in Aragon. A prominent painter of *retablos* who was a native of Girona, but resided in Barcelona from 1383 until his death in 1424, Borrassà was summoned to Saragossa by John I of Aragon (1387–1396) in June 1388 to collaborate in the preparations for his coronation festivities. Borrassà's presence in the city of Saragossa in 1388 could have marked the beginning of his influence on Aragonese painters, as evidenced by the imitation of his compositions on a number of local *retablos*. For instance, in the main altarpiece devoted to Saint Peter at the parochial church of Langa del Castillo, a village in the vicinity of Daroca (Saragossa), the scene depicting the encounter of Jesus with Saints Peter and Andrew on the Sea of Galilee faithfully reproduces the scene painted by Borrassà on the main *retablo* of the church of San Pedro de Tarrasa (Barcelona) commissioned in the year 1411. The artist of the Langa del Castillo *retablo* is known as the Maestro de Langa after this work; he was active in the city of Daroca and neighboring localities during the first third of the fifteenth century. Other Catalan painters, who are representative of the International Gothic style as practiced in the Crown of Aragon, created altarpieces for the cathedral of Huesca during the first half of the fifteenth century. Joan Mates, documented between 1391 and 1431, was the first artist from the circle of Lluís Borrassà to be active in Barcelona. In 1416 Mates created *retablos* for two chapels at the cathedral of Huesca—one altarpiece devoted to Saint Engracia, and a second dedicated to Saints Peter and Paul. The latter's central panel—with standing figures of the two apostles that follow traditional iconography—is preserved today in the Museo Diocesano of Huesca and features models used earlier by Mates on other *retablos*. The second artist is Pere Teixidor, a native of Lérida documented between 1397 and 1445, who painted *retablos* for the cities of Barcelona and Lérida. He also created an altarpiece devoted to Saint Catherine of Alexandria for her chapel in the cathedral of Huesca; it was completed in September 1445. The current location of the work is unknown. Around the same time other foreign painters arrived in Aragon, including the brothers Juan and Nicolás de Bruselas, who, beginning in 1379, worked on the decoration of the chapel of San Miguel Arcángel in the cathedral of Saragossa by commission of Archbishop Don Lope Fernández de Luna.

The first half of the fifteenth century is characterized by an abundance of Aragonese painters known to us both through documentation and through preserved *retablos* whose rich iconography reflects popular devotion. Juan de Leví stands out within the framework of the International Gothic stylistic trend. Member of a family of painters documented in Saragossa towards the end of the fourteenth century, Juan de Leví probably apprenticed with his uncle, Guillén de Leví (documented between 1378 and 1396), who, in February of 1388 named Juan his sole heir, willing him his entire estate.[5]

Juan de Leví is mentioned in Saragossa from 1388 until November of 1408. He died by 1410 according to a statement made by his widow, Doña Inés de Eslava. A number of contracts for the painting of *retablos* at various Aragonese localities in the provinces of Saragossa and Teruel testify to his activity for the twenty years between 1388 and 1408. In January of 1402, Juan de Leví signed a partnership agreement with the painter Pedro Robert, certifying that the two artists would work together for two years, sharing both a workshop and a residence in Saragossa.

Among the *retablo* commissions of Juan de Leví, the most important is, undoubtedly, the one received from Bishop Don Fernando Pérez Calvillo (1391–1405) for his funerary chapel in the cathedral of Tarazona (Saragossa) recorded in the capitulary document written in Saragossa and dated January 27, 1404. This large altarpiece is preserved, almost in its entirety, in situ. It is dedicated to Saints Lawrence, Prudentius, and Catherine of Alexandria. The predella is composed of nine panels, and the main part of the *retablo* has nine panels of three storeys each and an attic. Its iconography is of particular interest for the variety of settings and figures. In the case of Saints Lawrence and Catherine, who are both the subject of universal devotion, the selected scenes are easily identifiable yet infrequently featured. But the scenes related to Saint Prudentius, an Aragonese bishop from the period of Arab rule, are even more original. The work as a whole provides historians of medieval Aragon with highly valuable information about everyday life in the early fifteenth century.

Bonanat Zahortiga is an important Saragossan painter who is documented between 1409 and 1458.[6] He represents the International Gothic style at its apogee—a style of notable formal elegance—and his influence extended throughout the provinces of Saragossa, Huesca, and Teruel. In the year 1411 he created a *retablo* dedicated to Saint Mary Magdalen for Huesca's Convento de la Orden de Predicadores. Although the work is no longer in existence, we can imagine its magnificence judging by the great altarpiece begun by the artist in the following year for the funerary chapel of Don Francisco de Villaespesa, chancellor of King Charles III of Navarre (1387–1425), in the cathedral of Tudela. Dedicated to Nuestra Señora de la Esperanza (Our Lady of Hope), the *retablo* featured Saints Francis of Assisi and Giles Abbot with the noble donors, Don Francisco de Villaespesa and his wife Doña Isabel de Ujué, portrayed praying at the feet of the Virgin Mary. An altarpiece of great size, it is located at the front of a chapel situated at the east end of the church. It features a predella devoted to scenes of the Passion including the Entry to Jerusalem, the Last Supper, the Kiss of Judas, Jesus before Caiphas, the Flagellation, Jesus before Pilate, Jesus on the Road to Calvary, and the Crucifixion. Three different cycles are developed on the five panels of the *retablo*: a cycle devoted to the life of Saint Francis of Assisi (at left), one dedicated to the life of the Virgin Mary (at center) including its narrow flanking bands, *entrecalles*, and one devoted to Saint Gilbert Abbot. Four Evangelists and the Resurrected Jesus crown the main panels. A great narrative sense, with large groupings of figures depicted against backgrounds featuring detailed landscapes, characterizes the style of this Aragonese painter who left his signature—"[BONAN]AT ME PINTO" ([Bonan]at painted me)—at the foot of the image of the Virgen de la Esperanza.

An important commission carried out by Zahortiga in 1420 was the painting of the *retablo* of Saint Augustine for the saint's chapel in the cathedral of San Salvador (La Seo) in Saragossa, at the request of the Aragonese Benedict XIII, who served as pope in Avignon (1394–1422). The central panel of this *retablo,* preserved in the main sacristy of the cathedral, features the bishop of Hippo clad in his episcopal vestments, depicted in great detail. Later on, Zahortiga would paint another altarpiece for the chapel of Saint Augustine in the crypt underneath the main chapel of Huesca cathedral. This *retablo*'s side panels, devoted to Saints Lawrence and Vincent, are preserved in the Museu Nacional d'Art de Catalunya. Zahortiga also painted other *retablo*s in the first half of the fifteenth century of which a number of panels survive. Among them is an altarpiece for the hermitage of the Virgen de la Carrasca in the village of Blancas (Teruel), whose remaining central panel is today in the Museu Nacional d'Art de Catalunya (figure 17). The panel portrays the Virgen de la Misericordia (Virgin of Mercy) as the queen of heaven protecting men and women of diverse circumstances and social strata, who kneel at her feet, begging for help. Three panels of another *retablo* painted by Zahortiga for the parochial church of Villar del Cobo (Teruel) are extant. On them are depicted Saint Sebastian, a Crucifixion, and the head of a pontiff. The panels were preserved because they were inserted into a seventeenth-century baroque *retablo*, currently the church's main altarpiece.

Between 1465 and 1477, Bonanat Zahortiga's sons, Nicolás and Martín, painted the main *retablo* of the collegiate church of Santa María de Borja (Saragossa), which was located in the main chapel until the seventeenth century, and is today exhibited in the local museum. Preserved almost in its entirety, the altarpiece is devoted to scenes from the life of the Virgin Mary, patron of the church to which it was originally dedicated: from the Expulsion of Joachim and Anna from the Temple through the Pentecost (figure 19). The work is characterized by an abundant use of gold on the backgrounds and in the ornaments of the sacred figures (figure 18). Stylistically, the work belongs to a more advanced phase within the Gothic, known as Naturalistic Gothic, popular in the third quarter of the fifteenth century. Particularly beautiful is the main image of the Enthroned Virgin and Child accompanied by a number of female saints who were devotedly followed in Aragon during the fifteenth century: Justa and Rufina, Quiteria, Apollonia, Ursula, Catherine of Alexandria, Agueda, Lucy, Margaret, and Elizabeth of Hungary, women dedicated to sewing, embroidering, spinning, and other feminine crafts that accorded with the education received by Aragonese women in the fifteenth century.

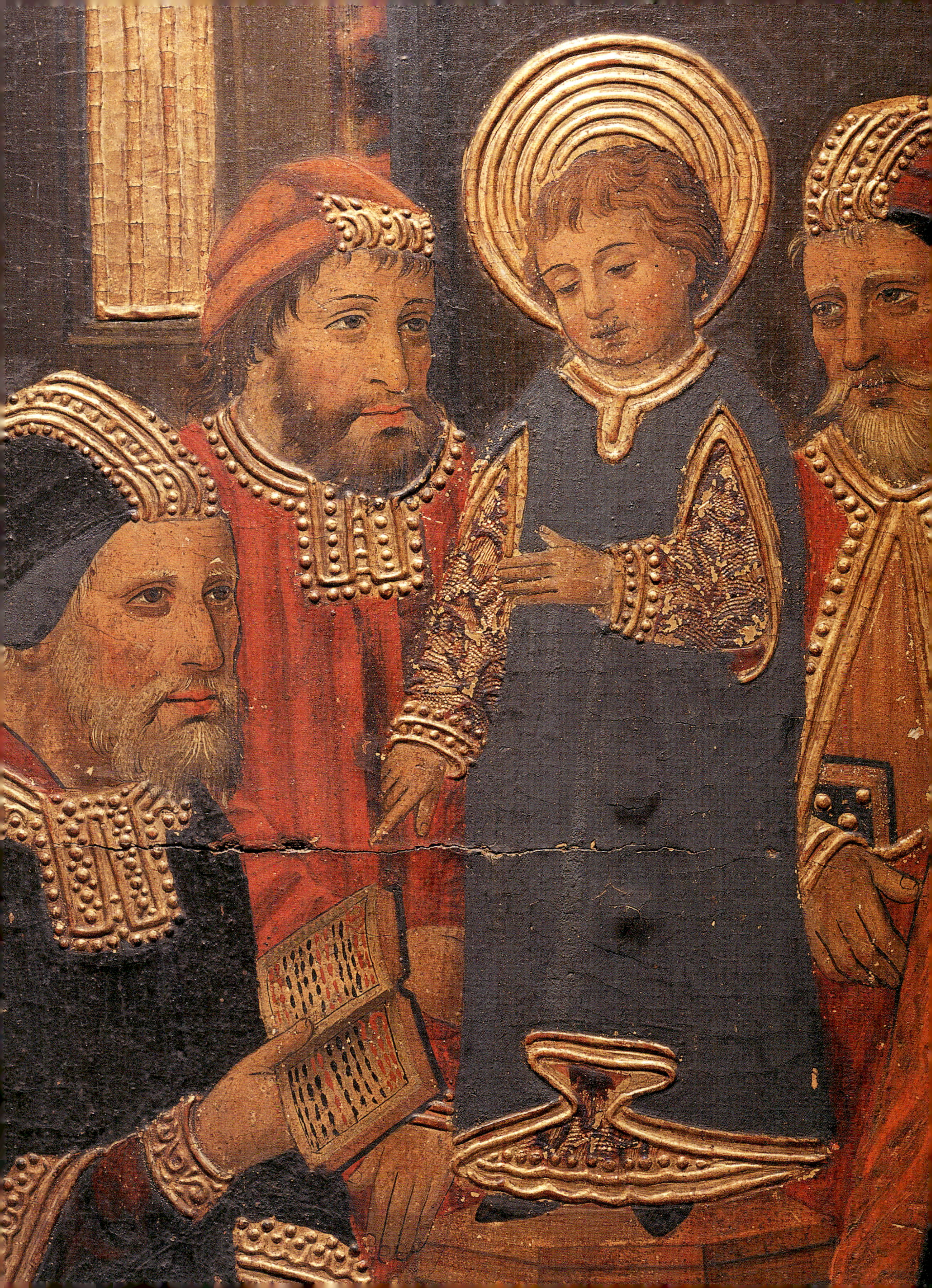

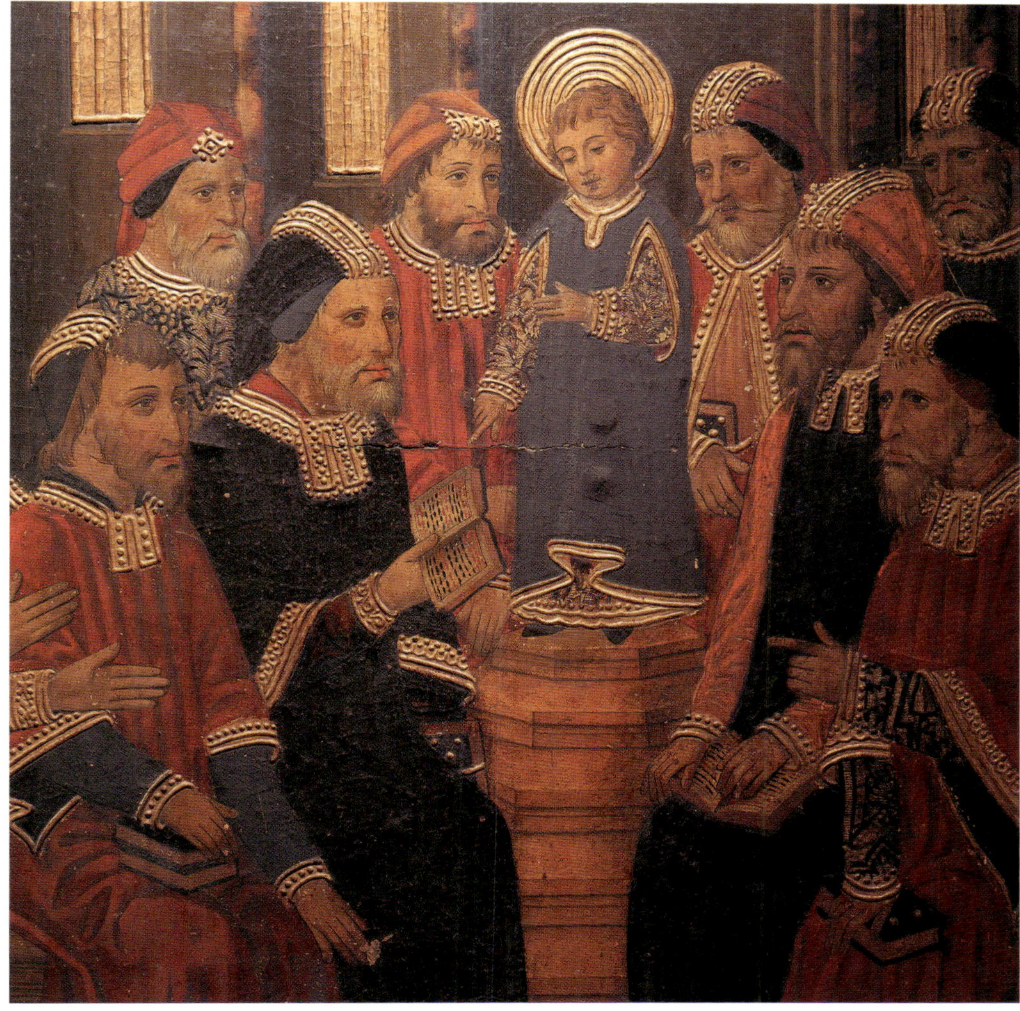

Benito Arnaldín is a well-known painter who created a *retablo* dedicated to Saint Martin of Tours that is located in the parochial church of San Félix in Torralba de Ribota (Saragossa). Its predella bears an inscription with his name: *BEN[E]DICTO ARNALDIN DEPINXIT ME* (Ben[e]dicto Arnaldin depicted me). It is a small size work, with a predella of five panels dedicated to Saint Mary Magdalen and Saint Andrew the Apostle, who flank an image of the Resurrection witnessed by the Virgin Mary and John the Evangelist. The body of the *retablo* is composed of three panels, the sides two-storeyed, and the center, a single storey. A Crucifixion is depicted in the attic and the remaining panels are devoted to the legend of Saint Martin of Tours based on the account of Saint Gregory of Tours, which was later popularized by Jacobus de Voragine in his *Golden Legend*. The anecdotal details

18. Nicolás and Martín Zahortiga
Altarpiece of the collegiate church of Santa María de Borja
Christ among the Doctors (detail)
ca. 1460
Oil on panel
Museo de Borja, Borja

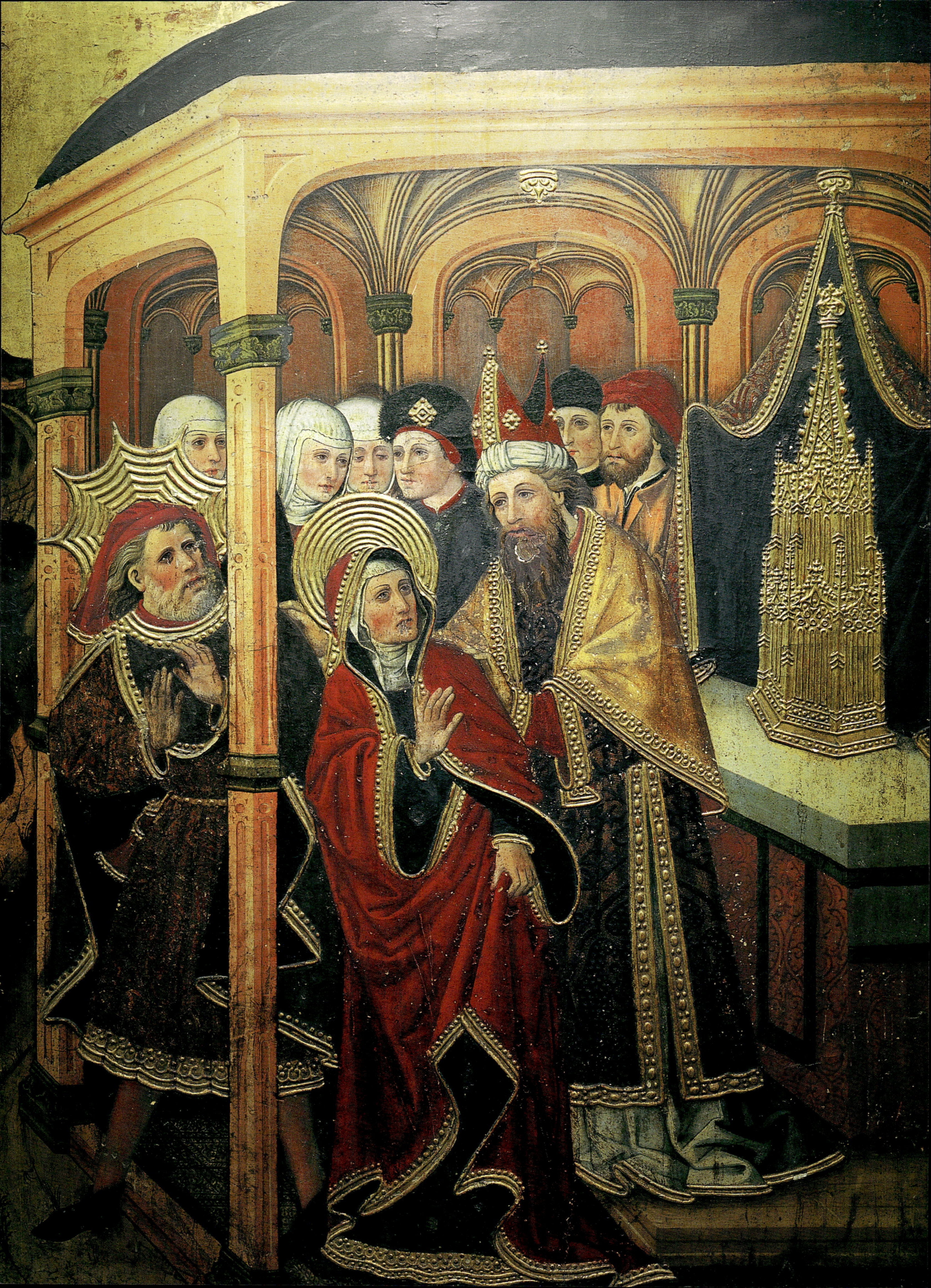

in the backgrounds and the delicacy of the figures are reminiscent of contemporaneous il-lumination. A painting of Saint Quiteria can also be attributed to Arnaldín, as it bears the inscription *BENEDYT ME PINTA* (Benedyt painted me). This work, once the central panel of a *retablo*, is today in a private collection in Barcelona.

Arnaldín, a native of Calatayud (Saragossa), was the head of a family of painters that included his sons Juan and Jaime who worked in Calatayud and Saragossa during the fif-teenth century. Only the father's style is known since none of the paintings created by his sons and grandsons have been identified. Arnaldín was a painter in the International Gothic style, who was dead by 1435. Since his sons appear to have trained with their father, it is reasonable to assume that their style was not unlike his. On the other hand, this assumption might be more applicable to Juan, the elder brother, than to his younger brother Jaime, who, in August 1433, was placed by Juan as an apprentice to the painter Pascual Ortoneda. In 1435, before conclud-ing his three-year training, Jaime committed to work as an assistant for Blasco de Grañén for a period of six years, which resulted in an ongoing relationship between the two families. For example, in February 1440, Juan Arnaldín is listed as witness in a letter of payment signed in Saragossa for part of the sum promised to Blasco de Grañén for his work on the main altarpiece of San Salvador at Ejea de los Caballeros (Saragossa). The Museu Nacional d'Art de Catalunya owns a painting on panel dedicated to Saint Ursula, with a donor at her feet—the central panel of a *retablo* that has not survived—bearing the following inscription at bottom: *JACOBUS ME FECIT* (Jacobus made me). Stylistically, the painting belongs to the Aragonese International Gothic, and it would not be a mistake to attribute it to Jaime Arnaldín.

The expressionist trend rooted in Franco-Flemish and Germanic art that charac-terized certain workshops of Gothic painting in Aragon and Valencia during the first decades of the fifteenth century is represented in Huesca by a painter who remains unidentified. He is known as the Maestro de Argüís after the altarpiece of Saint Michael the Archangel from the parish church of San Miguel Arcángel in Argüís (Huesca), currently preserved in the Museo del Prado. Undoubtedly also by the same painter is the small *retablo* of Saint Anne from the collegiate church of Santa María in Alquézar (Huesca); it was painted for the chapel of Santa Ana which was constructed in the church's cloister between 1437 and 1438.

In the south of the province of Saragossa, another painter identifiable by his ex-pressionism and his elongated figures is the artist known as the Maestro de Retascón, who created the *retablo* of the Virgin and Child in the parochial church of Retascón (Daroca) in collaboration with the so-called Maestro de Langa.

Much documentary information is available about Pascual Ortoneda (ca. 1423–1460), who resided in Huesca from 1423, the year of his marriage to Urraca Torrent, until 1428. He then spent a period of time in Saragossa, where he established an atelier and worked for a number of towns and cities in Aragon. Of the *retablos* created by him, only one panel from an altarpiece commissioned in 1437, depicting the Burial of Saint Paul the Hermit by Saint Anthony Abbot, is

19. Nicholás and Martín Zahortiga
Altarpiece of the collegiate church of Santa María de Borja
Expulsion of Joachim and Anna from the Temple
ca. 1460
Oil on panel
Museo de Borja, Borja

preserved in the Museu Nacional d'Art de Catalunya. In 1446 Pascual Ortoneda placed his son Bernardo as an apprentice in Master Bernardo Martorell's Barcelona workshop, for a period of four years. This clearly indicates the close relationship between painters in the Crown of Aragon during the late Middle Ages. Bernardo Ortoneda belongs to a later generation (ca. 1446–1489) and the work he carried out in the city of Huesca, where he resided, has not been identified.

Pedro de Zuera is one of the most representative painters of the second phase of the International Gothic style in the city of Huesca, where he is documented from 1430 until 1469, the year of his death. He created an altarpiece, the Coronation of the Virgin and All the Saints, for a chapel dedicated to the Virgin Mary in the cathedral, that is today in the Museo Diocesano in Huesca. This *retablo* bears the painter's signature at the bottom of the central panel: *AQUEST RETAULO PINTO PERE ÇUERA PINTOR* (This *retablo* was painted by Pere Çuera, the painter). Amongst his last documented works is the *retablo* of Saint Lucy which he painted toward the end of his life for the convent of Santa Clara at Huesca and whose central panel is preserved today at the Museo Arqueológico, in Madrid. To the same painter can be attributed, based on stylistic similarities, the small *retablo* of Saints Blaise and Mary Magdalen from the church of Nuestra Señora de la Violada, today in the parochial church of Almudevar (Huesca). Pedro de Zuera maintained a close professional relationship with Bernart de Aras, a Huescan painter documented between 1433 and 1472, with whom he created an altarpiece devoted to Saint Anne for the parochial church of Tardienta (Huesca) in 1448. The five remaining panels of the *retablo*—preserved in the Museo Diocesano in Huesca—include the main image of Saint Anne with the Virgin and Child, accompanied by the figure of the donor, Pascuala Clavero, kneeling with a prayerful gesture.

In 1449 Bernardo de Aras painted a *retablo* dedicated to Saint Hippolytus for Barbastro (Huesca). Preserved in the Archivo Histórico de Protocolos in Huesca is a sketch or design that once accompanied the contract for the 1461 commission of a *retablo* of the Virgin and Child for the church of Pompién (Huesca). Today damaged and incomplete, the Pompién *retablo* is preserved in the Museu Nacional d'Art de Catalunya. On the basis of the sketch and stylistic analysis, Bernardo de Aras can be identified as the painter of the *retablo* of Pompién, completed in 1463, and of two panels, Saint Vincent Martyr and a Crucifixion, that were once part of the main altarpiece at the church devoted to the Virgen de la Esperanza, Saint Lawrence, and Saint Vincent in the hospital of Huesca. In these two panels, preserved today in the Museo de Bellas Artes in Huesca, one can discern the mature artist's familiarity with mid-fifteenth-century naturalism, with which he may have become acquainted either in Saragossa or Huesca when he came into contact with other painters of his generation.

Blasco de Grañén, documented in Saragossa between 1422 and 1459, is one of the most original *retablo* painters of his era who worked in all regions of the Crown of Aragon with the help of collaborators and apprentices. First and foremost amongst his collaborators was undoubtedly his nephew Martín de Soria (documented between 1449 and 1487), who continued de Grañén's work, finishing a number of *retablos* that remained incomplete at the time of his uncle's sudden death in 1459, such as the main altarpiece of San Salvador at Ejea de los Caballeros. De Grañén's first apprentice was Jaime Arnaldín, younger brother of Juan Arnaldín of Calatayud. Many other painters may have trained with him. Noteworthy among those documented is Pedro García. A native of Benabarre (Huesca), he is listed as witness in a number of de Grañén's contracts dated between 1445 and 1447.

On the basis of existing documentation, an important number of works can be attributed to de Grañén. In addition, there are others which can be attributed to him on stylistic and technical grounds. Given his strong artistic personality, de Grañén may be considered the best exponent of Aragonese Gothic painting of the second quarter of the fifteenth century. His distinctive pictorial style makes him the great figure of late International Gothic, and his work refers to the world of manuscript illumination and to Franco-Flemish tapestries, to which he may have been exposed through his professional ties to both the high clergy and the nobility. In his last works, de Grañén reveals himself to be a follower of the Flemish naturalism characteristic of his time. He created a personal interpretation of religious iconography, evidenced by his important contribution to the subject of the Virgin and Child Enthroned and accompanied by small angelic musicians (figure 20).

Of the preserved large *retablos* painted by Blasco de Grañén the most important are, undoubtedly, the main altarpiece in Anento (Saragossa) and the main *retablo* of San Salvador at Ejea de los Caballeros, both still preserved in the churches for which they were painted. That in Anento has a triple dedication to Saint Blaise, the Virgen de la Misericordia, and Saint Thomas Becket. Its creation was due to the patronage of Achbishops of Saragossa Don Francesc Clemente Çapera (1415–1419) and Don Dalmau de Mur (1431–1456), as shown by the incorporation of their coat of arms on various parts of the *retablo*. The work is composed of a predella of ten panels featuring scenes of the Passion from the Entry to Jerusalem through the Entombment with a tabernacle at center. The body of the altarpiece consists of nine three-storeyed panels, with three panels devoted to each of the saints to whom the altarpiece is dedicated.

The altarpiece of the church of San Salvador at Ejea de los Caballeros marks the apex of de Grañén's career as a painter, without underestimating his other works.[7] It was commissioned on December 22, 1438 and was not completed until April 1476, with his nephew, Martín de Soria, taking over after de Grañén's death in 1459. The Ejea *retablo* consists of a predella with six panels devoted to the Passion, and a body of seven three-storeyed panels, and a polychrome wooden image of Jesus as Savior at center, carved by the Aragonese carpenters Domingo and Mateo Sariñena. The eighteen panels that form the body of the *retablo* constitute a singular case in Aragonese Gothic painting of the 1400s, given their large dimensions as well as the richness and variety of their iconography. Compositions devoted to the Life of Jesus, from the Adoration of the Shepherds to the Ascension, masterfully recreate both rural and urban life during the second third of the fifteenth century.

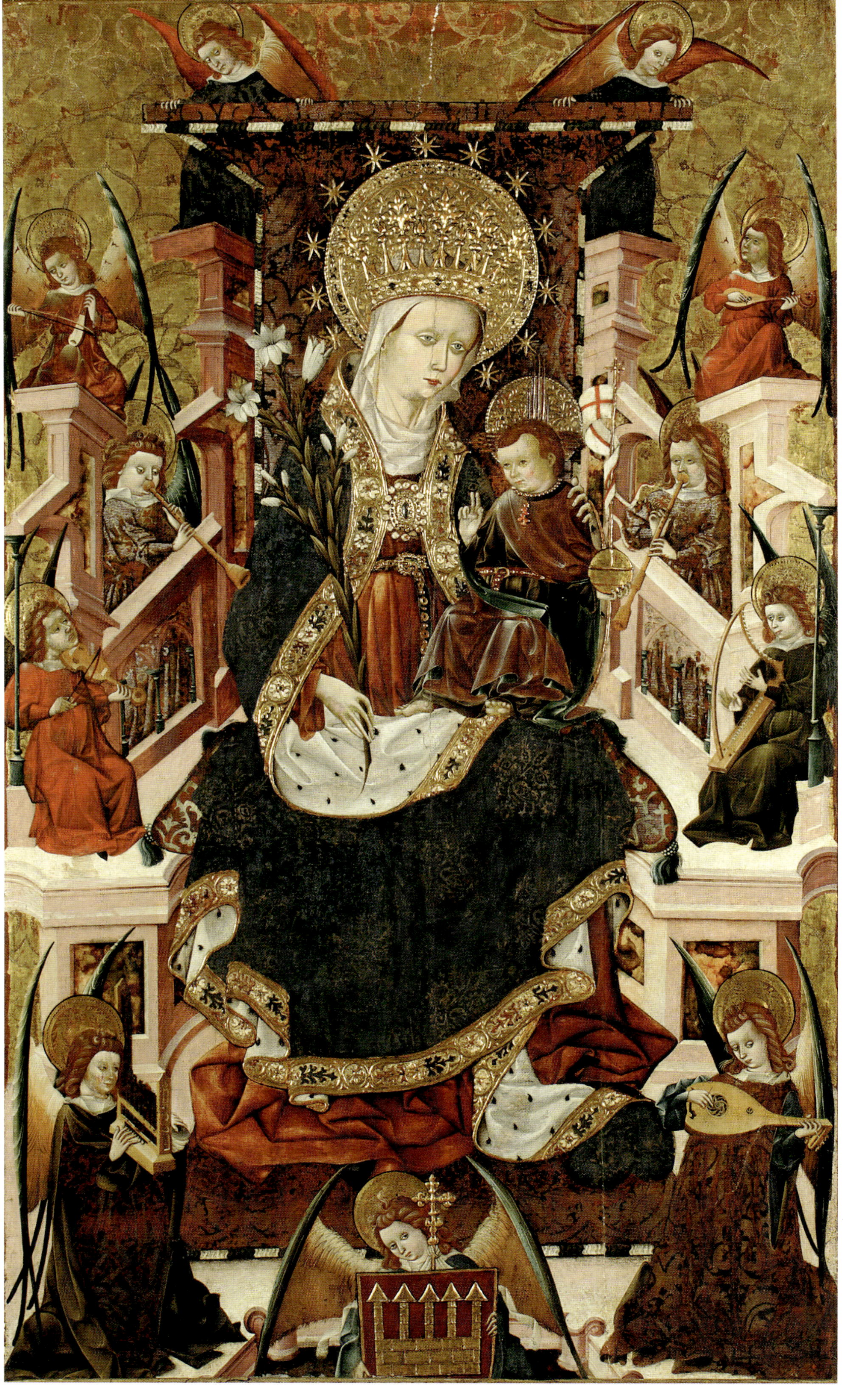

In the second half of the fifteenth century, the work of Aragonese painters drew closer to Flemish and Germanic naturalism through their use of oil painting, which became widespread by the end of the century. The presence of printers and booksellers of Germanic origin in the cities of Huesca and Saragossa led to familiarity with the engravings of Martin Schongauer (ca. 1450–1491), and resulted in a number of Aragonese painters using his prints as compositional models. An artist from Colmar, Schongauer had visited several cities in the Crown of Aragon during his youth, including Barcelona, Valencia, Daroca, and Saragossa.

One of the most important painters of *retablos* of the third quarter of the fifteenth century is Tomás Giner, documented in Saragossa between 1458 and 1480 (the year of his death). He is first mentioned in 1458, when he commits to work on the painting and gilding of the body and attic of an altarpiece whose socle and predella had been made in alabaster by the Catalan sculptor Francisco Gomar for the chapel of the archiepiscopal palace in Saragossa by order of Archbishop Don Dalmau de Mur (1431–1456). Of the three panels that composed the body of this *retablo,* two are preserved today in the archiepiscopal palace: the central panel, with the imposing figures of Saints Martin of Tours and Thecla, and a portrait of Archbishop Don Dalmau; and the panel that once occupied the left side featuring Saints Augustine and Lawrence. Missing are the panels with Saints Vincent and Valerius and the panel of the attic, which according to the contract would have featured a scene from the Passion. The artistic importance of Tomás Giner as a naturalistic painter can be appreciated in the two preserved panels. A year later, in 1459, he is cited in a document as the painter of the main altarpiece of the cathedral of Saragossa and as a resident of that city. The fact that Giner was given commissions of such magnitude as the *retablo* of the chapel in the archiepiscopal palace and the main *retablo* of the cathedral points to his having had an important early career, of which nothing is known from existing documents. His later appointment on November 3, 1473, as painter to the crown prince of the Crown of Aragon—Don Fernando, king of Sicily (the future King Ferdinand the Catholic of Aragon)—further demonstrates his successful professional trajectory. Documented among the altarpieces Giner made for the cathedral of Saragossa is the *retablo* of Saint Vincent Martyr for the chapel dedicated to the saint, the construction of which was ordered by the city council in 1460 (figure 21). Its main panel, with Saint Vincent and the donor, is preserved in the Museo del Prado. Giner's important status in Saragossan painting of the third quarter of the fifteenth century did not prevent him from collaborating with other artists. For instance, on June 16, 1466, he signed a three-year partnership agreement with the painter Arnal de Castelnou, although their collaboration had started some time earlier, since they had already worked on *retablos* for Santa Cristina de Somport (Huesca), La Virgen de Corona in Erla (Saragossa), and San Lorenzo Mártir de Magallón (Saragossa). The *retablo* of Erla is preserved in its parish church; its main panel is devoted to the Enthroned Virgin and Child accompanied by angelic musicians, clearly painted under the influence of the Flemish painter Jan van Eyck, as is the panel of the attic featuring the Coronation of the Virgin. Still in the parochial church

20. Blasco de Grañén
Central panel from the altarpiece of Queen Mary of the Angels
1437
Oil on panel
65 × 42 in.
Museo de Zaragoza, Saragossa

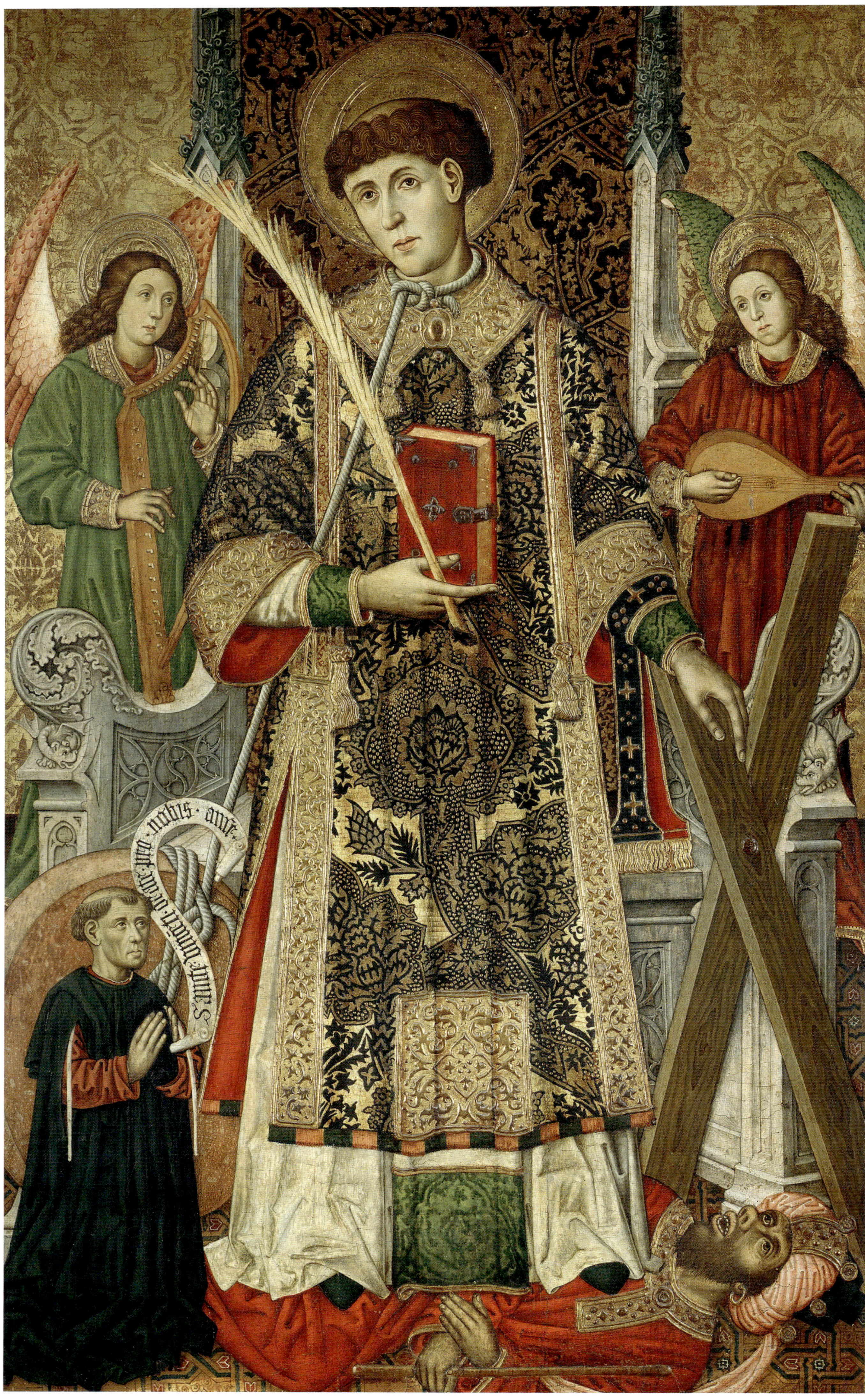
S· andreu· ora· pro· nobis· ante·

of Magallón is the central panel of the main *retablo*, with the figure of Saint Lawrence, as well as a number of minor panels with figures of prophets and portraits of the donors of the work. Around this time, Giner painted the *retablo* of the Epiphany for the collegiate church of Santa María in Calatayud that now hangs in its cloister, as well as the monumental Saint Christopher, which is preserved inside the same church, and the Resurrection today in the Museo de Federico Marés, Barcelona.

Another important painter was Martín de Soria of Saragossa, who was active in the three Aragonese provinces of Saragossa, Huesca, and Teruel. First cited in the year 1449, he is last documented on June 25, 1487, the date of his will, in which he requests to be buried in the convent of San Francisco in Saragossa. His uncle, Blasco de Grañén, could have facilitated de Soria's initial artistic career and supplied him with his first commissions. In September of 1452 de Grañén is in fact listed as agent for his nephew, who at that time was temporarily residing in Sariñena (Huesca). Years later, following the death of Blasco de Grañén in 1459, it was Martín de Soria who would complete the works left unfinished by his uncle, such as the main altarpiece in the church of San Salvador at Ejea de los Caballeros and the *retablo* of Saint James the Greater for the parochial church of Épila (Saragossa). The figure of Martín de Soria grew in stature with the discovery of his signature, *MARTIN DE SORIA PINTO* (Painted by Martín de Soria), and the date of completion—1485—on two scenes of the main altarpiece in the parish church of Pallaruelo de Monegros (Huesca). A large-size *retablo*, the altarpiece was composed of a socle devoted to biblical prophets considered to have foretold the birth of Jesus, a predella with scenes of the Passion (from the Garden of Gethsemane to the Crucifixion), and a body of five three-storeyed panels, devoted to the Life of Jesus, from his Birth to his Ascension, in addition to the Pentecost and the Final Judgment. The protecting frames or *polseras* featured figures of prophets, coat of arms, and angels bearing instruments of the Passion. In the seventeenth century the rudimentary tabernacle and its image that occupied the center of the predella was replaced by others in baroque style. Partially destroyed during the Spanish Civil War of 1936, all that remains of the work today are the predella and a panel featuring the scene of the Crucifixion preserved in the museum of Huesca cathedral.

Recent documentary findings confirm the attribution to Martín de Soria of a number of works that had hitherto been assigned to him on stylistic grounds, such as the panels of Saints Michael the Archangel and Catherine of Alexandria from the church of San Pablo in Saragossa. They were once part of an altarpiece commissioned in November 1459 by Miguel de Valtueña, a merchant, for his funerary chapel. Another altarpiece whose attribution is confirmed by the documents is the *retablo* of Nuestra Señora del Campo in Asín (Saragossa), preserved in its parish church and commissioned by the parishioners in February 1471. Other preserved works by the artist are the retablo of Saint Blaise in the parochial church of Luesia (Saragossa) which bears the date of its completion, 1464, and the recently discovered altarpiece of Saint Mary Magdalen in the parochial church of Zuera (Saragossa). His style represents

21. Tomás Giner
Saint Vincent Martyr
1467
Tempera on wood
Museo Nacional del Prado, Madrid

northern naturalism and a demonstrable familiarity with the engravings of Martin Schongauer, which de Soria interprets with great formal elegance. His work is distinguished by attention to the historical recreation of his subjects, both in the interior spaces that reproduce contemporary architecture of the second half of the fifteenth century, as well as in the dress of his protagonists—among them Muslims and Jews.

Another painter of the later fifteenth century, Juan de la Abadía "el mayor,"[8] is documented in the city of Huesca between 1469 and 1498, the year of his death. His work is outstanding for its quality. During his youth, Juan de la Abadía "el mayor" may have lived in Barcelona and collaborated with Pedro García de Benabarre and Miguel Nadal in the painting of the altarpiece of Saints Clare of Assisi and Catherine of Alexandria in the cathedral of Barcelona. By 1469 he had returned to Huesca and, in that year, he committed to paint an altarpiece for the city of Barbastro. From this date until his death, commissions ensued from parish churches and confraternities in Huesca and its province. De la Abadía may have already enjoyed a certain popularity by 1473, as is indicated by that year's commission for the main *retablo* in the cathedral of Jaca devoted to Saint Orosia, the city's patron saint. The altarpiece had been paid in full by 1469, but was inaugurated only in October of 1499, after the painter's death. Although the work is now lost, it undoubtedly influenced the number of commissions he received for other Huescan *retablos*, such as the altarpiece of the Virgin and Child for the parochial church of Sorripas, whose main panel is preserved today in the museum of Jaca cathedral.

In 1474 Juan de la Abadía "el mayor" created the *retablo* of Saints Vincent, Lawrence, and Michael the Archangel in the parochial church of Labuerda, which, fortunately, has been preserved. In 1490 he was commissioned to paint the altarpiece of Saint Catherine of Alexandria in the church of Santa María Magdalena, Huesca. A number of its panels have survived and are today in collections in Europe and the United States. This altarpiece is cited as a model in the contract for the *retablo* devoted to Saint Barbara for the hermitage of the martyrs Nunilo and Alodia of Huesca that was completed in 1493. Two of its panels are today in the museum of Huesca cathedral. Other undocumented *retablos* can also be attributed to the artist, since his style is easily identifiable. For example, the altarpiece of Saint Quiteria, originally from the church of San Pedro in Alquézar and today located in the collegiate church of Santa María in the same town, features compositions found in his documented *retablos*.[9]

The painter Pedro García was a native of the village of Benabarre (Huesca) who is documented living in Aragon and Catalonia between 1445 and 1483. His pictorial style is known from the main panel of the *retablo* of the Virgin of Bellcaire (Lérida), today in the Museu Nacional d'Art de Catalunya, which bears an inscription confirming his authorship: *PERE GARCIA MA PINTAT ANY 14…*(Pere Garcia painted me in the year 14…). His significant professional activity, made possible by a workshop populated with collaborators and disciples, resulted in the proliferation of his style in eastern Aragon until the beginning of the sixteenth century.

His career had begun in Saragossa, where he is first mentioned between the years 1445 and 1447 as a witness to contracts of Blasco de Grañén who was probably his master. To the period of Pedro García's training in de Grañén's workshop can be attributed three altarpieces, now damaged, that are preserved in the church of San Pedro de Siresa (Huesca). These *retablos*, devoted to the Holy Trinity, to Saint Stephen, and to Saint Blaise, are part of the church's Gothic furnishings, along with the *retablos* of Saint James the Greater and Saint John the Evangelist painted by Blasco de Grañén. The influence of Blasco de Grañén is also apparent in the main *retablo* of the church of the Virgen del Rosario in Villarroya del Campo (Saragossa), recently attributed to García's early period.

In June 1446 Pedro García was commissioned to paint a *retablo* for a small village near Barbastro (Huesca). In 1449, in Saragossa, he painted an altarpiece for Villar de los Navarros, near Daroca (Saragossa). In February of 1452 he was residing in Benabarre, his town of birth. By that time he had relations in Barcelona and maybe even with the prominent Barcelonese painter of *retablos*, Bernardo Martorell, who in 1437 had created an altarpiece for the church of Santa María del Romeral in the small village of Monzón (Huesca), a locality very close to Barbastro and not too far from Benabarre. In November 1455 Pedro García signed a contract with Bernardo Martorell's widow and son, Bernardo, for a period of five years, to complete works that were unfinished at the time of Martorell's death. To the period of García's collaboration with the workshop of Bernardo Martorell belong a number of panels from the *retablo* of Saints Clare of Assisi and Catherine of Alexandria for the cathedral of Barcelona on which he worked with the Catalan painter Miguel Nadal.[10]

In 1460 García was living in Benabarre, where he is documented until 1469. During this period, he painted two *retablos* for the churches of San Francisco and of San Salvador in Barbastro (Huesca). Toward the end of his life, García lived in Barbastro where he had a workshop and painted a *retablo* of Saints Benedict and Victoria for the parish church of Graus (Huesca) and the altarpiece of the Virgin and Child originally in the church of Montañana (Huesca), now in the Museu Nacional d'Art de Catalunya and private Catalan collections. Between May 1481 and September 1483, he painted the main *retablo* for the convent of San Francisco in Barbastro, in collaboration with the artists Joan Reg and Francisco Juan Baget.

Bartolomé de Cárdenas, called "el Bermejo," was a painter of *retablos* of Cordoban origin. From documents covering his professional life during the second half of the fifteenth and the beginning of the sixteenth centuries, he seems to have lived a nomadic artistic life working in the cities of Valencia, Daroca, Saragossa, and Barcelona, and possibly in Flanders where he would have studied new painting techniques. The artist's sojourn in Daroca documented in 1474 marks the beginning of his long career as a painter of *retablos* in Aragon. On September 5 of that year, he signed a contract for the main *retablo* of the church of Santo Domingo de Silos (Daroca), although he undoubtedly had resided there for some time and had carried out other commissions, including an altarpiece for the chapel of merchant Don Juan de Loperuelo in the

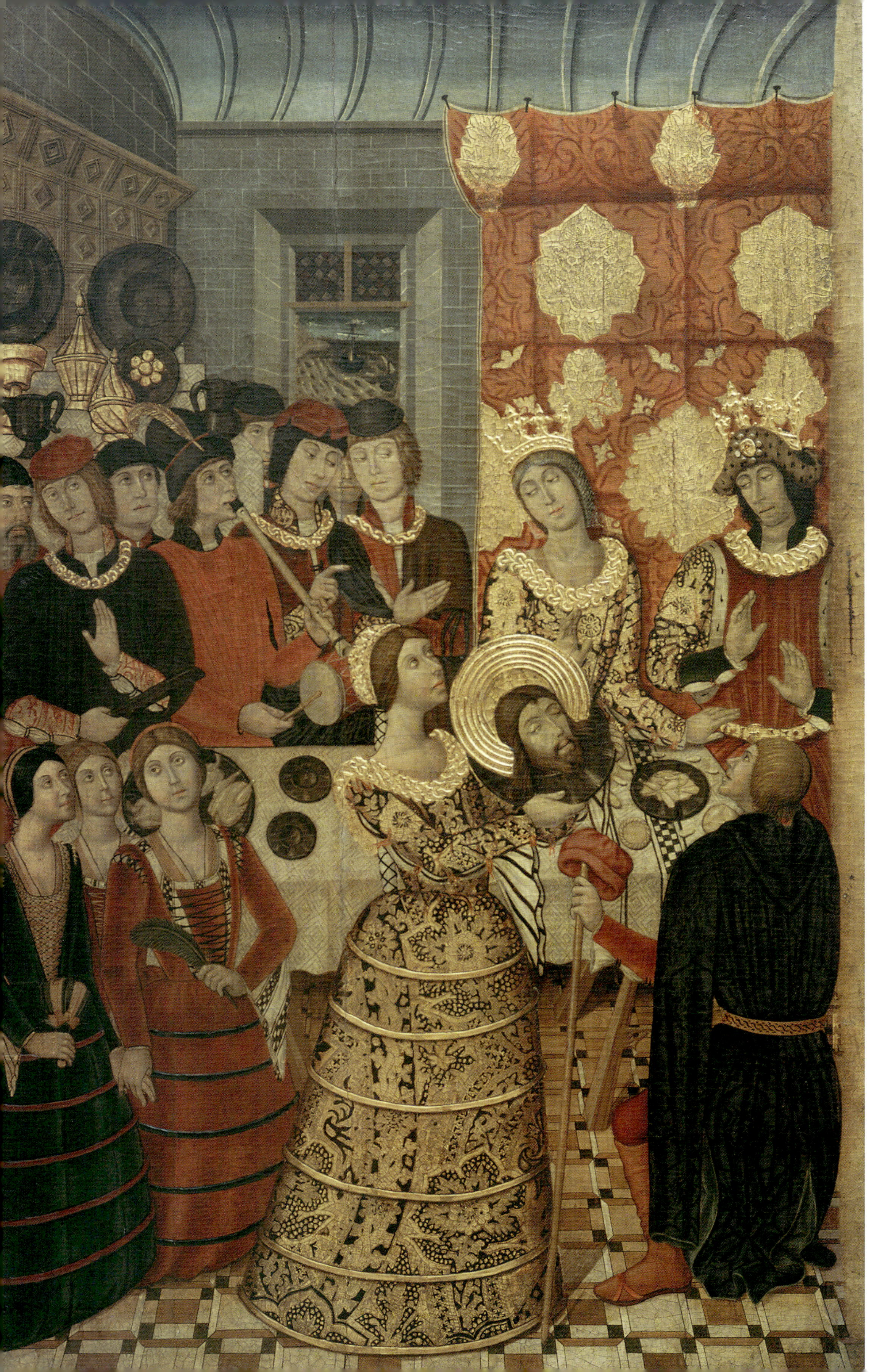

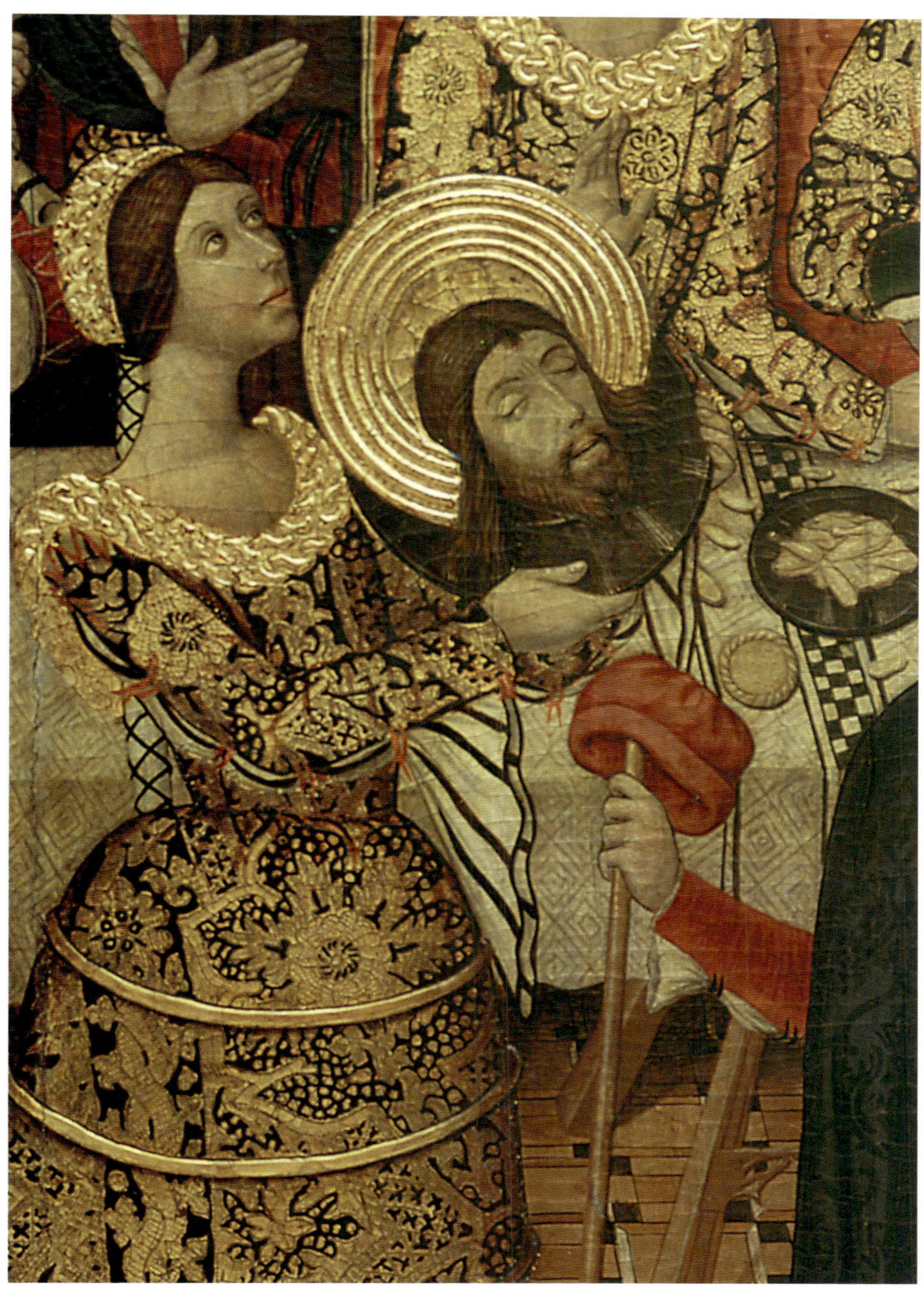

22. Pedro García de Benabarre
Altarpiece of Saint John
The Banquet of Herod, with the Figure of Salomé and the Head of John the Baptist
ca. 1470
Tempera on wood
78 × 49 × 3 in.
Museo Nacional d'Art de Catalunya, Barcelona

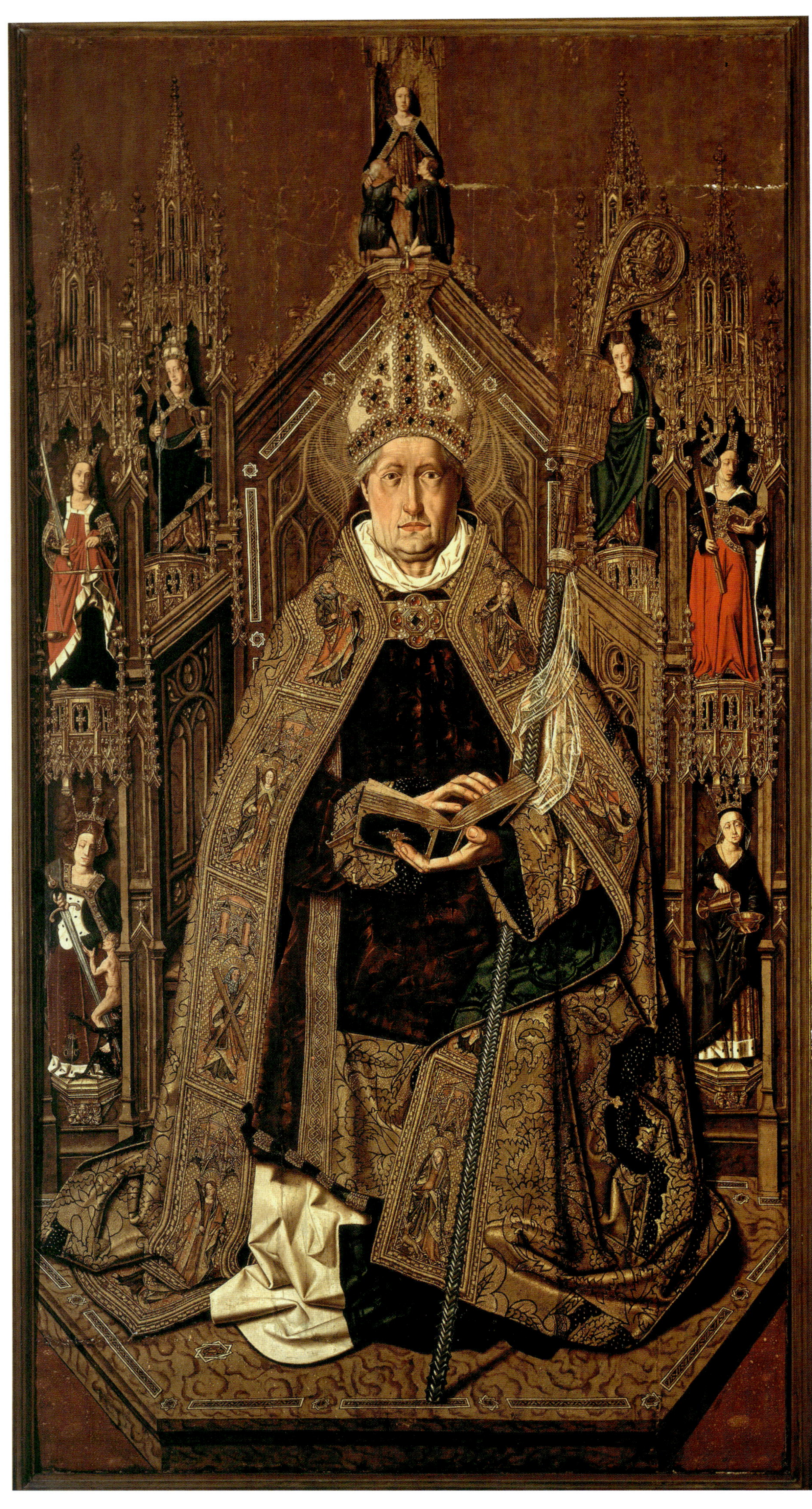

convent church of San Francisco, mentioned as an example in the Silos contract. He also created a *retablo* in Daroca devoted to Saint Engracia, a Saragossan martyr from the reign of Diocletian, of which a number of panels have survived and are today in the Museo de la Colegiata, Daroca, the Museo de Bellas Artes, Bilbao, the Isabella Stewart Gardner Museum in Boston, and the San Diego Museum of Art. By 1477 de Cárdenas resided in Saragossa where, on November 17, he undertook to paint the altarpiece of Santo Domingo de Silos in Daroca, then still unfinished, in collaboration with Martín Bernat, the Saragossan painter (figure 23).

Two years later, Bermejo agreed to paint an altarpiece devoted to the Virgen de la Misericordia for the chapel of merchant Don Juan de Lobera, in the cloister of Santa María del Pilar in Saragossa, with the collaboration of Martín Bernat, which signifies the continuous professional relationship between the two painters. This *retablo*, of which a number of panels have survived, including the main one preserved today at the Grand Rapids Art Museum, was completed a year after the contract was signed (figure 24). In fact, on December 10, 1479, Juan de Lobera, Martín Bernat, and Bartolomé Bermejo declared their mutual agreement satisfied, indicating that the commission had been already fulfilled.

From May 1, 1482, until May of the following year, Bermejo is one of the painters who worked on the restoration of the main *retablo* of the cathedral of San Salvador in Saragossa. Work on the altarpiece, whose polychromy had been damaged in an accidental fire in May 1481, took a year and a half. Documents preserved in the cathedral's archive indicate the costs of the restoration as well as the names of the artists involved, all of them well-known painters of Aragonese *retablos*: Bartolomé Bermejo, Miguel and Bartolomé Vallés—a father and son of Castilian origin—Martín Bernat, and Miguel Jiménez, from Castile. That Bermejo charged a higher fee for his work than his colleagues and had the privilege of his own room at the work site indicate the high professional recognition he enjoyed among his contemporaries. Bermejo's stay in Aragon lasted more than ten years. Nevertheless, a number of questions remain unanswered concerning his arrival in Daroca from Valencia, the cause of his removal from Daroca to Saragossa, and the ultimate reason for his departure to Barcelona, where he is documented as living from October of 1486 until May 1501. These moves might have been for professional or personal reasons.

Bermejo's works are exemplary for the brilliancy of their polychromy, created in oil with a Flemish technique, and for his use of light and chiaroscuro to faithfully reproduce the material quality of depicted objects. His religious compositions recreate, with elegant realism, the period in which he lived—Spain under the rule of the Catholic Kings. His work thus becomes a source of information about the society of his time, which, not undeservedly, was one of the most fascinating of the fifteenth century.

Martín Bernat is documented in the city of Saragossa between 1445 and 1505, the year of his death. Painter of *retablos* for the three Aragonese provinces—Saragossa, Huesca, and Teruel—he enjoyed a rather privileged position in his native city that enabled him to

23. Bartolomé Bermejo
Altarpiece of Saint Dominic of Silos
Saint Dominic of Silos enthroned as a Bishop
1474–77
Oil on panel
95 × 51 in.
Museo Nacional del Prado, Madrid

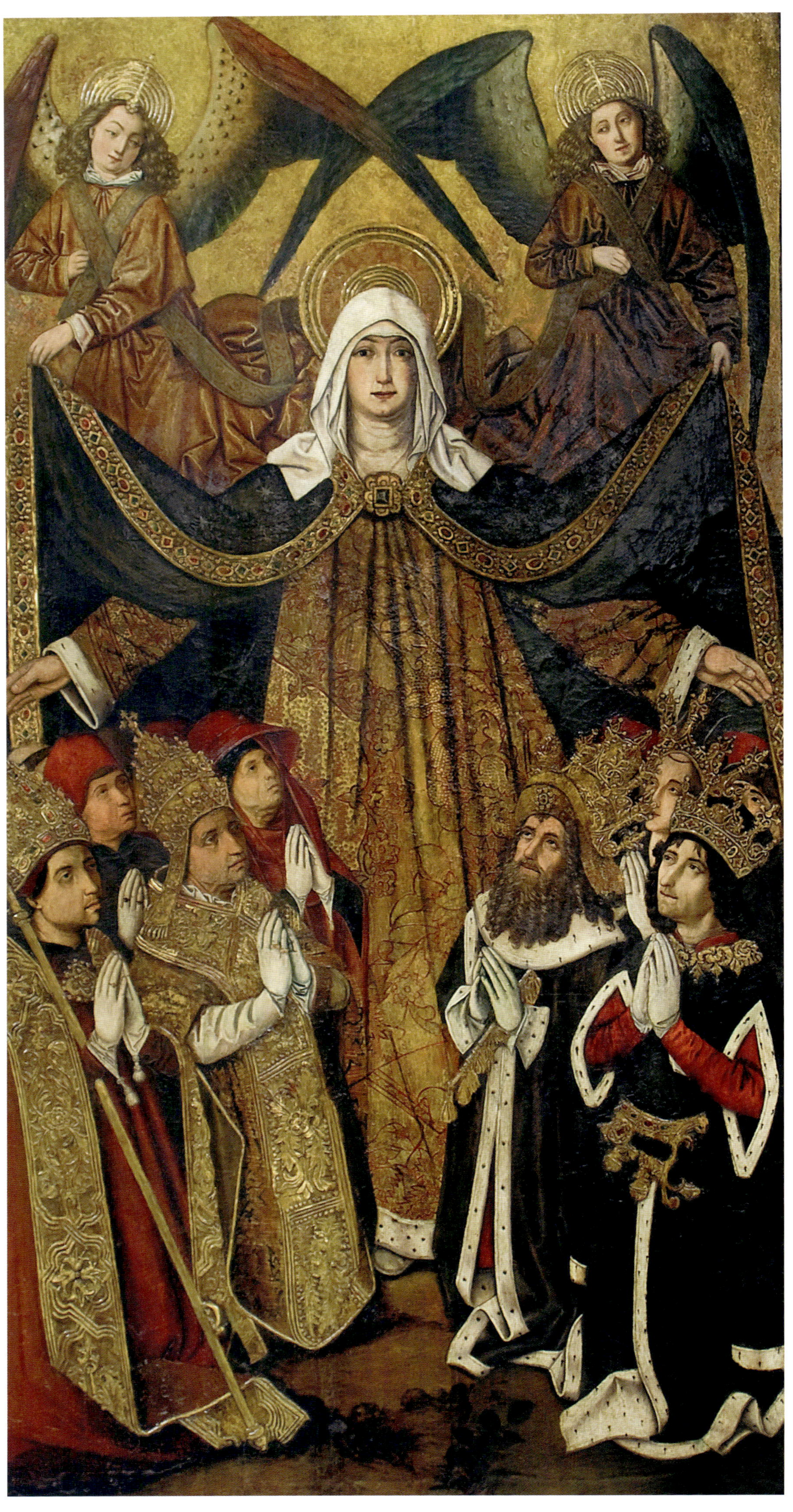

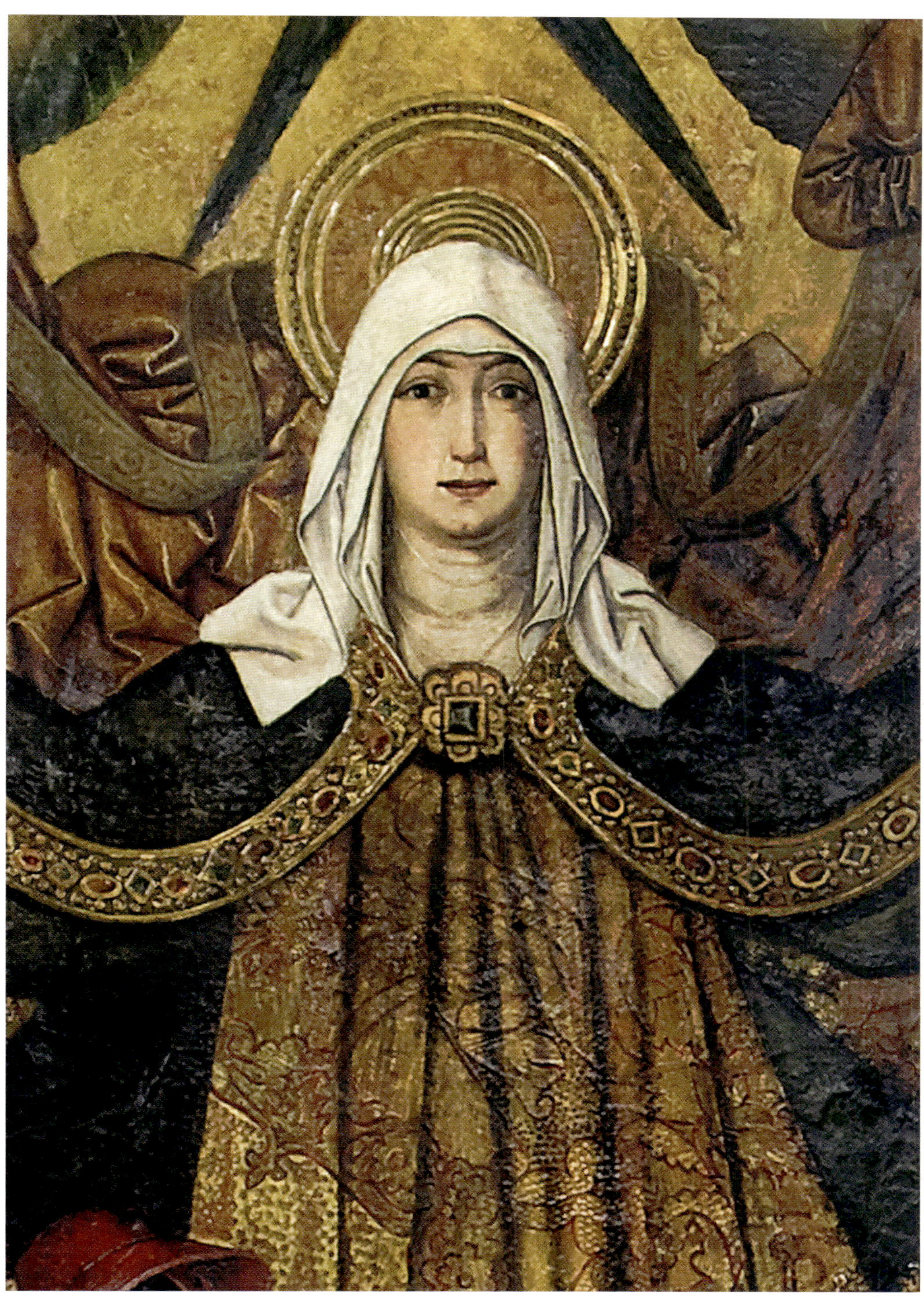

24. Bartolomé Bermejo and Martín Bernat
Virgin of Mercy from the church of Santa María del Pilar, Saragossa
1479–80
Oil on panel
78 × 45 ⅜ in.
Grand Rapids Art Museum, Michigan

come into contact with prominent figures in the art field, such as sculptors, engravers, and painters. His collaboration with the painter Bartolomé Bermejo gave him access to the latter's models, as evinced by Bernat's Virgen de la Misericordia, the main image of the altarpiece of the Talavera family in the cathedral of Tarazona (Saragossa), in which the artist returned to a composition he had created with Bermejo for the chapel of merchant Don Juan de Lobera in Santa María la Mayor of Saragossa. This is also true for the central panel of the main *retablo* from Santo Domingo de Silos in Daroca (today in the Museo del Prado), and in the panel of Saint Victorián in the cathedral of Barbastro, and in the figure of Saint Blaise in the parochial church of Lécera (Saragossa).

Martín Bernat proved to be more original in his depiction of Saint John the Baptist, once the principal panel of the main altarpiece of the church in Zaidín (Huesca), painted between 1493 and 1495, and today in the Museo Diocesano y Comarcal of Lérida; and in the *retablo* of the Virgin of Montserrat in the church of San Miguel Arcángel in Alfajarín (Saragossa). In both these compositions, as well as in the one devoted to the Temptation of Saint Anthony, Bernat demonstrates his knowledge of the engravings of Martin Schongauer. In his frequent collaborations with Miguel Jiménez, such as the main altarpiece for the church of Santa Blesa (Teruel)—the most important of their surviving joint works—Bernat's style is clearly discernible for being more traditional, and thus more Gothic, than that of his partner. Painted between 1481 and 1487, this large altarpiece is devoted to the Finding of the True Cross by Saint Helena, mother of Emperor Constantine, and to several episodes from the Passion (figure 25). Martin Schongauer's engravings were used as models for certain scenes, for example Jesus before Caiphas, while others recreate urban scenes populated by figures elegantly dressed according to the fashion of the Catholic Kings. The altarpiece is preserved almost in its entirety in the Museo de Bellas Artes in Saragossa.

Martín Bernat's well-designed and brilliantly colored paintings belong to the late Gothic style in Aragon that was imbued with influences from the Low Countries and Germany, received through engravings such as Schongauer's which Bernat could have seen at the workshop of his friend Pablo Hurus, a Saragossan printer and book dealer.

Miguel Jiménez, a painter of Castilian origin, settled in the city of Saragossa in 1462 and lived there until his death in 1505. He occupied the post of painter to King Ferdinand the Catholic, following the death of Tomás Giner. Jiménez's professional collaborations with Bermejo were not as frequent as those with Bernat, but the two painters had worked together on the restoration of the polychromy of the main altarpiece of the cathedral of Saragossa between 1482 and 1483. Jiménez's joint projects with Bernat included sizable altarpieces, such as the main *retablo* for the church of San Gil Abad in Saragossa, commissioned in 1477 and now lost, and the altarpiece of Saint Peter the Apostle for the cathedral of San Salvador in Saragossa, commissioned in 1482 and known from a drawing today in the Archivo Histórico de Protocolos Notariales in Saragossa that was presented by the two art-

25. Miguel Jiménez and Martín Bernat
Altarpiece of the True Cross
Saint Helena Meeting with the Jews (detail)
1485–87
Oil on panel
61 × 45 in.
Museo de Zaragoza, Saragossa

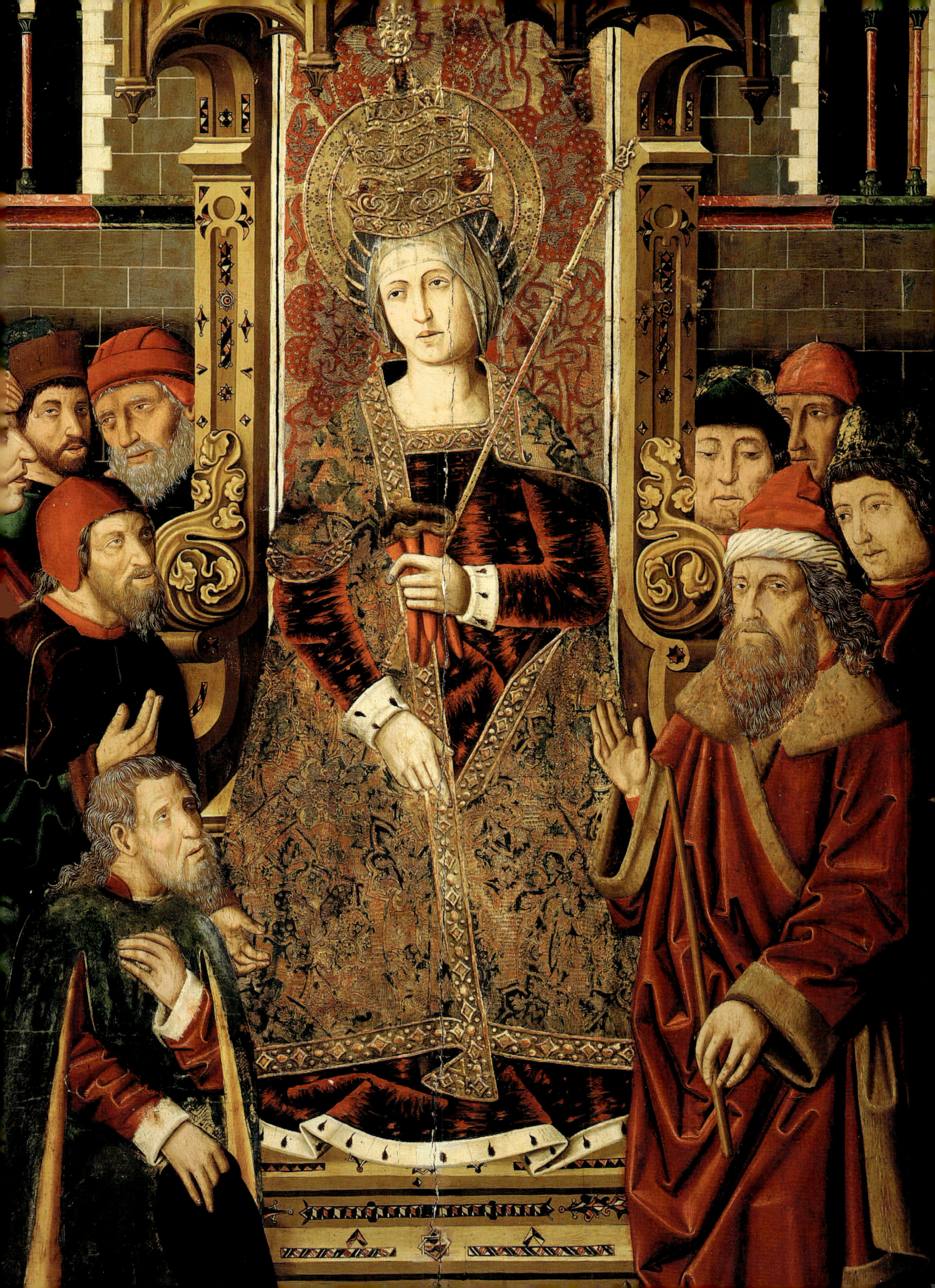

ists as a model, at the time the contract was signed. Other important joint works include the main altarpiece of the parochial church of Blesa (Teruel), previously mentioned; the main *retablo* of the convent of San Agustín in Saragossa, commissioned in 1489, whereabouts now unknown, and the main *retablo* of the church of Salvatierra in Escá (Saragossa), commissioned in 1496. The latter's tabernacle, as well as one panel depicting the Resurrection, have survived and are kept in the parochial church in Escá. Jiménez and Bernat also painted the doors of the organ box at the church of San Pablo in Saragossa in 1482. Either alone, or in conjunction with others, such as his son Juan, Miguel Jiménez painted *retablos* that display a pictorial style of great formal elegance and carefully applied polychromy.

One of the last works created by Jiménez in collaboration with his son is the main *retablo* of the church of Tamarite de Litera (Huesca), commissioned in 1500, of which a number of panels have survived, including one featuring Saint Michael Archangel, which is preserved in the Philadelphia Museum of Art. Also by Jiménez is the *retablo* depicting Saint Martin of Tours between Saint John the Evangelist and Saint Catherine of Alexandria, created in 1498 for the church of San Pablo in Saragossa, of which three main panels are preserved in the city's Museo de Bellas Artes. The central panel is devoted to Saint Martin's charity and shows him dividing his cloak into two halves in order to give one part to a poor man he had encountered at the outskirts of the French city of Amiens. It is notable for its background featuring a cityscape. Miguel Jiménez also painted the *retablo* of Saint John the Baptist between Saints Fabian and Sebastian that was commissioned in 1494 for the monastery of Santa María in Sijena (Huesca), and is today at the Museu Nacional d'Art de Catalunya. The altarpiece featuring a Pietà between Saint Michael Archangel and Saint Catherine of Alexandria, created for the church of Santa María at Ejea de los Caballeros, is also by Jiménez, as is indicated by the signature inscribed in the predella: *MIGEL XIMENEZ ME PINTO* (Migel Ximenez painted me). The *retablo*'s panels are currently distributed between the Museo del Prado and the archiepiscopal palace of Saragossa.

In the late Middle Ages, the Crown of Aragon sustained a rich cultural life. The complex and beautiful altarpieces of the period are witnesses to the flourishing of the arts in the fourteenth and fifteenth centuries.

ENDNOTES

1   The medieval Kingdom of Aragon was called the Crown of Aragon.

2   In the province of Huesca, the most important groups of mural paintings are to be found in the diocesan museums of the cities of Jaca, Barbastro, and Huesca, and in the churches of San Miguel Arcángel in Barluenga, San Fructuoso de Tarragona in Bierge, San Miguel Arcángel de Foces in Ibieca, and Nuestra Señora del Monte in Liesa. In the province of Saragossa, the most noteworthy mural paintings are preserved in the village of Sos del Rey Católico (in the church of San Esteban, in the church of Santa Lucía—previously known as San Miguel Arcángel—and in the chapel of San Martín de Tours in the Palacio de Sada) and in the city of Daroca (in the church of San Juan Bautista or San Juan de la Cuesta and in the church of San Miguel Arcángel). Also significant are the paintings later discovered in churches of neighboring localities, such as those in the parochial church of Saint Blaise in Anento and in the church of the Virgen del Rosario in Balconchán. Important mural paintings are also preserved in the church of Santa María de Cabañas in La Almunia de Doña Godina, and in the church of San Nicolás in Azuara.

3   The Noli me Tangere is the name given to the New Testament episode in which the risen Christ meets Mary Magdalen and commands her not to touch him (John 20:11–17).

4   The altarpiece is missing the panels that once constituted the predella, as well as one part of the left panel—possibly depicting the Epiphany—and the frames that once protected the paintings. In addition, the lower section of the panel in the attic was severed, damaging the Crucifixion depicted there.

5   Editor's note: The Levís were probably *conversos* or descendants of *conversos*. (See Mann's essay in this volume, p. 89.)

6   Editor's note: The Zahortiga painters were *conversos*. (See Mann's essay, p. 90.)

7   For example, the *retablos* created for the collegiate church of Santa María la Mayor of Saragossa and for the churches of both Lanaja and Ontiñena, dependencies of the monastery of Santa María de Sijena (Huesca).

8   Juan de la Abadía was called "el mayor" to differentiate him from his son of the same name and trade, who both alone and sometimes in collaboration with his father and other artists (such as the Catalan Francisco Joan Baget) painted numerous *retablos* for the province of Huesca.

9   Other works that can be attributed to Juan de la Abadía "el mayor" are the panels featuring Saint Michael Archangel and Saint Sebastian, once part of the main *retablo* of the church of San Esteban de Aniés (Huesca) and today in the Museo Lázaro Galdiano in Madrid, and the panel with Saint Michael Archangel originally from the church of Liesa (Huesca), now preserved in the Museu Nacional d'Art de Catalunya.

10 From the same period is the *retablo* of Saints Quiricus and Julita, originally from San Quirce de la Serra, and located today in the Museo Diocesano, Barcelona. García's works of the following period, when he alternated his residence between Benabarre and Lérida, include the beautiful altarpiece from the church of San Juan del Mercado in Lérida whose panels are now distributed in private collections, the Museu Nacional d'Art de Catalunya, and the Isabella Stewart Gardner Museum, Boston; the altarpiece of Bellecaire; and the *retablo* of the Virgin and Child with Saint Vincent Ferrer originally from the church of the Dominican convent in Cervera (Lérida) and today in the Museu Nacional d'Art de Catalunya. The altarpiece of Saint Anne from the collegiate church at Ainsa (Huesca) and several panels devoted to the Life of the Virgin Mary, to Saint Catherine of Alexandria, and to Saint James the Greater from the parochial church of Benabarre are today in various Catalan museums and collections.

JEWS AND ALTARPIECES IN MEDIEVAL SPAIN

— Vivian B. Mann

INTRODUCTION

At first glance, the title of this essay may seem to be an oxymoron, but the realities of Jewish life under Christian rule in late medieval Spain were subtle and complicated, even allowing Jews a role in the production of church art. This essay focuses on art as a means of illuminating relationships between Christians and Jews in the fourteenth and fifteenth centuries. Historians continue to discuss whether the *convivencia* that characterized the earlier Islamic rule on the Iberian Peninsula continued after the Christian Reconquest, the massacres following the Black Death in 1348 and, especially, after the persecutions of 1391 that initiated a traumatic period lasting until 1416. One view is that the later centuries of Jewish life on the Peninsula were largely a period of decline that culminated in the Expulsion from Spain in 1492 and the Expulsion from Portugal four years later. As David Nirenberg has written, "Violence was a central and systematic aspect of the coexistence of the majority and minorities of medieval Spain."[1] Other, recent literature emphasizes the continuities in Jewish life before and after the period 1391–1416 that witnessed the death of approximately one-third of the Jewish population and the conversion of another third to one half.[2] As Mark Meyerson has noted, in Valencia and the Crown of Aragon, the horrific events of 1391 were sudden and unexpected; only in Castile can they be seen as the product of prolonged anti-Jewish activity.[3] Still the 1391 pogroms were preceded by attacks on Jews during Holy Week, for example those of 1331 in Girona.[4]

      Nearly twenty years ago Thomas Glick defined *convivencia* as "coexistence, but... [with] connotations of mutual interpenetration and creative influence, even as it also embraces...

26. Pere Serra, Guerau Gener, and Lluís Borrassà
Altarpiece of the Virgin of Santes Creus
1403–11
Tempera and gilding on wood
216 × 135 in.
Monastery of Santes Creus, Tarragona

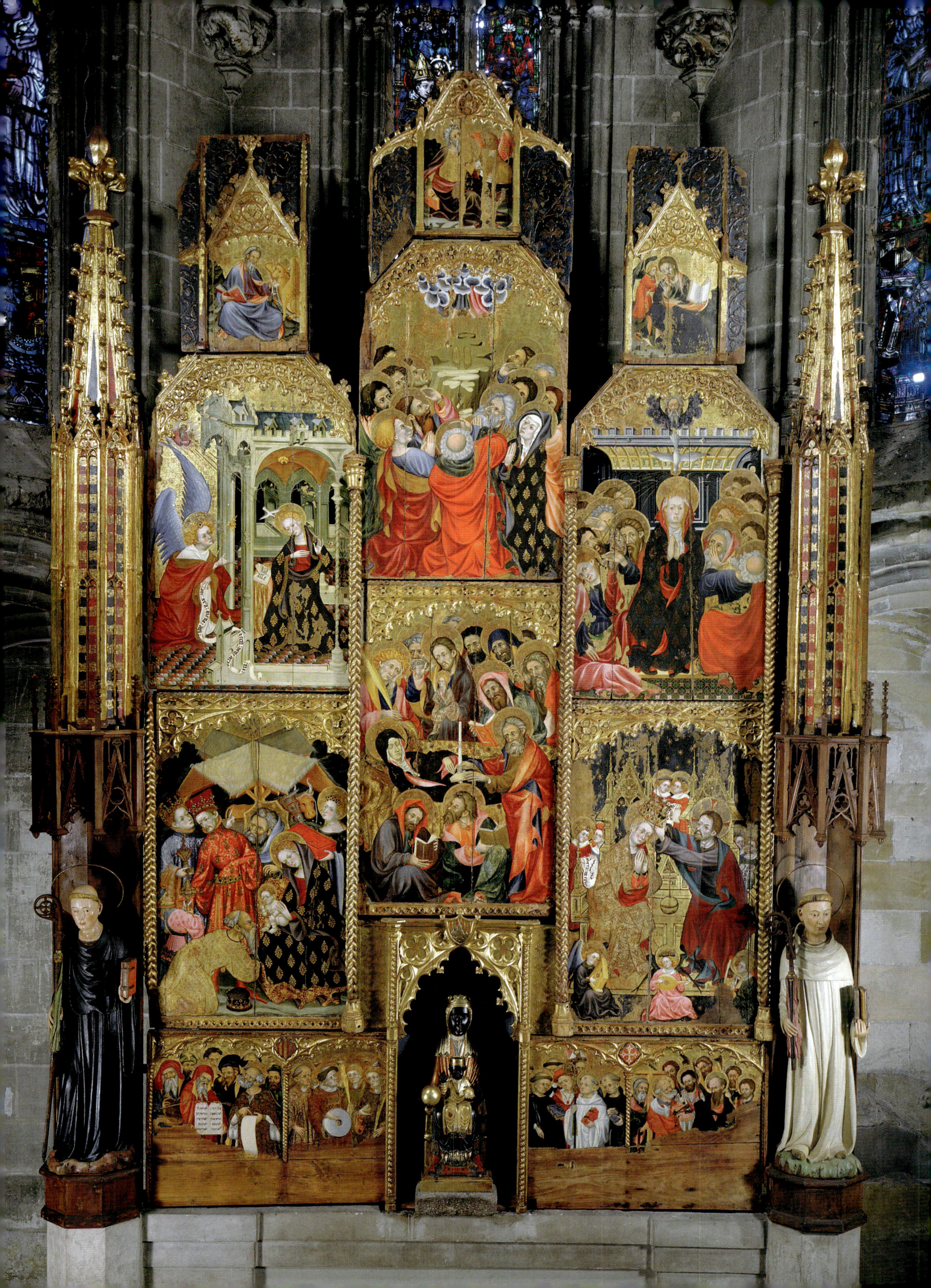

mutual friction, rivalry and suspicion."[5] His definition is still considered applicable to the relations between Christians and Jews in late medieval Spain.[6] The study of art produced in the last centuries of Jewish residence on the Peninsula may nuance our understanding of this *convivencia*.

None of the historians concerned with the nature of Jewish–Christian coexistence in the fourteenth and fifteenth centuries have analyzed the art of the period and the history of its production as a source for understanding relationships between Christians and Jews, or as evidence for knowledge of one another's religion. Despite the fact that Jews worked as artists for Christians, which suggests they were knowledgeable about Christian history and beliefs, and that Christian artists demonstrated an intimate knowledge of Jewish life by setting scenes from the Gospels and Christian lore within Jewish architectural and ceremonial contexts, the implications of these artistic themes have been ignored.[7] The failure to exploit this historical source may be due to a lack of knowledge of the arthistorical methodologies necessary to an understanding of medieval works of art, which are more than a product of the artist's imagination. The modern model of an artist who creates sculpture or painting according to his own ideas and design and then seeks a buyer for the finished piece could not be further removed from that of his medieval counterpart whose patrons, either individuals or institutions, initiated the production of a work, and specified its subject, constituent materials, and even its composition in detailed contracts. Consider for example this 1483 contract written for a painter, Pere Cabanes, who was to create an altarpiece in a Valencian funerary chapel:

> First, in the center, the image of the most glorious Virgin Mary that is [the same as the image of Mary] in the *retablo mayor* of the Cathedral of Valencia... and at the side...there is to be the image of Saint Augustine robed, I say robed with the chasuble and dalmatic and with ornaments in the dalmatic and on the shirt, all brocaded in fine gold...with the church in his hand, and from his hand should issue rays of gold...in addition it is agreed that the image of Saint Catherine Martyr is to be dressed with a beautiful ceremonial mantle, of beautiful folds, all brocaded in gold, the field of green, and the skirt below is to be of fine gold brocade on a carmine ground, and with its beautiful borders of garnishings of fine gold, and with the gold chain around her neck, and gold crown in her hair.[8]

This extract from the contract demonstrates the patron's role in choosing the subject of the altarpiece, its composition—that is the placement of the figures—and the manner in which they were to be represented. Again and again, the use of gold is stressed, an indication of the importance of this costly material. The contract further indicates how a medieval work was embedded in a tradition of representation linked to its subject matter, as when the text demands that the Virgin be based on the depiction of the same figure in the main altarpiece in the cathedral of Valencia.[9]

27. Anonymous
Scenes from the Life of Saint Martin
The Mass of Saint Martin
ca. 1401–99
Tempera on panel
44 × 37 in.
The Hispanic Society of America, New York (A9/1)

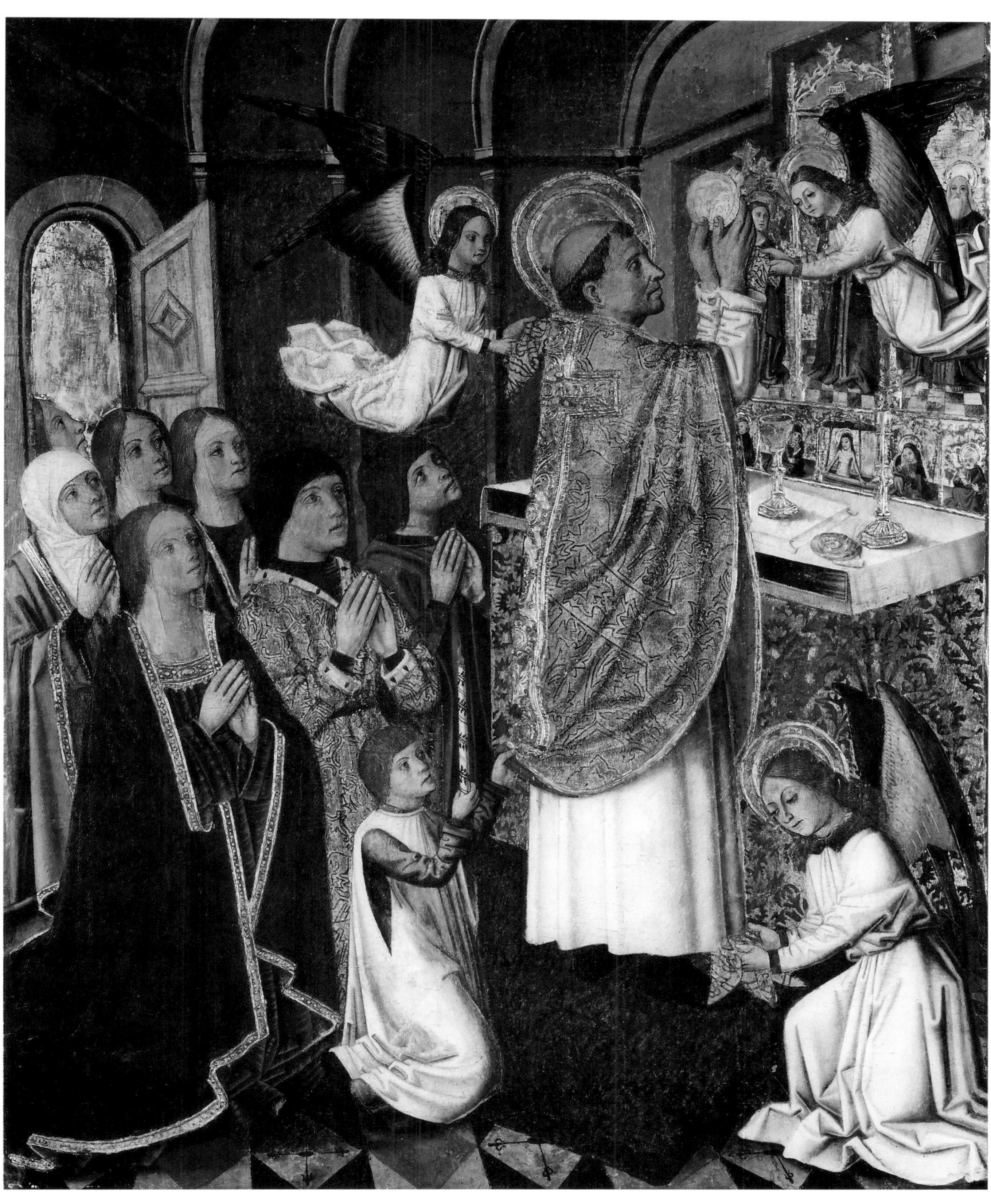

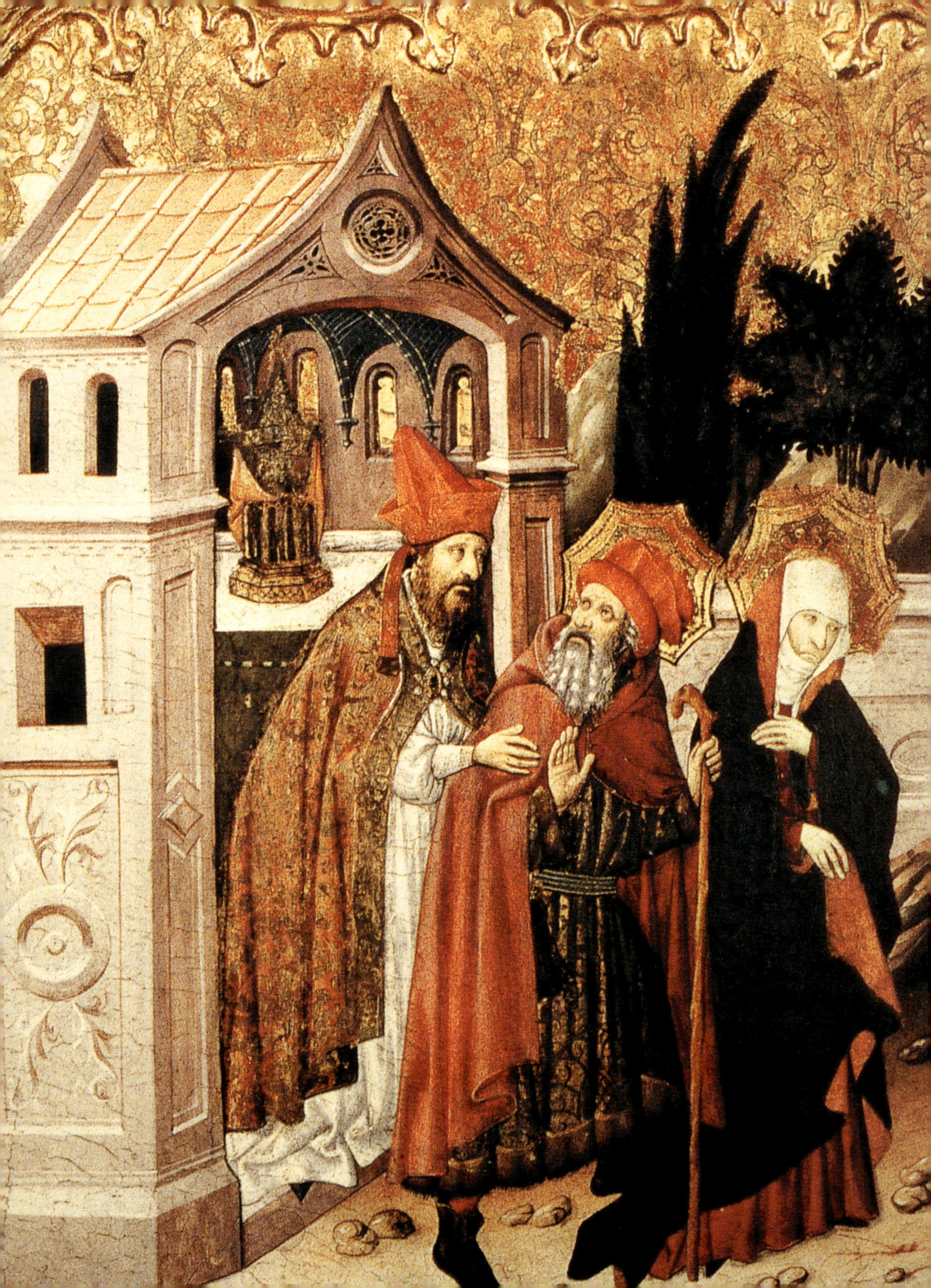

The existence of detailed contracts and traditional compositions did not prevent an artist from being innovative, however, introducing new elements that reflected contemporary concerns.[10] In fact, the innovations in a work that diverge from the conventional model are "red flags" calling attention to new content, although only a thorough knowledge of the available models allows the art historian to perceive what is innovative. When elements such as clothing, architectural settings, or the physiognomy of figures can be matched against contemporary textual descriptions, surviving buildings or objects, and comparative visual representations, the conclusion may be reached that painted scenes mirrored the reality before the artist's eyes, as Richard Ettinghausen noted in discussing Islamic miniatures: "Manuscripts inform us better than...any other medium about contemporary daily life in the Arab world."[11] The same is true of *retablos* according to Carmen Lacarra Ducay.[12]

Painters of altarpieces may have been compelled to introduce new subjects or contemporary details because of a change in form that was created in Spain around the second quarter of the fourteenth century. Acting to implement the ruling of the Fourth Lateran Council of 1215 requiring congregants to see the moment of Transubstantiation during mass, the churches moved their paintings off the altar to a position behind it (figure 27). The *retablos*, as they came to be called, were thereby freed from the spatial constraints of ordinary altarpieces, and grew in size, often reaching the height of the church vaults as at Teruel and Ejea de los Caballeros. This new art form allowed for many more panels and subjects surrounding the central depictions of saints or holy figures. The artists responsible for creating *retablos* were challenged to provide more complex iconographic programs than before, and the manner in which they met this challenge forms part of the present discussion.

Of course, the added scenes included Christian subjects, some of which necessarily involved Jewish characters, for example the Expulsion of Joachim and Anna—the parents of Mary—from the Temple on an altarpiece painted by the workshop of Blasco de Grañén between 1435 and 1445 (figure 28).[13] The expanded corpus also encompassed episodes from the Hebrew Bible, such as scenes of the Creation of the World, the Crossing of the Red Sea, and depictions of Jewish worthies like Kings David and Solomon and the Prophets (figure 29). Themes from the Apocrypha also took pictorial form, for example the conversion of Anianus,

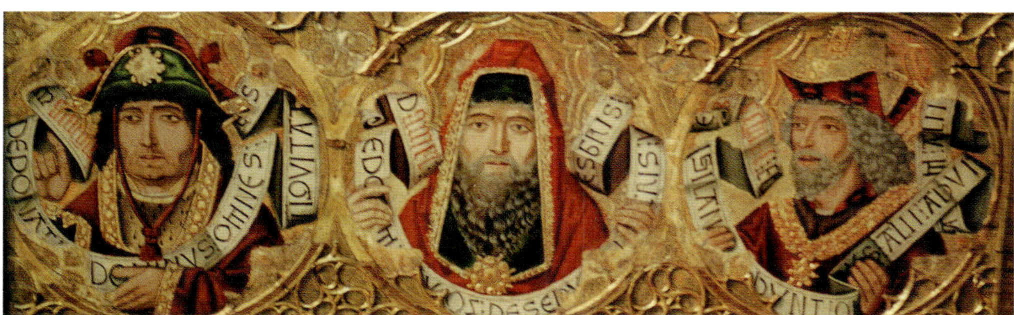

<table>
<tr><td>

28. Workshop of Blasco de Grañén
Altarpiece of the Virgin and Child
Expulsion of Joachim and Anna from the Temple (detail)
1435–45
Tempera on wood
47 ¼ × 29 ¹⁵⁄₁₆ in.
Parish church of Nuestra Señora del Rosario, Villarroya de Campo

</td><td>

29. Miguel Jiménez and Martín Bernat
Altarpiece of the True Cross
The Prophets Malachi, Daniel and Ezekiel
1485–87
Oil on panel
61 × 45 in.
Museo de Zaragoza, Saragossa

</td></tr>
</table>

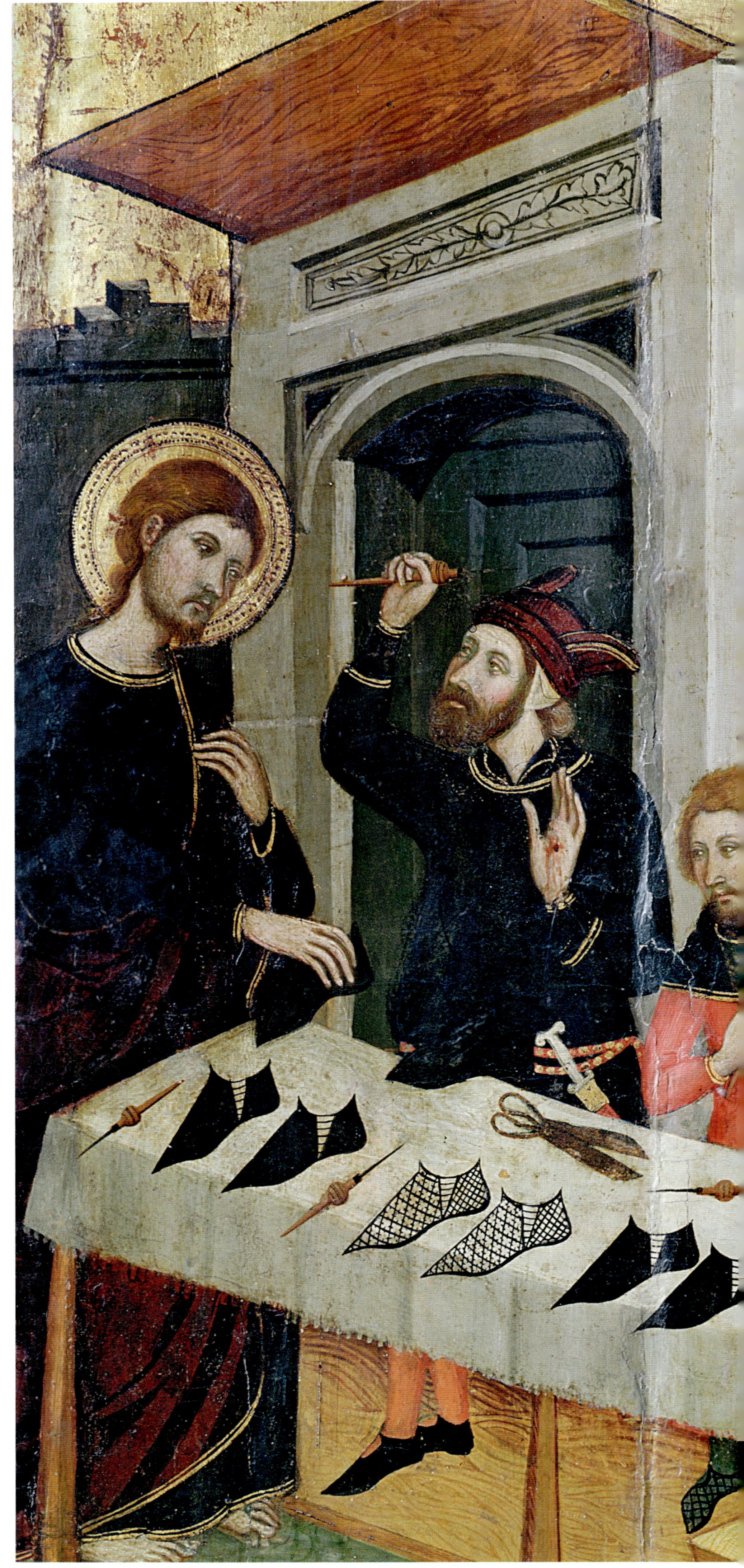

30. Arnau Bassa
    Altarpiece of Saint Mark
    A Shoemender's Stall
    1346
    Oil on panel
    89 × 94 in.
    Cathedral of Manresa, Catalonia

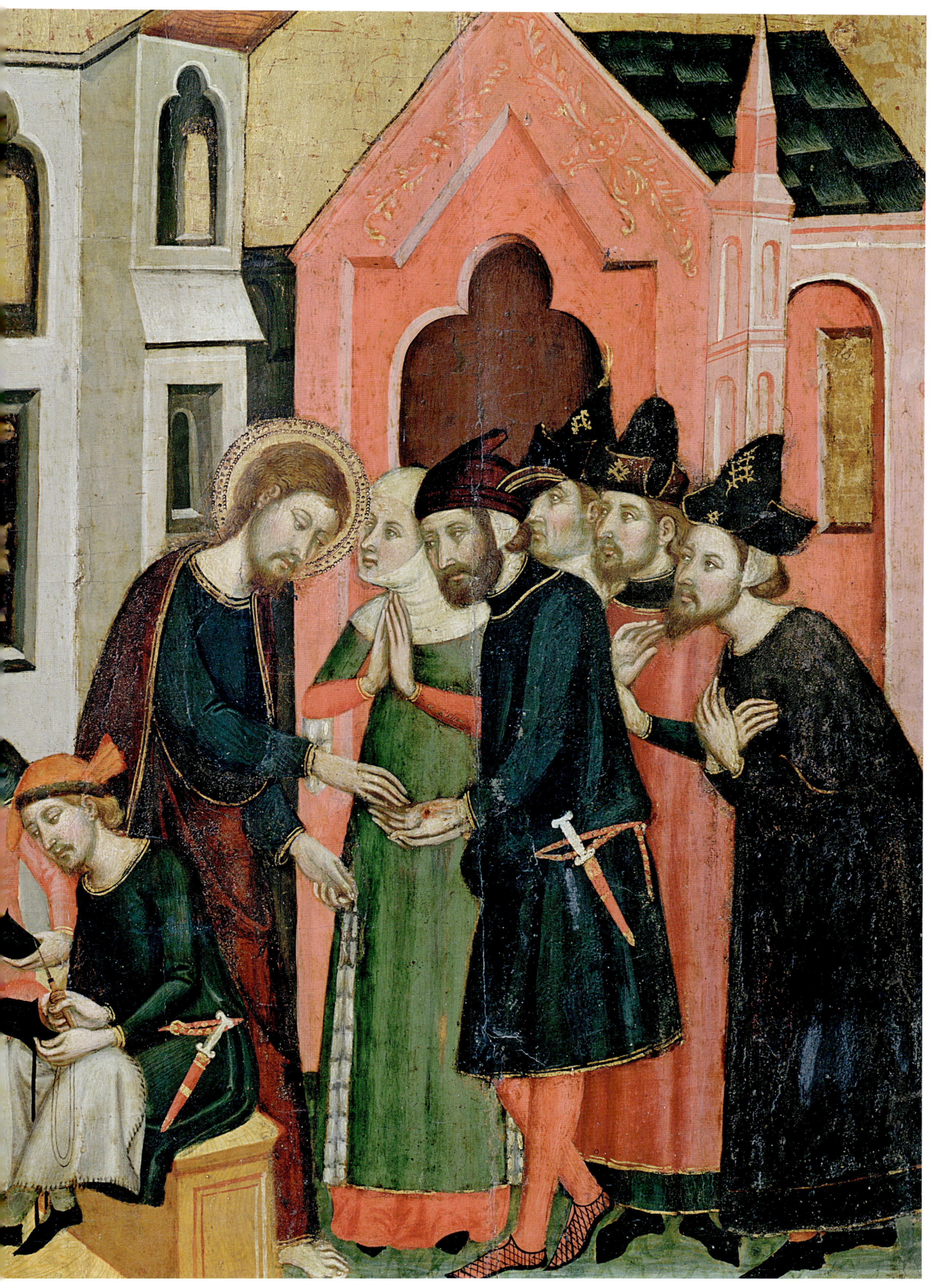

who became Saint Mark's successor as bishop of Alexandria ca. 61 C.E. According to the apocryphal Acts of Saint Mark, as the saint entered Alexandria his sandal strap broke and he sought a shoemaker to mend it. He found Anianus who pierced his own hand while mending the sandal.[14] The shoemaker cried out in pain to the One God, prompting Mark to heal Anianus' wound and then to preach to him and his family. Many of the listeners wear the pointed hats common to representations of medieval Jews of western Europe, but unusual in Spain. Anianus and his wife were then baptized.

All three episodes are portrayed on a *retablo* by Arnau Bassa. His depiction of the story emphasizes Anianus' profession as a shoemaker by placing him within an atelier that includes two other cobblers; their wares are spread out before them. This detailed history of Saint Mark's encounter with Anianus is explained by the role of the Shoemakers' Guild of Barcelona in commissioning the altarpiece in 1346–7; Saint Mark was their patron saint.[15] The role of the patrons is emphasized by the pattern of shoes on the robes of Anianus as he is consecrated as a bishop by Saint Mark in the central panel and by the carved shoes on the vertical frames that divide the *retablo* into three zones. Interestingly, the shoemakers shown in the first episode seem to be all Jews, recognizable by their beards and their red hair, long considered a sign of evil (figure 30).[16] Their depictions are a reflection of the large number of Jews engaged in shoemaking in medieval Spain, and represent an instance of transposing events from the life of Jesus and the saints to the period when the altarpiece was painted.[17] The scene showing Anianus and his wife being baptized also had contemporary relevance, since the pogroms accompanying the Black Death of 1348,[18] which occurred while the altarpiece was in process, led to the conversion of Jews such as Anianus (figure 31).[19] His baptism referenced contemporaneous conversions and exemplifies another category of altarpiece subjects involving Jewish figures—scenes of religious conflict between Jews and Christians.[20] Other such subjects are conversionist sermons, disputations, and the Host Libel.

In the thirteenth century, anti-Jewish libels involving young boys became widespread in Spain. The Host Libel, the charge that Jews desecrated the host by stabbing it, thereby symbolically killing the Christian god, developed in the late thirteenth century and appeared on Spanish altarpieces around the time of the Black Death, 1349–50, for which the Jews were blamed.[21] Two *retablos* from the monastery of Vallbona de les Monges created at that time show various scenes of host desecration: the host is stabbed; it is placed in a pot of boiling liquid; Jews are punished by being burned alive or they are converted.[22] Slightly later, 1363–70, is the more elaborate narrative on an altarpiece of the Virgin painted by the Serra atelier, a family workshop whose principals were Jaume (ca. 1358–90) and Pere (ca. 1360–1407) (figure 32).[23] The main predella scene, centrally placed, is the Last Supper; scenes of desecration are at both sides. At left, a Jew with red hair who is also dressed in red throws a wafer into the sea (figure 33). A more detailed sequence of events unfolds at right. A

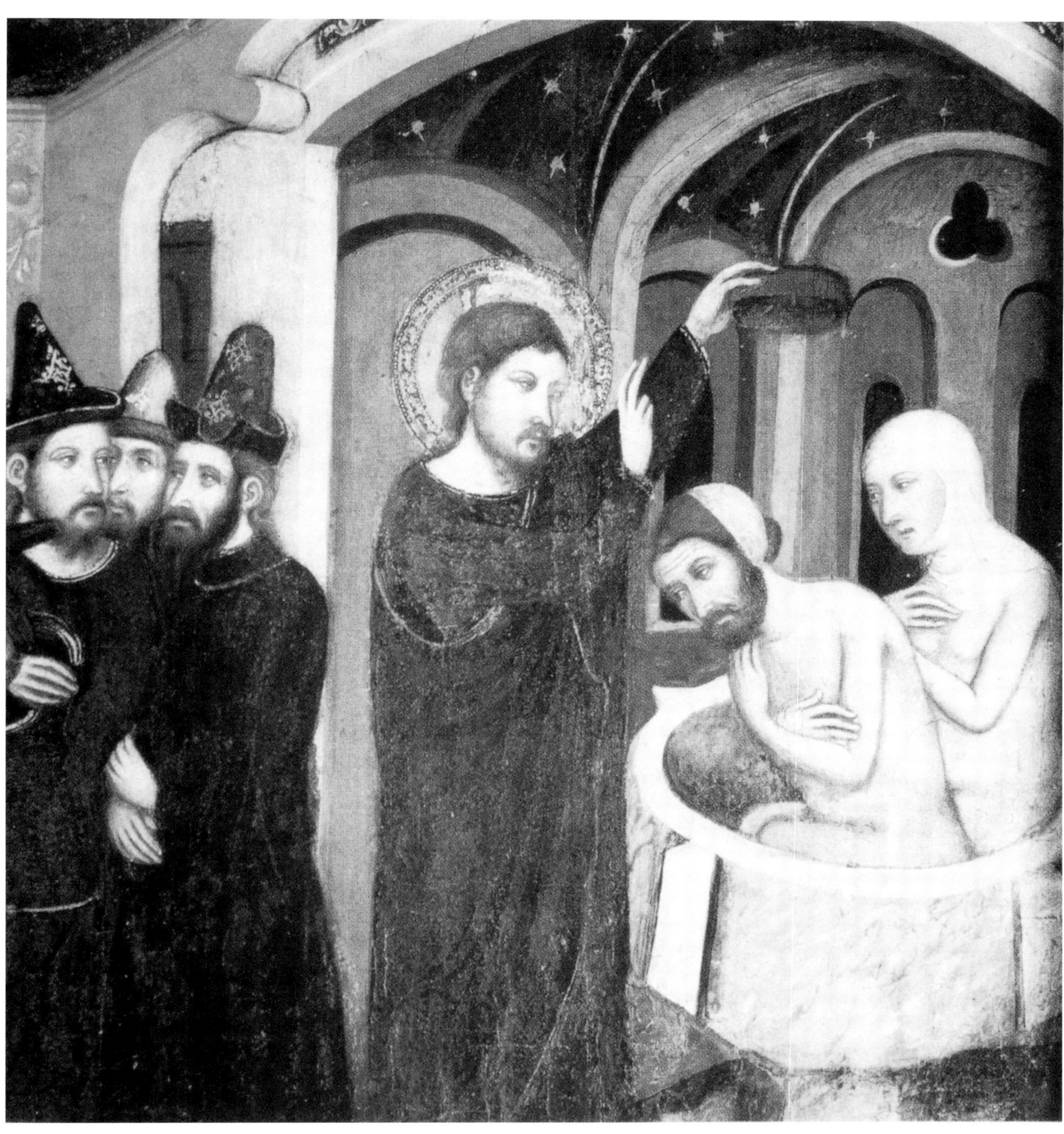

31. Arnau Bassa
     Altarpiece of Saint Mark
     Saint Mark Baptizing Anianus and his Wife (detail)
     1346
     Oil on panel
     Cathedral of Manresa, Catalonia

Christian woman presents a host to a Jewish man. He reappears in the main space piercing the host with a knife; blood streams forth. Simultaneously, a host that was thrown in a vat of boiling liquid is transformed into the Child. A Jewish woman identified by her distinctive headdress watches with emotion and restrains a young boy in the foreground whose gestures draw attention to the scene. Presumably, their actions express recognition of the truth of Transubstantiation, a major step on the road to conversion. At far right a woman who was originally Jewish as seen by her red hair receives communion from a cleric. The conversion of Jews is likewise a component of the written Host Libel narratives.[24]

Another scene expressing the uneasy relationship between Jews and Christians in the late Middle Ages is "A Disputation between Moses and Saint Peter," a panel from the predella of an altarpiece dedicated to the Mother of God painted for the monastery of Santes Creus by Pere Serra, Guerau Gener, and Lluís Borrassà in the early fifteenth century (figure 10).[25] The subject is based on actual debates between church prelates and rabbis in which Jews were forced to participate. Two of the most important disputations occurred in Barcelona in 1263 between the convert Pablo Christiani and the esteemed scholar, Moses ben Naḥman (Naḥmanides) and in Tortosa in 1413.

JEWISH ARTISTS WORKING FOR CHRISTIANS

Research in the archives of the Crown of Aragon has revealed the names of Jewish artists engaged in a variety of métiers.[26] Perhaps the most interesting for an essay devoted to *retablos* is the information on Abraham de Salinas, a painter in Saragossa who was commissioned by the cathedral of San Salvador (known as La Seo) to paint a *retablo* on the Life of the Virgin in 1393, just two years after the worst pogroms in Spanish history, although it must be noted that the Jewish community of Saragossa was one of two spared these attacks. Bonafós Abenxueu, a Jewish silversmith, contracted to provide the frame. Later, Abraham created two other *retablos* for the church of San Felipe in Saragossa, one on the Life of Saint Matthew and another devoted to Saint John the Baptist. He also painted a *retablo* for the parochial church of La Puebla de Alborton in the province of Saragossa, and a second altarpiece for the same church with six scenes depicting the story of the Annunciation to Mary. That Abraham de Salinas was given the commissions just mentioned, including repeat commissions from the same churches, testifies both to the fact that he was esteemed as a painter, and that he was able to produce various Christological themes that satisfied his patrons. Recently, Robert Chazan analyzed Hebrew polemical literature and concluded that Jewish polemicists knew Christian religious literature and utilized that knowledge in their arguments with Christian debaters.[27] Abraham's commissions suggest that the same was true for Jewish artists. They must have had sufficient visual models like those cited in the Cabanes contract, or a model book on Christian iconography, or they may have known a Christian textual source.

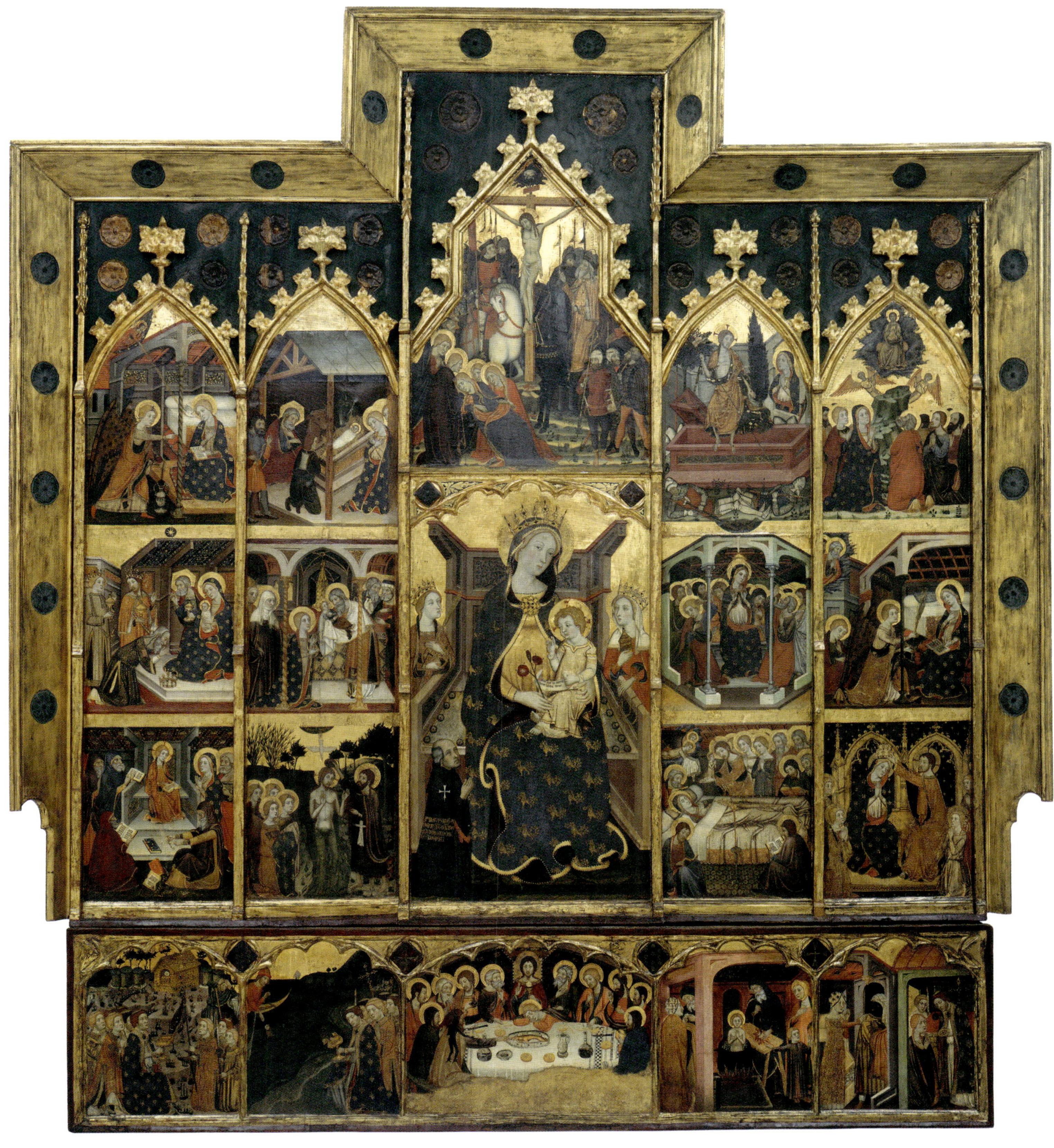

32. Pere Serra
     Altarpiece of the Virgin
     1362–75
     Tempera on panel
     135 × 128 in.
     Museu Nacional d'Art de Catalunya, Barcelona
     MNAC/MAC 15916

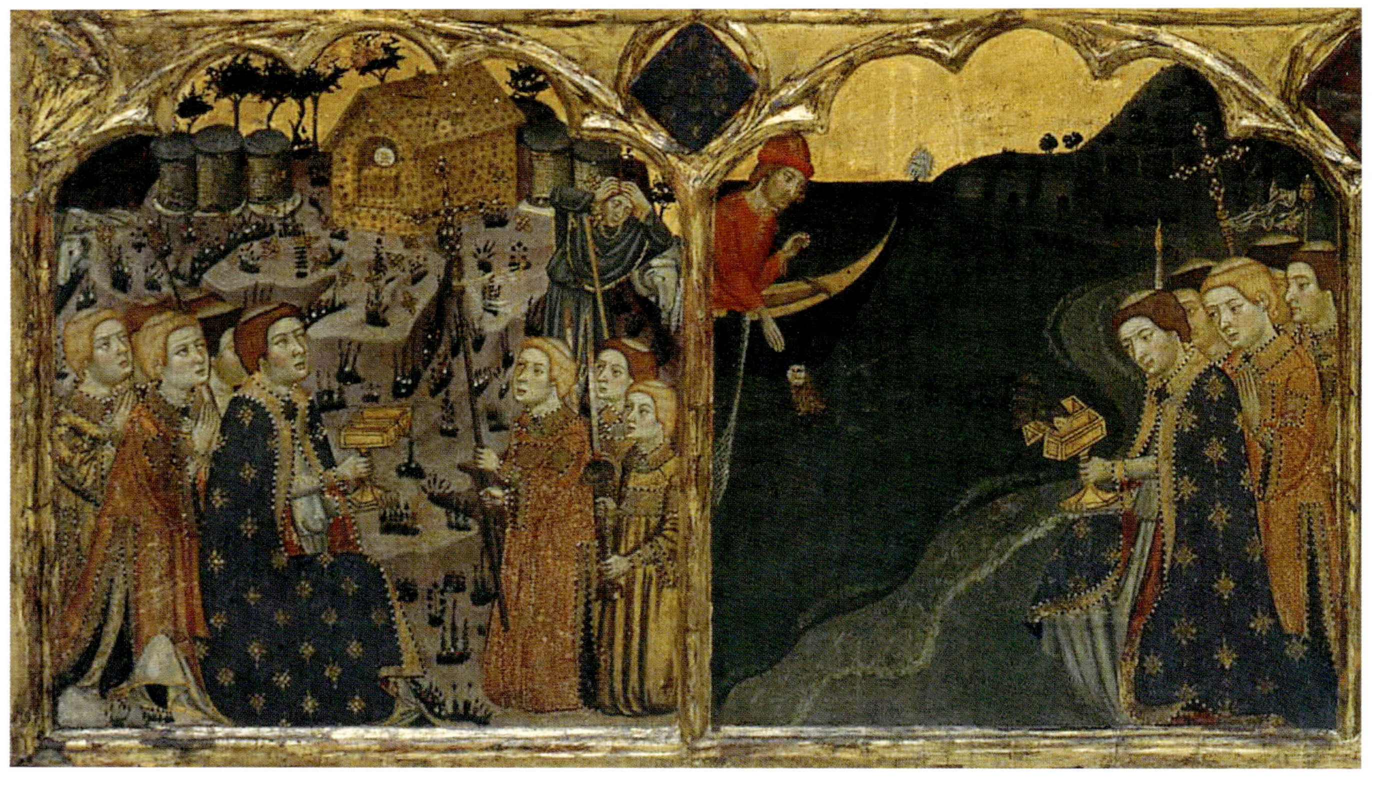

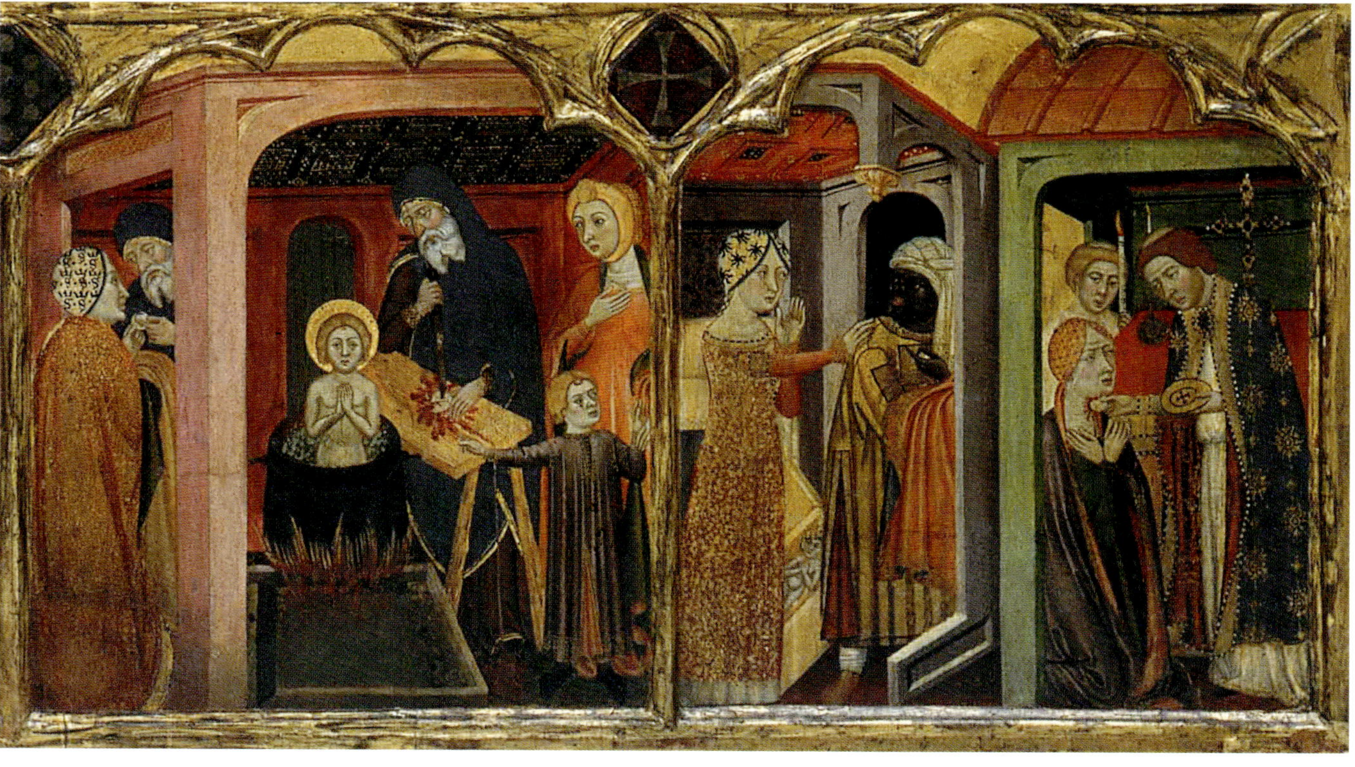

33. Pere Serra
Altarpiece of the Virgin
Predella with scenes of the Blood and Host Libels (detail)
1362–75
Tempera on panel
Museu Nacional d'Art de Catalunya, Barcelona
MNAC/MAC 15916

Bonafós Abenxueu, who made the frame for the La Seo altarpiece, was a silversmith, one of the many Jewish silversmiths of Saragossa who were numerous enough to support their own synagogue.[28] Confraternities of artists and craftsmen, both Jewish and Christian, organized to protect their religious concerns and for mutual support in areas of social welfare, were more numerous in Aragon than elsewhere in Christian Spain, and most Jewish confraternities were in Aragon, particularly in Saragossa.[29] The earliest recorded silversmith in Morella, Aragon, was the Jew Mose Alafoydar, nicknamed "the Jewish silversmith" in documents of 1334–35.[30] Mose had two brothers, Salomon and Caquo, who were also silversmiths. The Santalinea family of silversmiths who flourished in Morella during the second half of the century were *conversos*. In fourteenth- and fifteenth-century Morvedre (Aragon), silversmiths were the foremost artists in the Jewish community; indeed their work was so highly esteemed that they established branch workshops in other locales to which they regularly traveled, and apprentices from other cities came to study with them.[31] The prominence of Jews in silversmithing may be a legacy from their roles in areas previously under Muslim rule, since the *hadith*, the religious traditions of Islam, viewed metalworking as degrading and left it to Jews. Their knowledge of the forms of church vessels could have been acquired during the times that church silver was pawned with Jews or from works given to them as models for new commissions. In 1380 the sister of the bishop of Tarazona and the sacristan of the church in Borja pawned a silver cross, a reliquary, a censer, and an incense vessel with its ladle of silver with the Jew Yuçe Francés.[32]

Just as silversmiths became *conversos*, so did painters of altarpieces. Born and educated in the Jewish community, they later converted to Christianity, taking their Jewish educations with them. Among them were an uncle and nephew, Guillén and Juan de Leví, whose family name indicates a Jewish origin.[33] Nothing is known of Guillén until the 1380s when he is listed as a painter. Juan is undocumented until 1388 when he is named Guillén's heir. The lack of early records may be another indication of Jewish origins. Juan de Leví created a *retablo* for the tomb of the bishops of Tarazona, Pedro and Fernando Pérez Calvillo, brothers who succeeded one another in office. The existing biographical information on the Pérez Calvillo brothers begins only at the point of their service to the Church, which raises the possibility that they, too, were converts.[34] The brothers owned many houses in the Jewish quarter of Tarazona, the rents from which were used for the rebuilding of the cathedral. It is well known that *conversos* often had dealings with one another, and a similar sense of fraternity may have led Bishop Fernando to commission the altarpiece for his brother's tomb from Juan de Leví in 1408.

In the church of Rubielos de Mora is a *retablo* dated ca. 1420 that seems related to those of the de Leví atelier. The proportions of the panels and the Gothic framing devices are similar to those of the Tarazona altarpiece and the palette appears similar, for example the use of red clay earth in outdoor scenes.[35] The facial type of Jesus in the scene among the Doctors at Rubielos (figure 34) is similar to that of Saint Prudentius preaching in Calahorra (figure 35).

Both have pudgy faces, arched eyebrows, small eyes and mouths, features that appear to sit on the surface rather than emerging from the planes of the face. Their idealization contrasts with the Jewish figures in the scene of Christ among the Doctors, whose faces are individualized by features such as large noses, and whose purple robes signify their potential status as penitents.[36] All sit in a contemporary Gothic building. The Jews hold books with accurately formed Hebrew letters that suggest the texts were written by someone who had studied the Hebrew language (figure 36), which is not surprising if the painter was connected with the de Leví atelier. The *sottobanco*—the lowest register of the altarpiece at the viewers' eye level—is devoted to the depiction of twelve Hebrew prophets, an unusually large number on one *retablo* and a reflection of the significance of prophetic writings in Christian attempts to convince Jews to convert (figure 37).

In addition to painting *retablos,* Juan de Leví was also known for fabricating glass and his uncle, Guillén, produced paintings on clear and colored glass; for example, glass with the figures of the kings of Armenia, Norway, Bosnia and others.[37] Guillén was also a painter on panel and documents record a *retablo* of his as well as portraits of nobility. Nicolás and Bonanat Zahortiga who worked in the first quarter of the fifteenth century were also *converso* painters of *retablos.*[38] With continuing study in the Spanish archives more names of Jewish artists will probably emerge, although establishing a link to actual works may be difficult.

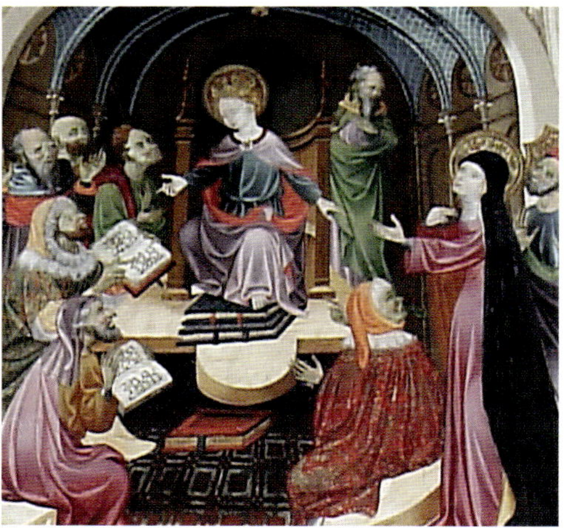

Fig. 34

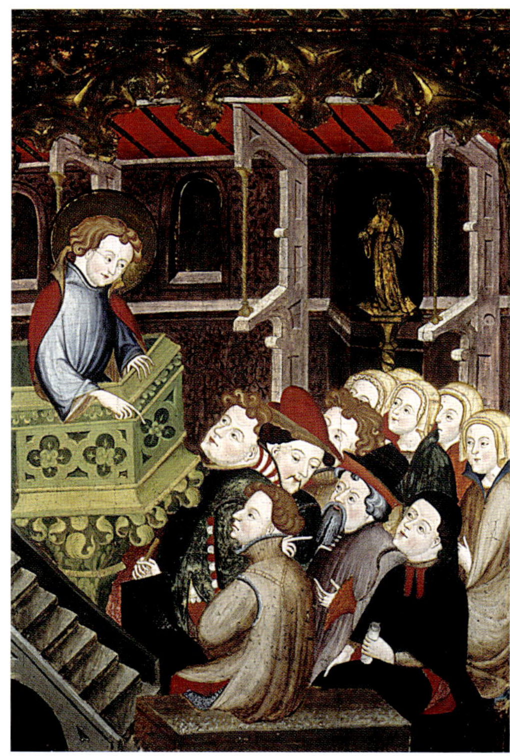

Fig. 35

34. Gonçal Peris
     Altarpiece of Christ and the Virgin
     Christ among the Doctors (detail)
     ca. 1420
     Tempera and gilding on wood
     Parish church of Rubielos de Mora

35. Juan de Leví
     Altarpiece in the Pérez Calvillo chapel in Tarazona
     Saint Prudentius Preaching in Calahorra (detail)
     1403–8
     Tempera and gilding on wood
     Cathedral of Tarazona, Tarazona

All of the artists discussed above can be identified as Jewish from their names or personal histories. The inclusion of correctly written Hebrew inscriptions in a *retablo* scene definitely indicates the participation of a Jewish or *converso* artist or scribe. A striking example is the Disputation between Moses and Saint Peter mentioned earlier, which was probably inspired by the *Dialogi* or *Dialogues* written by the *converso* Petrus Alfonsi in the early twelfth century (figure 10). The great popularity of the *Dialogi* is indicated by the fifty-six manuscript copies that date prior to the advent of printing.[39] Alfonsi's text is patterned on classical dialogues, as were most polemical tracts written in the Middle Ages, since this literary genre allowed authors to present claim and counterclaim in an easily understandable format.[40] Its subject is the relative merits of Judaism versus Christianity. The choice of protagonists symbolized the two phases of Petrus Alfonsi's life. He was Moses before conversion and Peter afterwards. Saint Peter's empty scroll indicates the artist's ignorance of Latin, but that he was knowledgeable about Hebrew is shown by the Commandments inscribed on Moses' tablets.

There are Hebrew inscriptions on other *retablos*. One decorates the tomb of Jesus on a panel of a Pietà in Daroca painted ca. 1470 by Bartolomé de Cárdenas known as "el Bermejo".[41] The inscription is clear but not perfectly written. Still it can be translated "Through his death, he made an end to death." Interestingly, Hebrew letters occur on other works by Bermejo, for example, on the canopy over Mary's bed in a Dormition, and on the tomb of a Resurrection dated 1468–71.[42] In contrast, other artists producing scenes requiring Hebrew texts painted pseudo-letters, for example on Saint Stephen Preaching in a Synagogue, a fourteenth-century *retablo* by Jaume Serra (figure 50).[43] The prayer books held by the Jewish worshippers are inscribed with gibberish.

Bartolomé de Cárdenas' use of Hebrew letters becomes even more striking when one considers his incorporation of Jewish genre elements into his paintings for the Church. One is a Jew on horseback depicted to the left of the Virgin's head in a Pietà of 1490 in the Museo Diocesano of Barcelona.[44] Another is men with *pe'ot* (side locks), which cover an area that men were forbidden by Jewish law to shave.[45] The repeated inclusions of Jewish script and details in his art may indicate that Cárdenas was of *converso* stock.

Another inter-religious relationship involved a Christian patron hiring a Jew to oversee the production of a work of art. In 1422 Don Guzman, Master of the Order of Calatrava, commissioned a new translation of the Hebrew Bible into Castilian from Rabbi Moses of Arragel, which became known as *La Biblia de Alba* (Madrid, Palacio de Liria, no. 399).[46] Don Guzman wished the text to be accompanied by a commentary and illustrations, but the rabbi was reluctant to violate what he understood to be the biblical prohibition against images. In response, Don Guzman agreed to hire several illuminators from Toledo and to provide them with a model manuscript from the cathedral. In all, Don Guzman wrote to the rabbi three times and amended his commission until Rabbi Moses agreed to participate in the translation project. The *Biblia de Alba*'s prefatory text tells the history of the commission and is testimony both to the use of models in the production of medieval art, and to the persistence of Christian–Jewish dialogue, *convivencia*, in the century of the Expulsion.

To sum up what has been outlined so far, there were Jewish and *converso* artists living in Spain in the fourteenth and fifteenth centuries who worked for the Church and produced what has always been termed Christian art. That it was Christian in concept and use is certainly true, but in the multiethnic society of medieval Spain, the artist could be of another faith.

CHRISTIAN ARTISTS DEPICTING JEWISH LIFE

In a similar fashion, Christian artists portrayed Jewish life with an astonishing fidelity, but always within a Christian context. If Jewish characters were required for a scene from Christian history, the artist cast his Jewish contemporaries in the roles of their ancestors who lived at the time of Jesus and the Apostles, recalling Saint Augustine's view that Jews were witnesses to the veracity of the Old and New Testaments.[47] The small size of cities and towns whose churches commissioned large altarpieces from major artists, like Ejea de los Caballeros and Rubielos de Mora, were places where Jews formed a significant portion of the population and were easily accessible as models for paintings. Representations of contemporary reality infiltrated scenes set in the distant past like episodes from the Life of Jesus and the early saints that were placed around the central image of the holy figure to whom an altarpiece was dedicated. For example, late medieval Jews appear in a Presentation of Jesus in the Temple,

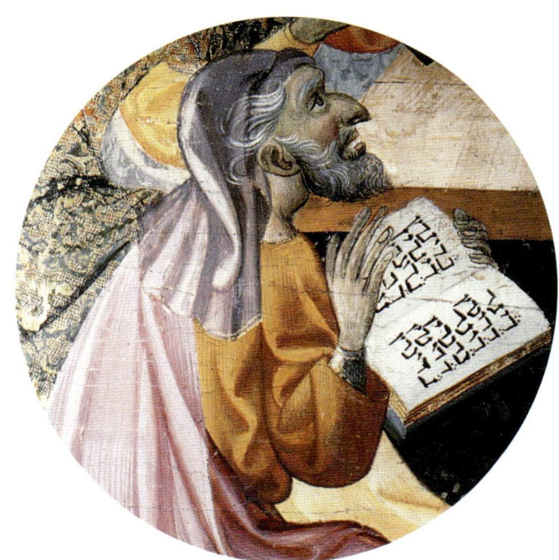

36. Gonçal Peris
Altarpiece of Christ and the Virgin
Christ among the Doctors (detail)
ca. 1420
Tempera and gilding on wood
Parish church of Rubielos de Mora

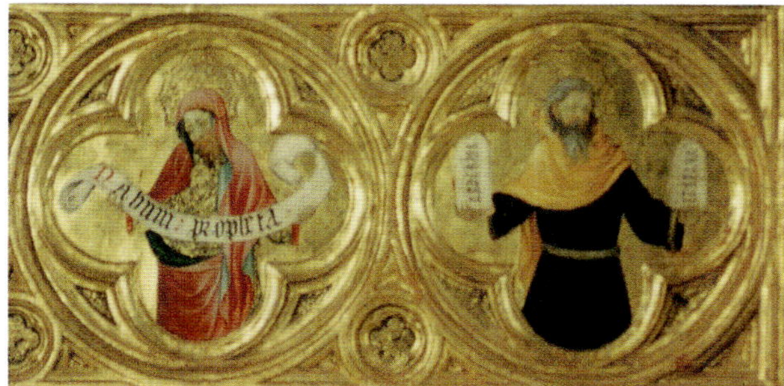

part of the *retablo* in the church of San Salvador in Ejea de los Caballeros painted by Blasco de Grañén from ca. 1440 until his death in 1459 (figure 38).[48]

In the Presentation of Jesus in the Temple from Ejea, the primary Christian figures of Jesus and Mary are idealized in their form and dress and crowned by circular haloes whose shape symbolizes perfection. The Jewish figures of the narrative, Joseph and the High Priest, possessed of a lesser degree of holiness, wear cusped haloes above faces that are individualized, portrait-like and different from the ethereal, blemish-free figures of Jesus and Mary. The Jews' appearance also reflects discriminatory regulations enacted by the kings of Aragon after the Lateran Council of 1215 that were intended to prevent sexual relations between Jews and Christians by marking the non-Christian.[49] The Law Code of Alfonso X of Castile (1252–84), which was later adopted in all of Spain in 1348, elaborates on this point:

> Many crimes and outrageous things occur between Christians and Jews because they live together in cities, and dress alike; and in order to avoid the offenses and evils which take place for this reason, we deem it proper and we order that all Jews, male and female, living in our dominions shall bear some distinguishing mark upon their heads so that people may plainly recognize a Jew, or a Jewess.

King James I of Aragon decreed in 1263 that his Jewish subjects wear a dark cloak out of doors emblazoned with a rotulus and, in 1412, Jews and Muslims were prohibited from trimming their hair and beards so that unkempt hair became a compulsory sign of alterity. Wild hair was a sign that also marked heretics in the *Bible Moralisée*, the large picture Bibles written and illuminated in the first half of the thirteenth century for the kings of France. Jews were often conflated with heretics.[50] The imposition of these restrictions provoked the following response from the Spanish Jew Solomon Alami (1370–1420):

> We have suffered measure for measure. Because we adopted their dress, they dressed us in different vestments so that we would seem to be strangers among them, and because we shortened the corners of our hair and bears, they forced us to let our hair grow as if we were plunged into deep mourning.[51]

The presence of recognizable Jews in Christological scenes served to underscore the Christianity of holy figures, much as black figures in exotic clothes emphasized the European character

37. Gonçal Peris
     Altarpiece of Christ and the Virgin
     Predella with prophets
     ca. 1420
     Tempera and gilding on wood
     Parish church of Rubielos de Mora

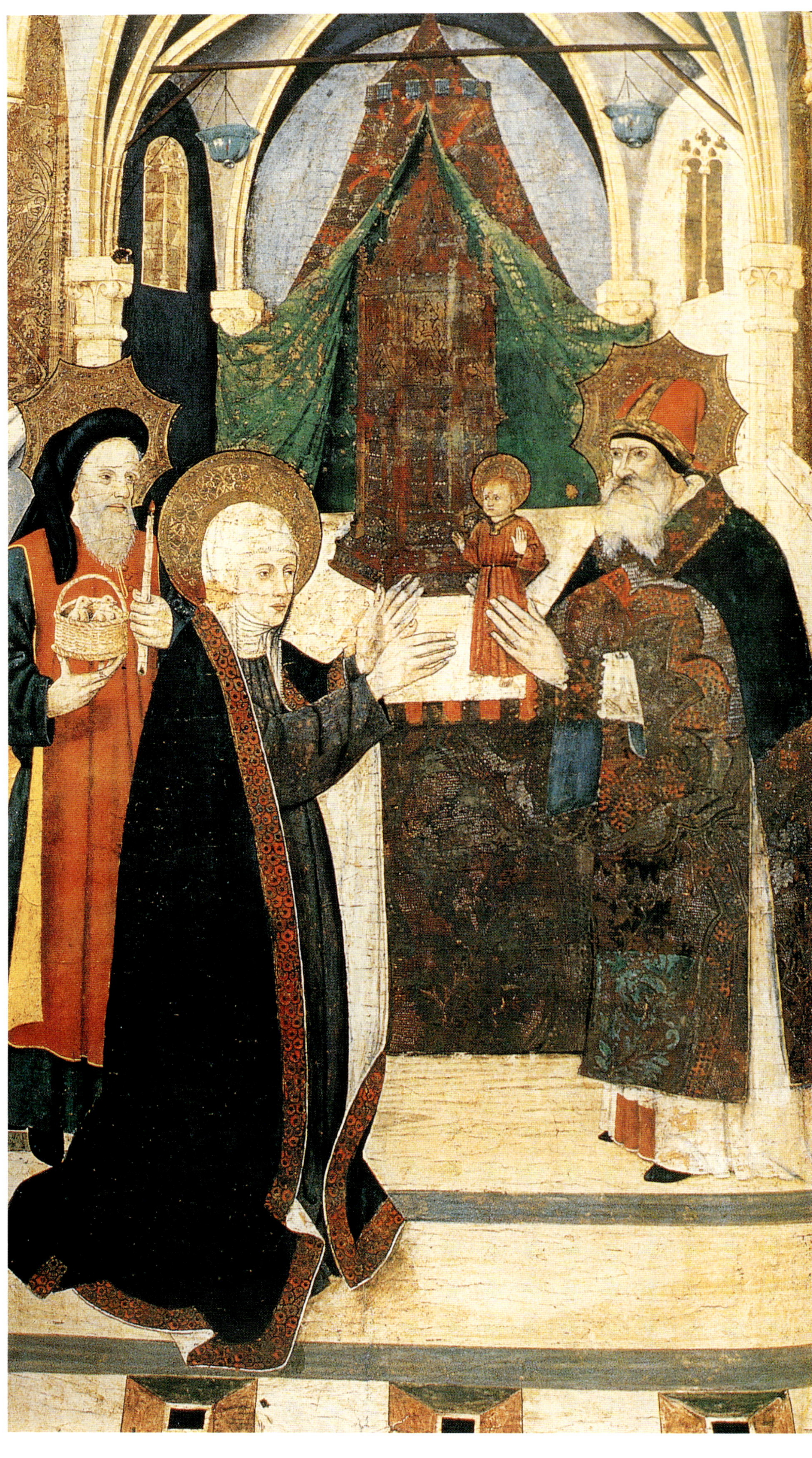

of those who sat for portraits during the Renaissance.[52] The differences in the clothing or appearance of the Jews also reinforced their Otherness.

That these regulations were necessary suggests the visual homogeneity of the Spanish population, a homogeneity that required artificial means of differentiation.[53] In other words, Jews and Christians looked very much alike. On the Iberian Peninsula, sartorial differentiation had first been instituted by the Muslim rulers of Al-Andalus to signify the subordinate status of *dhimmi* or protected minorities, peoples who had a sacred text.[54] Some articles of dress required by the Muslims, such as the *zunnar*, a rope belt, appear in the later Christian art of Aragon, for example, in the scene of the Expulsion of Joachim and Anna from the Temple discussed earlier (figure 28). The designation of clothing as a symbol of minority status was part of a general medieval view of dress as denoting class or occupation. Ann Rosalind Jones and Peter Stallybrass describe medieval and Renaissance clothing as material mnemonics.[55] Clothes signified an individual's place in society, and were not "fashion" in the contemporary sense of the term. Livery, for example, marked an individual as in the service of another, more powerful person. The dingy clothing and wild hair of Jews were signs of their exclusion from Christian society and of their defeat by a victorious Christianity.

The presence in the Ejea Presentation of Jesus in the Temple of these discriminatory markers are a contemporary intrusion into the subject, as is the setting of the scene in a Gothic building whose representation includes detailed pier capitals and a triforium. That the building is not a church but a synagogue is indicated by the Torah case or *tik* that is on the altar. A cylindrical case of wood or silver to hold a Torah scroll upright in the synagogue first came into use in the eleventh century in the Maghreb, at the same time that the Koran box became a feature of mosques.[56] It was used in Spain until the Expulsion, alternatively with textile coverings (mantles) for the Torah scroll. That the case was understood as a Jewish appurtenance is explicit in a 1515 scene of Christ among the Doctors on the main altarpiece in the royal monastery de Santa María de Sijena.[57] There the case is shown partially open revealing two round-topped Tablets of the Law with five lines of "writing" on each, corresponding to the Ten Commandments. Another detail of the Ejea panel, Joseph's basket with two doves, the post-partum Temple offering of a woman of modest means, indicates that the architecture is meant to be understood as the Temple, although its form reflects contemporary synagogues. In other words, if the Jews of the late Middle Ages could be construed as representatives of Jews alive during the early history of the Church, by the same reasoning the contemporary Jewish house of worship could serve as a stand-in for the Temple of antiquity. In a Presentation of Jesus in the Hispanic Society of New York, further contemporaneous details are included: a curved circumcision knife and a beaker to hold wine blessed after the actual circumcision (figure 40).[58]

In fact, all scenes on the *retablos* that were supposed to have taken place in the Temple are shown in synagogue spaces: the Presentation of Jesus in the Temple (sometimes represented as his Circumcision), the most commonly depicted Temple narrative; Christ among

38. Blasco de Grañén
Main altarpiece of Christ the Savior
Presentation of Jesus in the Temple (detail)
Tempera on wood
San Salvador, Ejea de los Caballeros

the Doctors; the Annunciation to Zacharias, the father of John the Baptist; and the Expulsion of Joachim and Anna from the Temple. All of these scenes are staged in Gothic buildings that are sometimes a combination of nave-like spaces and apses or are simply rectangular halls as in the Expulsion of Joachim and Anna. One *retablo* includes another detail, an outside staircase leading to a second storey,[59] presumably the balcony for women that is found in the Cordoba synagogue, El Tránsito in Toledo, in the Hijar synagogue and at Lorca. The identification of the painted buildings depends on the placement of the *tik* on the altar and the absence of any Christian accoutrements such as a cross. In the Expulsion of Joachim and Anna, a noteworthy detail of the *tik* is its decoration with a scarf or cloth, a custom still practiced in the Sephardi diaspora and also by eastern Jewish communities today.

The scene of the Annunciation to Zacharias while he is serving in the Temple appears on *retablos* dedicated to Saint John the Baptist. According to Christian lore, Zacharias was an ordinary Temple priest, but on an altarpiece in The Cloisters, he acts as the High Priest in the Holy of Holies on Yom Kippur, the holiest day of the Jewish year. His garb is a mix of that worn by all priests, for example the headdress and linen belt, but with the addition of elements from the High Priest's regalia such as the pendant bells and pomegranates along the hem. Another extraordinary detail of this scene that indicates Zacharias is acting as the High Priest is the rope wound around his leg and held by a priest who stands outside the Holy of Holies. The rope allowed the High Priest's body to be removed in the event that he died in the Divine presence for not having performed his duties correctly. The service depicted in this extremely detailed and particularized scene is based on the talmudic tractate, Yoma. Yet, as in other *retablo* depictions of the Temple, there is a Torah case on the altar, which is a synagogue appurtenance. The wealth of the detail from Jewish lore suggests that the artist, Domingo Ram (ca. 1464–1507), came from a *converso* background or had a Jewish assistant.

Excavations near the fortress in Lorca in 2003 prove the accuracy of the synagogue architecture painted on some *retablos*. The remains of the Lorca synagogue consist of a vestibule leading to a rectangular hall whose perimeter is surrounded by stone benches.[60] The ruins of the Torah ark are on one of the short ends and the center of the hall is filled with the remains of the reader's desk or *teivah* that was reached by a flight of steps. A painted version of this synagogue type appears on a *retablo* panel now in the Metropolitan Museum in New York, where the scene is enlivened by Jewish worshippers seated along the walls and by Mary and Joseph watching Jesus ascend the steps of the *teivah* (figure 42). The space is illuminated by glass "mosque" lamps and, in a case of life imitating art, a large cache of glass shards from "mosque" lamps was found beneath the *teivah* at Lorca and reconstructed.[61]

The substitution of "modern" synagogue buildings for the ancient Temple may be attributable to the fact that the actual appearance of the Temple was unknown to medieval men and women.[62] Or the substitution may have been encouraged by a common Jewish usage that terms the synagogue a "small sanctuary" (*mikdash me'at*), a play on the name of

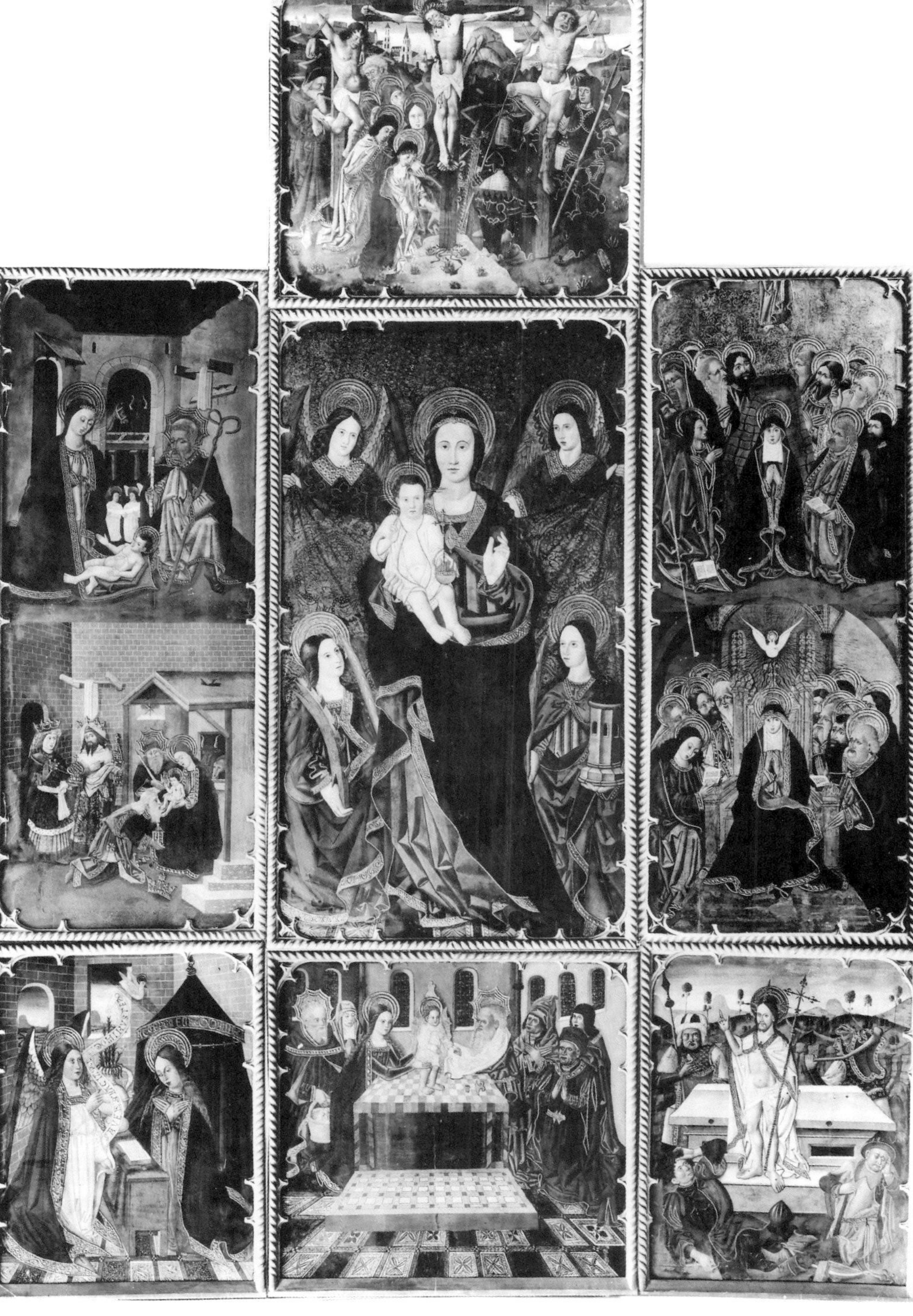

39. Anonymous
   Altarpiece of the Virgin and Child
   Castile, 1450–99
   The Hispanic Society of America, New York (A1)

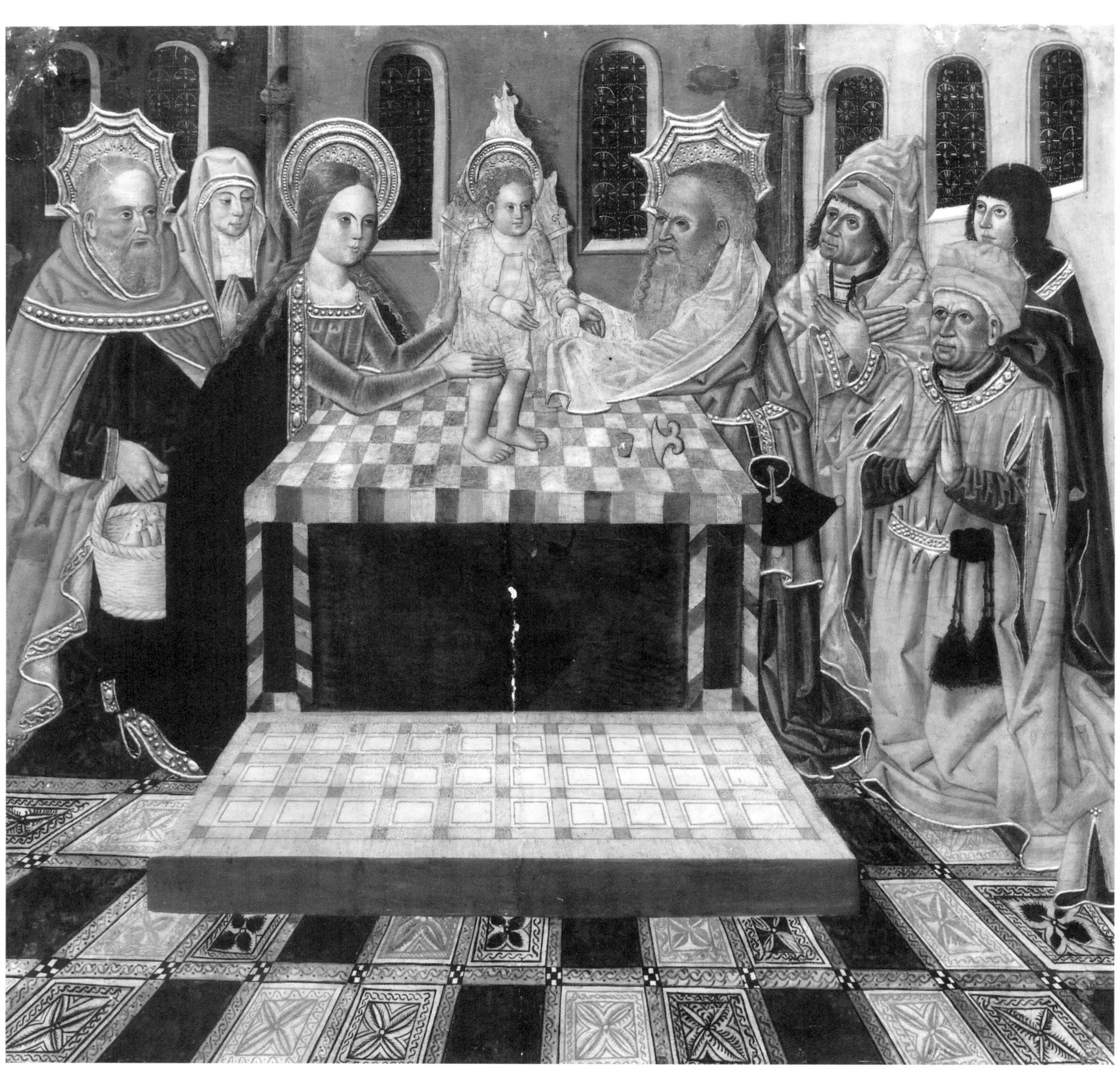

40. Anonymous
Altarpiece of the Virgin and Child
The Circumcision of Christ
Castile, 1450–99
37 × 41 in.
The Hispanic Society of America, New York (A1/6)

the Temple in Jerusalem, the *beit ha-mikdash*. In medieval Spain, the phrase is used in the Hebrew dedicatory inscription of the Cordoba synagogue:

> Isaac Mehab, son of the honorable Ephraim, has completed this lesser sanctuary (*mikdash me'at*) and he built it in the year 75 [1314–1315] as a temporary abode. Hasten, O God, to rebuild Jerusalem.[63]

The impact of the term "lesser sanctuary" is emphasized by Isaac Mehab's characterization of the synagogue as a temporary abode, accompanied by his prayer that the true House of God, the Jerusalem Temple, will soon be rebuilt.

The one exception to the modeling of the Temple on local synagogues is a scene of the Presentation of Jesus on an altarpiece in Palencia, in which all the figures stand in an hexagonal structure with a domed roof.[64] Medieval circular or polygonal structures were thought to imitate the Church of the Holy Sepulchre, the most important Christian building in Jerusalem.[65]

Of the architecture associated with Jewish life in the Kingdom of Aragon, the most common form still standing is the arcuated gate to the *judería*, the Jewish quarter. The use of this defining structure to situate an episode from fourth-century Christian history within the ambience of late fifteenth-century Jewish life is evident in a portrayal of Saint Helena in the Holy Land questioning Judas, a Jew who claimed to have knowledge of the burial spot of the True Cross (figure 43). The scene is part of an altarpiece devoted to the True Cross by Miguel Jiménez and Martín Bernat painted in 1485–87 for the parish church of Santa Cruz de Blesa in Teruel. The scene is staged on local Jewish turf, just inside the arcuated gate to an Aragonese *judería*, while the house behind is based on the architecture of Jewish houses still existing in former Jewish quarters. In this painting, the *judería* symbolizes the land of the Jews, the Holy Land.

The scene of Saint Helena is remarkable for its representation of fifteenth-century dress. The Jew Judas is dressed in the dark cloak mandated by the decree of Peter III of Aragon in 1263; his hair and beard grow wild because of the decree of 1412. But Helena and her ladies are dressed in rich silks and jewels. She wears a red gown with ermine cuffs and hem, a brocade cloak of silk and gold threads, and an elaborate crown. The lady directly behind her wears a headdress with pearls. In the high Middle Ages, scarlet cloth gave status to the wearer and was reserved for the elite, while silk brocade was a mark of royalty.[66] Various sources indicate that wealthy Jews were able to wear clothing similar to the robes of royalty depicted on the altarpieces. In 1268 a Jew from Játiva bought his wife an exemption from the dress regulations which specifically allowed her to wear scarlet and "snow white" clothes. According to the sumptuary laws passed at a meeting of Castilian Jews convened at Valladolid in 1432:[67]

> No woman unless unmarried or a bride in the first year of her marriage shall wear costly dresses of gold-cloth, or olive-colored material (a Chinese silk) or fine linen or silk, or of fine wool. Neither shall they wear on their dresses trimming of velvet

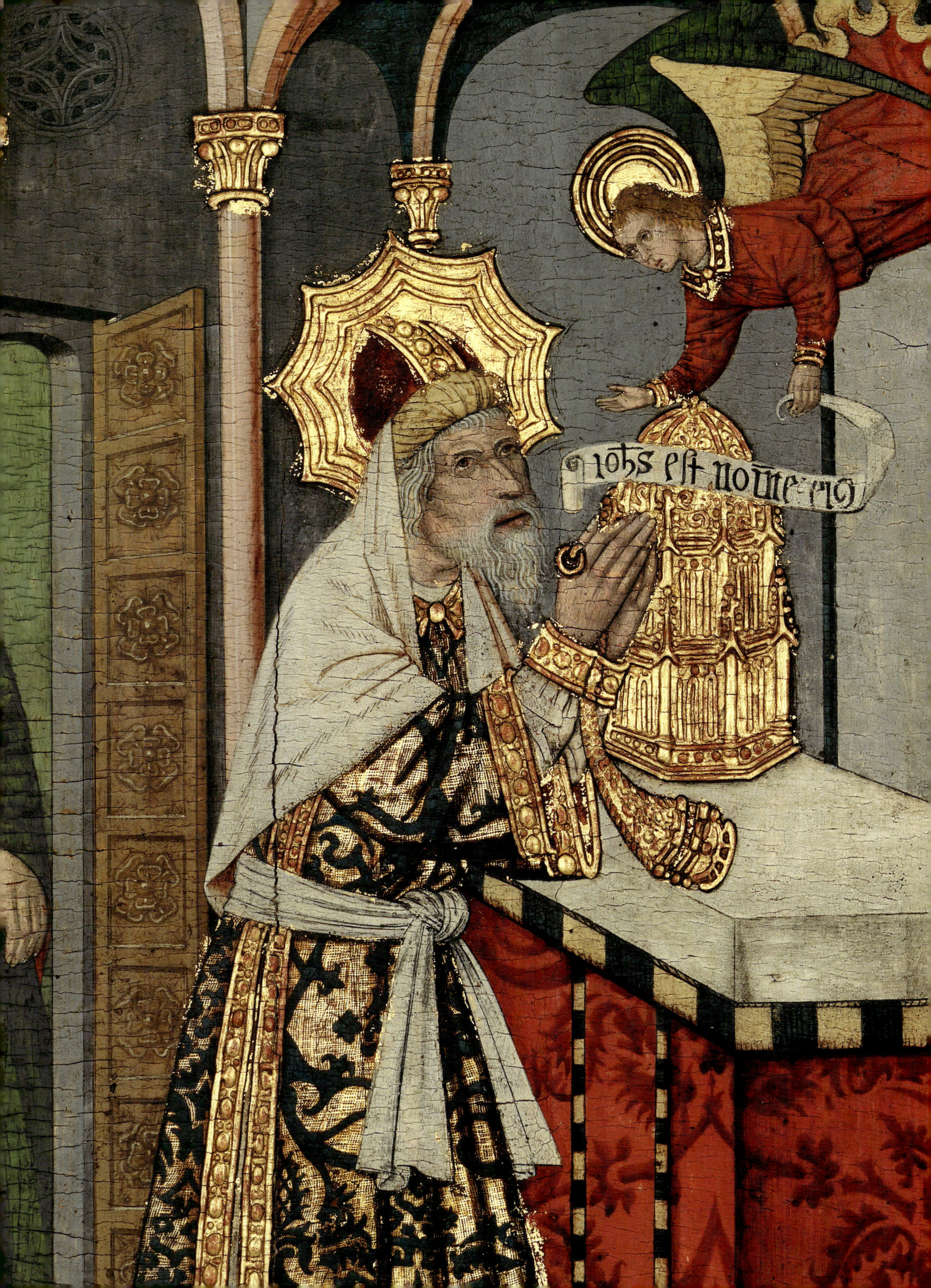
iohs est nome eig

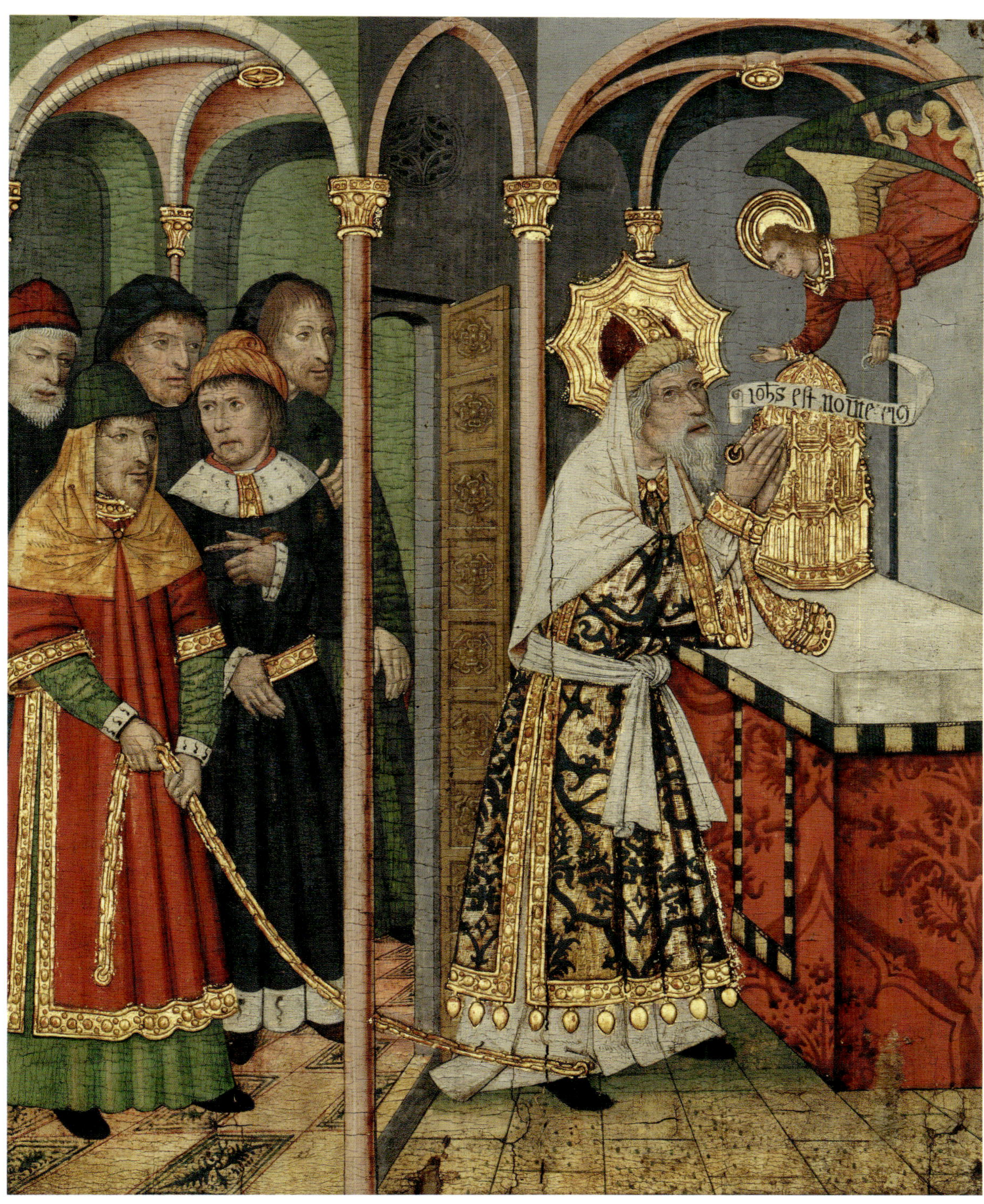

41. Domingo Ram
Altarpiece of Saint John the Baptist with Scenes from his Life
Annunciation to Zacharias
1464–1507
Tempera on wood
59 ½ × 28 ⅝ in.
The Cloisters, Metropolitan Museum of Art, New York
MMA 25.120.929

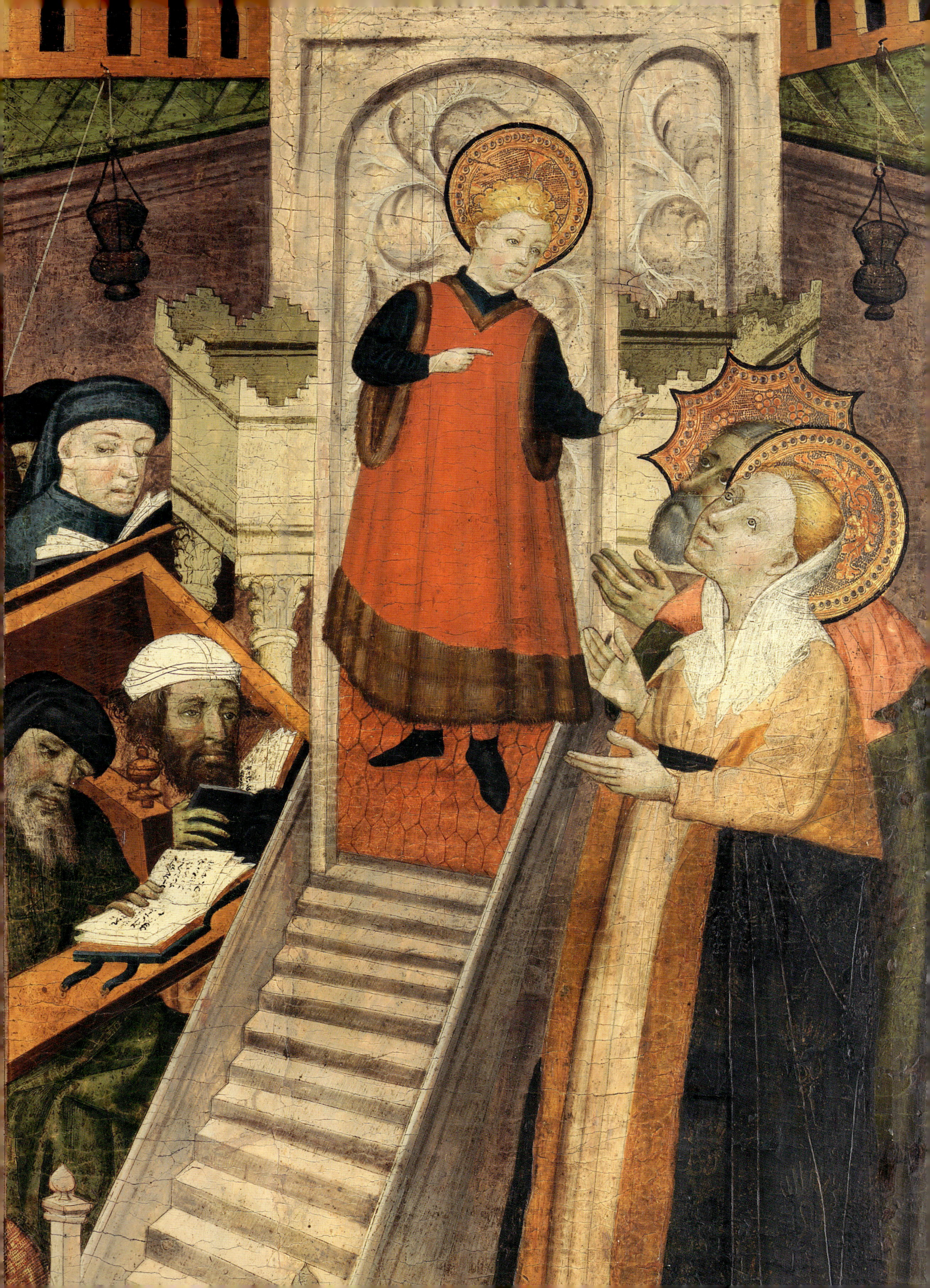

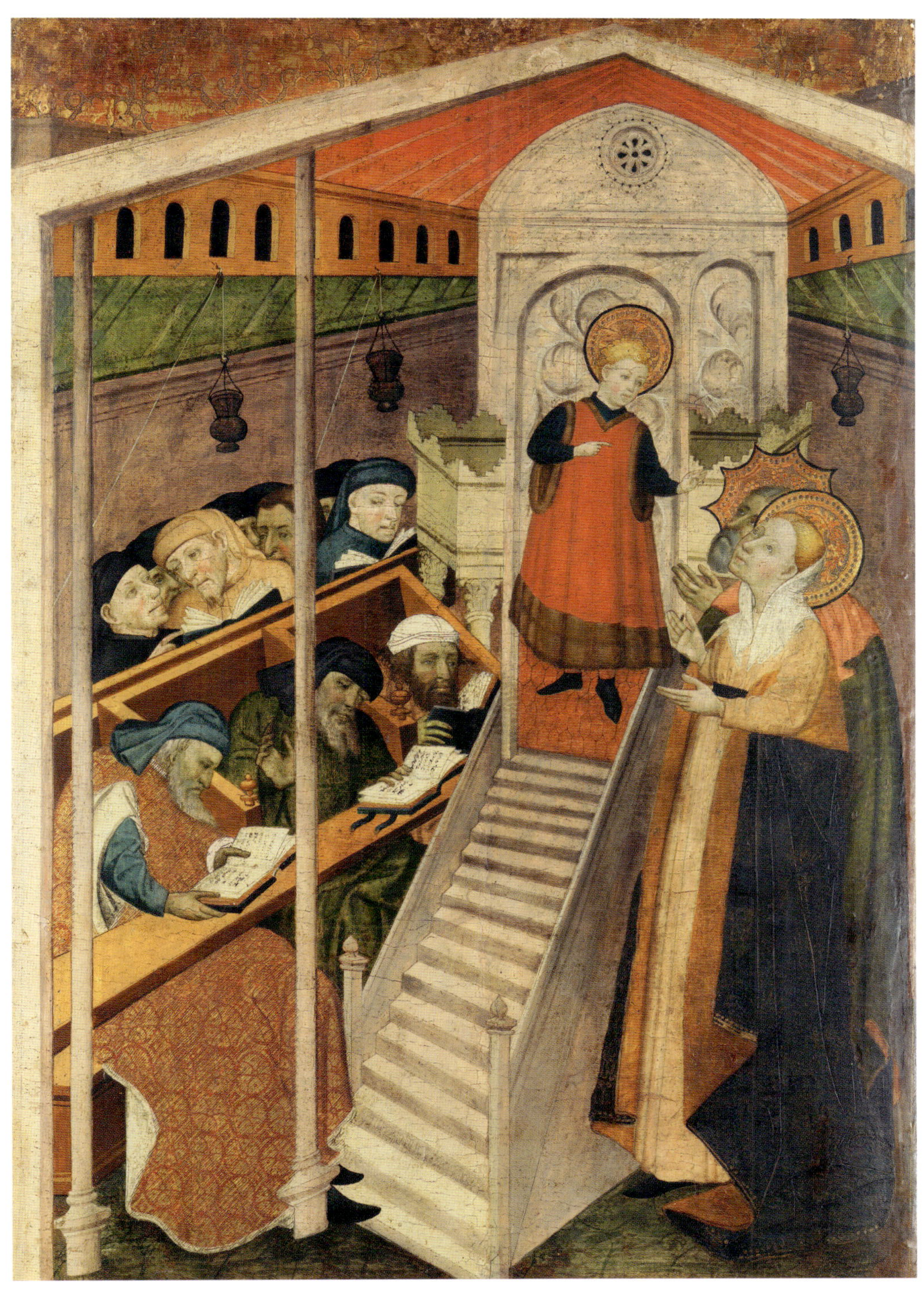

42. Anonymous
Christ among the Doctors
Early fifteenth century
Tempera and gold on wood
44 × 30 in.
Metropolitan Museum of Art, New York
MMA 32.100.123

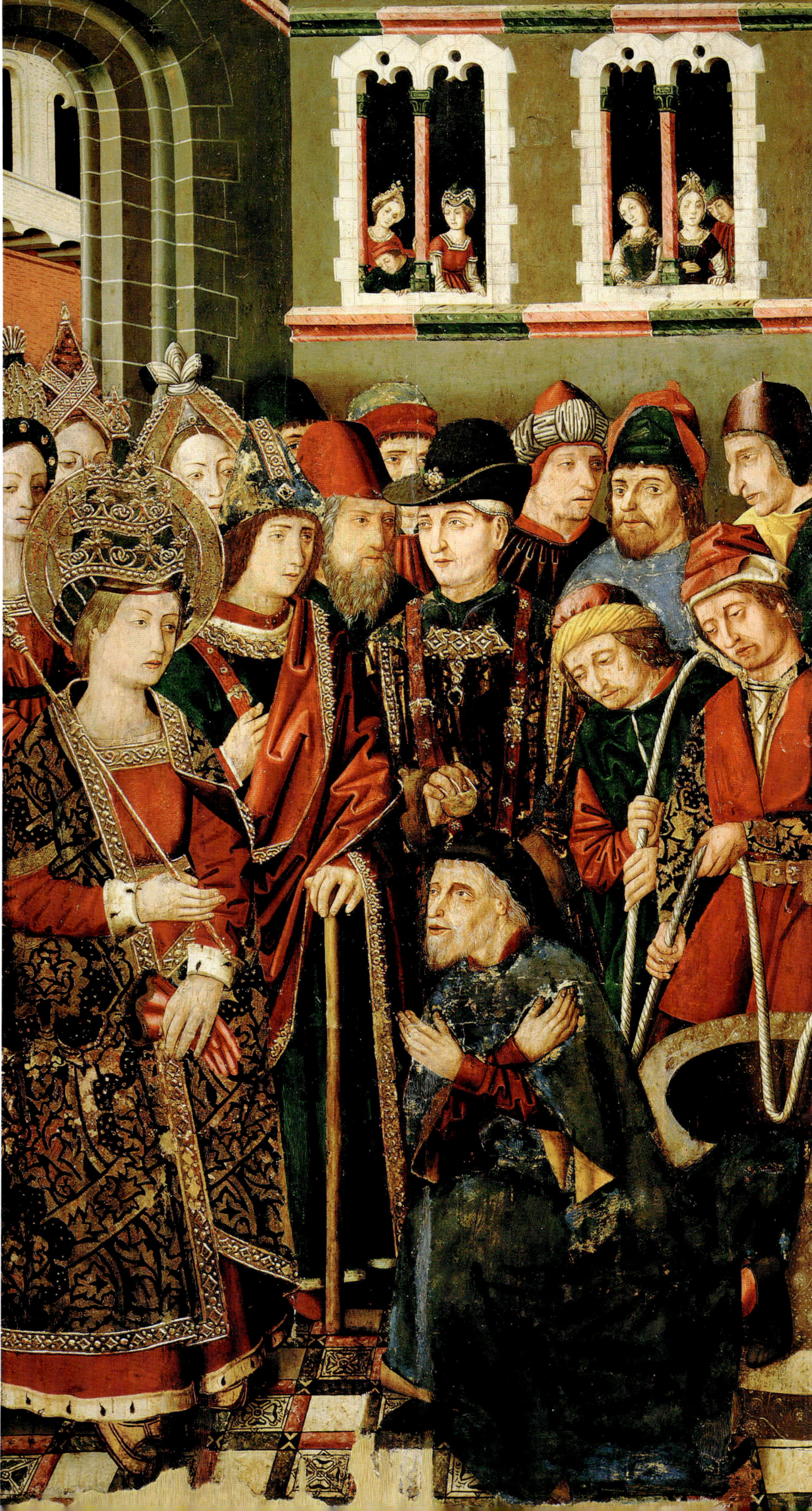

> or brocade or olive-colored cloth. Nor shall they wear a golden brooch nor one of
> pearls, nor a string of pearls on the forehead, nor dresses with trains on the ground
> more than one third of a *vara* in measure, nor fringed Moorish garments, nor coats
> with high collars, nor cloth of high reddish color, nor a skirt of *hermeia* thread...
> nor shall they make wide sleeves on the Moorish garments of more than two palms
> in width, but they may wear jewelry like silver brooches and silver belts provided
> that there is not more than four ounces of silver on any of them.

Although not identified as such in the sumptuary laws, the bridal costumes described are similar to the royal dress of Helena and her courtiers. In contrast, the Jewish women in the open windows in the background of the scene wear subdued dresses and headgear. The artist created a single, nuanced facial type and then used it for all four women, but varied their dresses, which have different necklines and trim and are of differently colored textiles. Emphasis is given to the rendering of the white silk sleeves that appear to be a separate garment worn together with the women's gowns, like those described in the sumptuary laws.

Despite the rich details on these panels, there is an air of tension to the confrontation between Helena and Judas that is generated by the sober expressions of all figures. As a result, the depiction of the Christian Queen Helena interrogating the Jew, Judas, may have been intended to represent the activities of the Inquisition, established in Aragon in the second half of the thirteenth century.

In the case of Jewish women's dress, we are fortunate to have representations in other works of art to corroborate what is known from the *retablos*. Prior to the late medieval examples that are the subject of this chapter, the number of Jews depicted in Spanish art was small and nearly all were male.[68] During the fourteenth and fifteenth centuries, however, Jewish women were depicted in both Jewish and Christian art.

In Jewish art, women appear in some ten illuminated haggadot (or service books for Passover) that were created in Barcelona and its environs between 1300 and 1360. These manuscripts contain an illuminated text of the Seder, the home ceremony for Passover, and some include a prefatory series of biblical and genre scenes. In the Seder scene of the Sarajevo Haggadah (Sarajevo, National Museum) and in that of the manuscript known as the Sister of the Golden Haggadah (London, British Library, Ms. Or. 2884, fol. 18r) (figure 44), the women wear elaborate pleated head coverings with a raised flower-like element in the center of the forehead. Otherwise their indoor dress is nondescript, essentially the flowing robes that hide the body in much Gothic art. In depictions of the synagogue service that preceded the Seder, both men and women wear the long, hooded cloaks that were required dress out of doors (e.g. London, British Library, Barcelona Haggadah, Add. 14761, fol. 65v.).[69]

The identification of Jewish women in Christian art of the fourteenth and fifteenth centuries depends on their clothing and the narrative context in which they are seen, since they lacked the identifying beards of Jewish men and their hair was generally covered.

43. Miguel Jiménez and Martín Bernat
Altarpiece of the True Cross
Saint Helena Interrogating Judas (detail)
1485–87
Oil on panel
77 × 45 × 5 in.
Museo de Zaragoza, Saragossa

One of the scenes from the Hebrew Bible, an Exodus from Egypt included in the *retablo* of Saint Bernard and the Guardian Angel of 1462–82 (Barcelona, Museu de la Catedral), is the work of a painter from the atelier of Jaume Huguet (figure 45).[70] The panel preserves the traditional v-shaped composition in which the drowning Egyptians appear in a lower corner, while the Israelites stride along the Red Sea, a composition that appeared in early Christian art.[71] A manuscript or copy book may have been the means by which this iconography was transmitted from Rome to medieval Spain. Although composed traditionally, the Israelites are represented as contemporary Jews. The painter took great care to individualize the faces of the Israelites and to vary their dress. The foremost Jewish figures, Moses and Aaron, are thought to be portraits of the leading Jewish residents of Banyoles where the *retablo* first hung. The figure guided by the Guardian Angel is tentatively identified as Bonjuà Cabrit, who was doctor-surgeon to the Royal House of Barcelona.[72] He wears a striped garment over his head, probably a *tallit* or prayer shawl and a gold-bordered cloak, and carries a codex with gilt edges. Although most of the women leaving Egypt wear simple scarves over their heads, one near the end of the procession wears an elaborate headdress with chin strap that forms a roll around her head and has a protruding element at top dotted with pearls. Attention is drawn to this elaborately dressed woman by her bright red cloak, which visually links her to the man at the head of the procession and suggests she is his wife.[73] Above the scene of the Exodus is a panel representing a parallel event, the Guardian Angel leading Lot, his wife and daughters out of Sodom.[74] The wife, wearing a white tunic that foreshadows her fate, turns back toward the city. The same angel redeems Lot's family and the Israelites of Egypt.

An identical headdress to that worn in the Exodus scene appears in Christian sculptures and on altarpieces to identify Jewish women, suggesting that this headdress was considered distinctive. It appears, for example, on a *retablo* panel of the Massacre of the Innocents dated 1390–1400, now in the Museo de Zaragoza,[75] and worn by a group of women on a fourteenth-century capital in the cloister of Barcelona cathedral.[76]

OTHER RELATIONSHIPS BETWEEN JEWISH AND CHRISTIAN ARTISTS

The relationship between the iconography of the haggadot manuscripts and that of the altarpieces, which goes beyond the matter of dress, is key to understanding another facet of the relationship between Christian and Jewish artists in fourteenth- and fifteenth-century Spain.

We have examined evidence that Jewish artists worked to produce Christian art, specifically works of silver and altarpieces, and that Christian artists were knowledgeable about Jewish life, which they depicted on *retablos* when appropriate to the subject matter. This common knowledge was due, at least in part, to ateliers that included both Christians and Jews. A responsum of Maimonides (Cordoba 1138—1204 Cairo) indicates that mixed workshops existed as early as the twelfth century in North Africa:

44. Anonymous
Sister of the Golden Haggadah
Seder scene
ca. 1350
Ink, gouache, and gold on parchment
9 × 8 in.
British Library, London
Ms. Or. 2884, fol. 18r

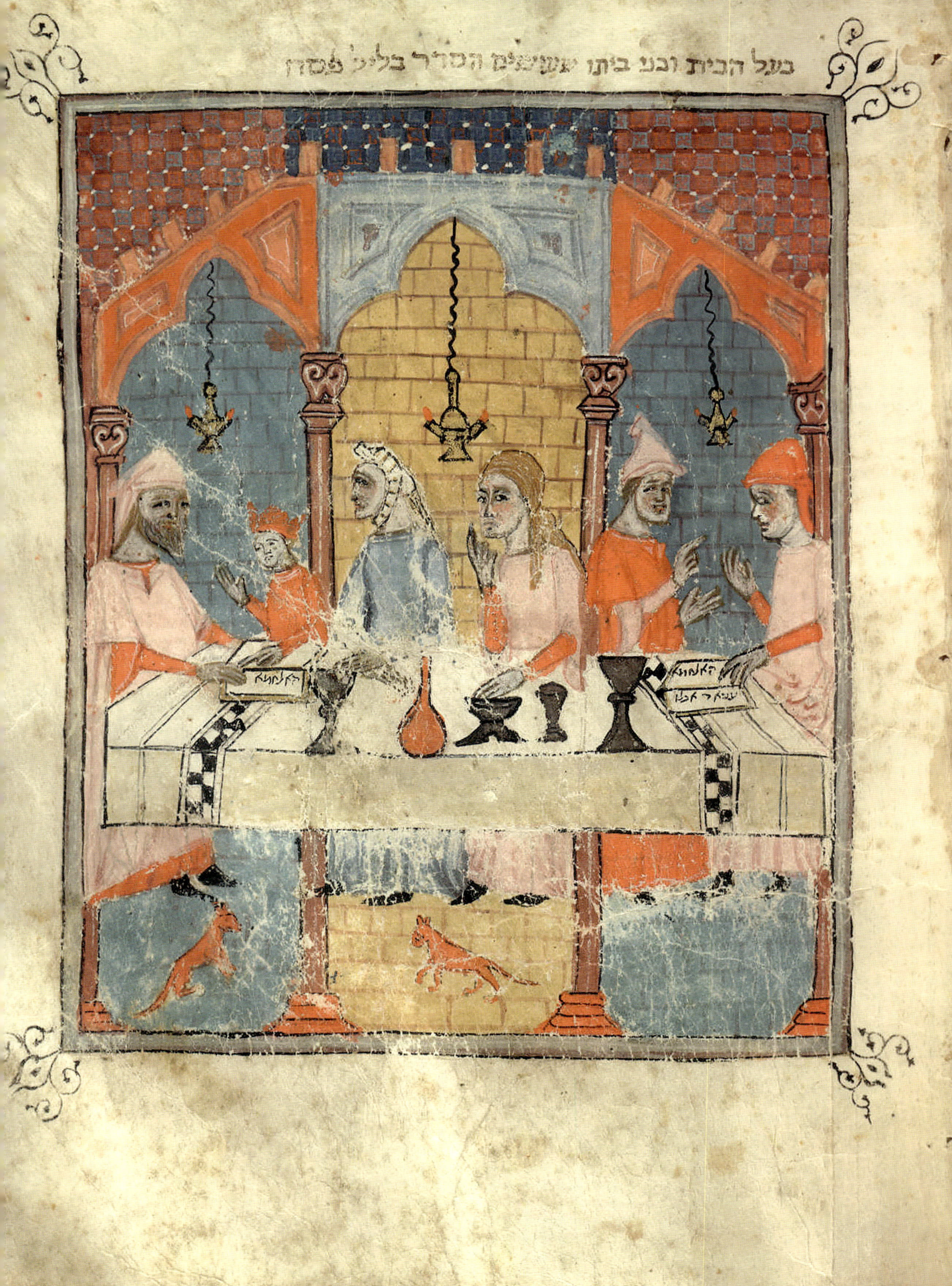

בעל הבית ובני ביתו יעשים הסדר בליל פסח

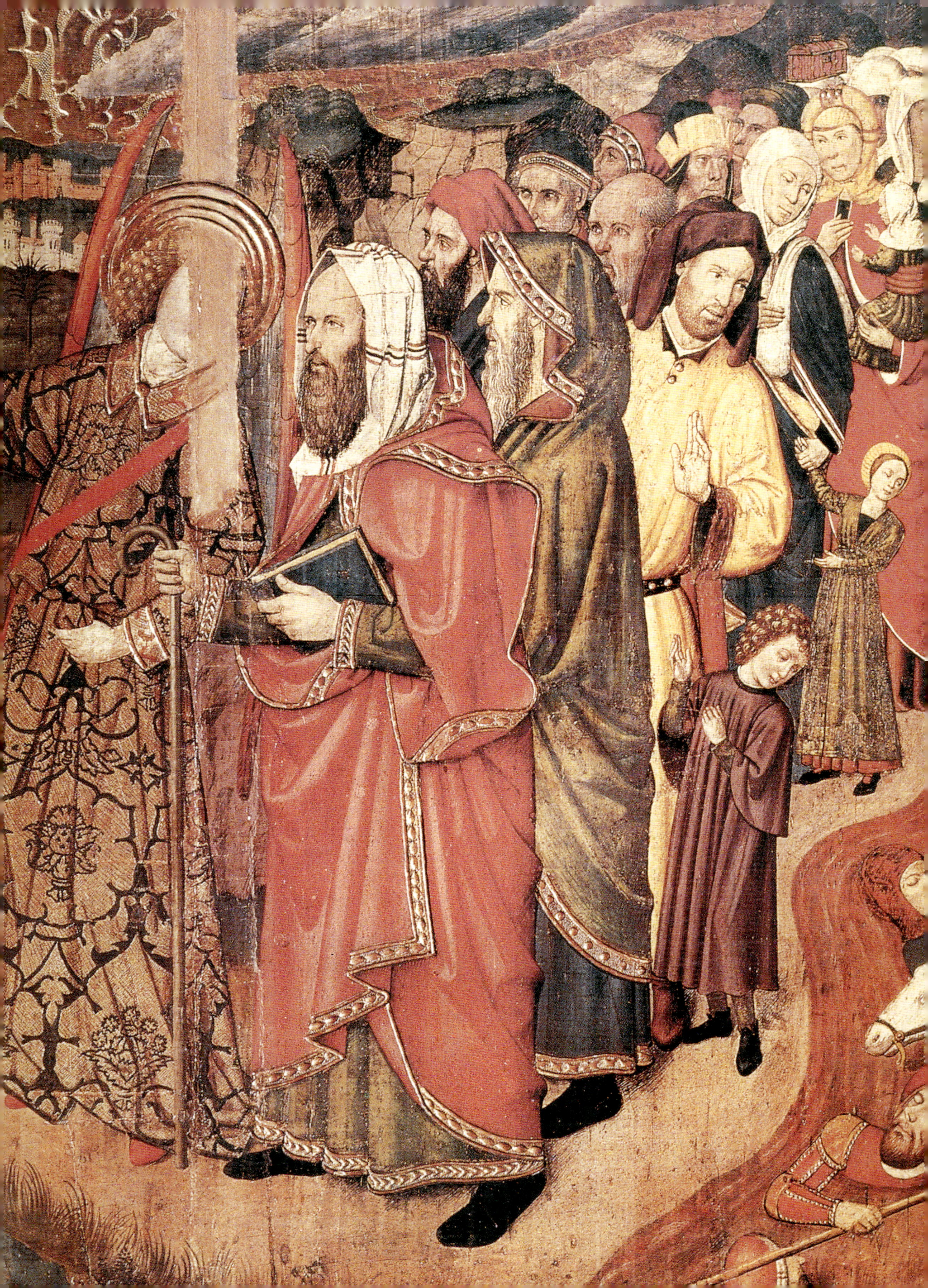

What does our Master say with regard to partners in a workshop, some being Jews and some Muslims, exercising the same craft. The partners have agreed between themselves that the [gains made on] Friday should go the Jews and those made on Saturday to the Muslims. The implements of the workshop are held in partnership; the crafts exercised are in one case goldsmithing, in another the making of glass.[77]

Maimonides allowed the arrangement as long as the Jewish craftsmen did not benefit from revenues earned on Saturday. Although the text is not specific, the Jew was in all likelihood the goldsmith, as the *hadith* (Muslim legal traditions) viewed these professions as unclean, better left to the *dhimmis*, the Jews. Another mixed shop mentioned in a Geniza document was that of a Jewish silk weaver who employed Muslims, a Jew, and a Jewish convert to Islam.[78]

That inter-religious ateliers also existed in Spain was first suggested by the renowned art historian Millard Meiss. In 1941 Meiss published an article in which he linked a *retablo* dedicated to Saint Mark, now in the Morgan Library, New York (figure 46) to several manuscripts, including Peter IV the Ceremonious's *Ceremonial de la consagración y coronación de los reyes y reinas de Aragón* (Madrid, Museo Lázaro Galdiano).[79] On the basis of their similarity in style Meiss argued that the altarpiece and the manuscript were produced by artists working in the same atelier.[80] A few years later, Francis Wormald added a Hebrew translation of Maimonides' *Guide to the Perplexed* (figure 9) to the manuscripts produced in the same atelier on the basis of its figure style and decorative motifs, thereby establishing the participation of both Jews and Christians in one workshop that produced manuscripts for both religious communities.[81] One result of the inter-religious character of this workshop is that both Christian and Jewish models must have been available, since a miniature of the Maimonides manuscript is based on a Byzantine composition of the four Evangelist symbols.[82] The simultaneous presence of the same creatures in Jewish lore (Ezekiel 1) must have facilitated the transfer of the composition to Maimonides' *Guide*. At the very least, Meiss and Wormald proved that Hebrew scribes provided manuscripts for the same illuminators who decorated Christian texts. The chief illuminator is now identified as Ferrer Bassa (d. 1348).[83] The fact that this atelier created both small-scale works of art (the manuscript miniatures) and large-scale altarpieces allows us to draw connections between both types of works.

The existence of the San Marco atelier is of great significance when considering the genesis of the illuminated haggadot produced in Spain during the second and third quarters of the fourteenth century. These haggadot have always been viewed as a unique phenomenon within Spanish Jewish art, whose origins in the second quarter of the fourteenth century have never been satisfactorily explained.[84] When the biblical and genre scenes, however, are viewed in the context of the altarpieces, and their style is considered, the place of the haggadot within Spanish art becomes more apparent.

An early haggadah, a late thirteenth-century "Hispano-Moresque" manuscript in the British Library (figure 1) is related stylistically to scenes from the Life of Christ on a

45. Workshop of Jaume Huguet
Altarpiece of Saint Bernard and the Guardian Angel
Exodus from Egypt (detail)
1462–82
Tempera on wood
Museo Diocesano, Barcelona

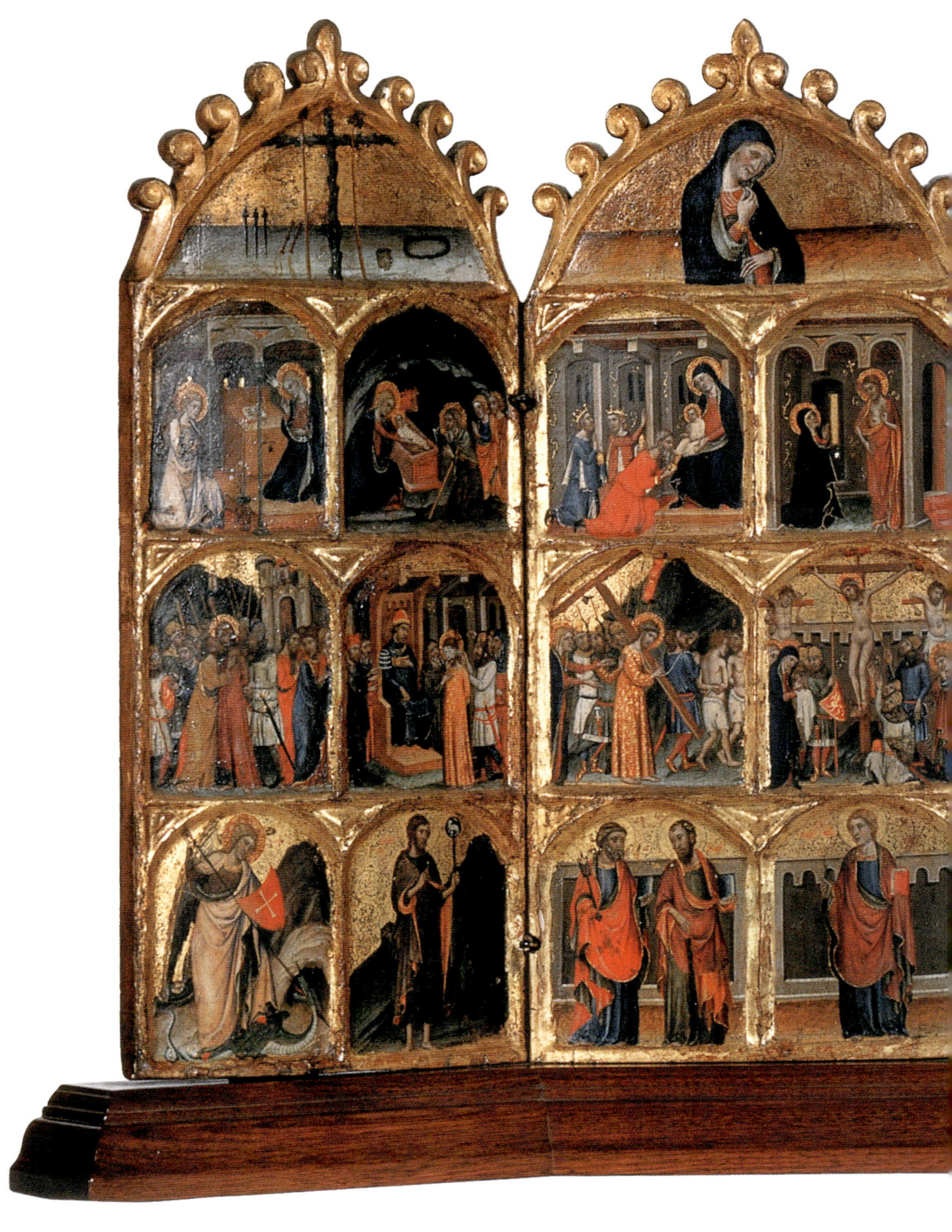

46. Workshop of Ferrer Bassa
Altarpiece of Saint Mark
Fourteenth century
Paint on wood
22 ½ × 44 ¼ in.
The Morgan Library, New York
AZ071

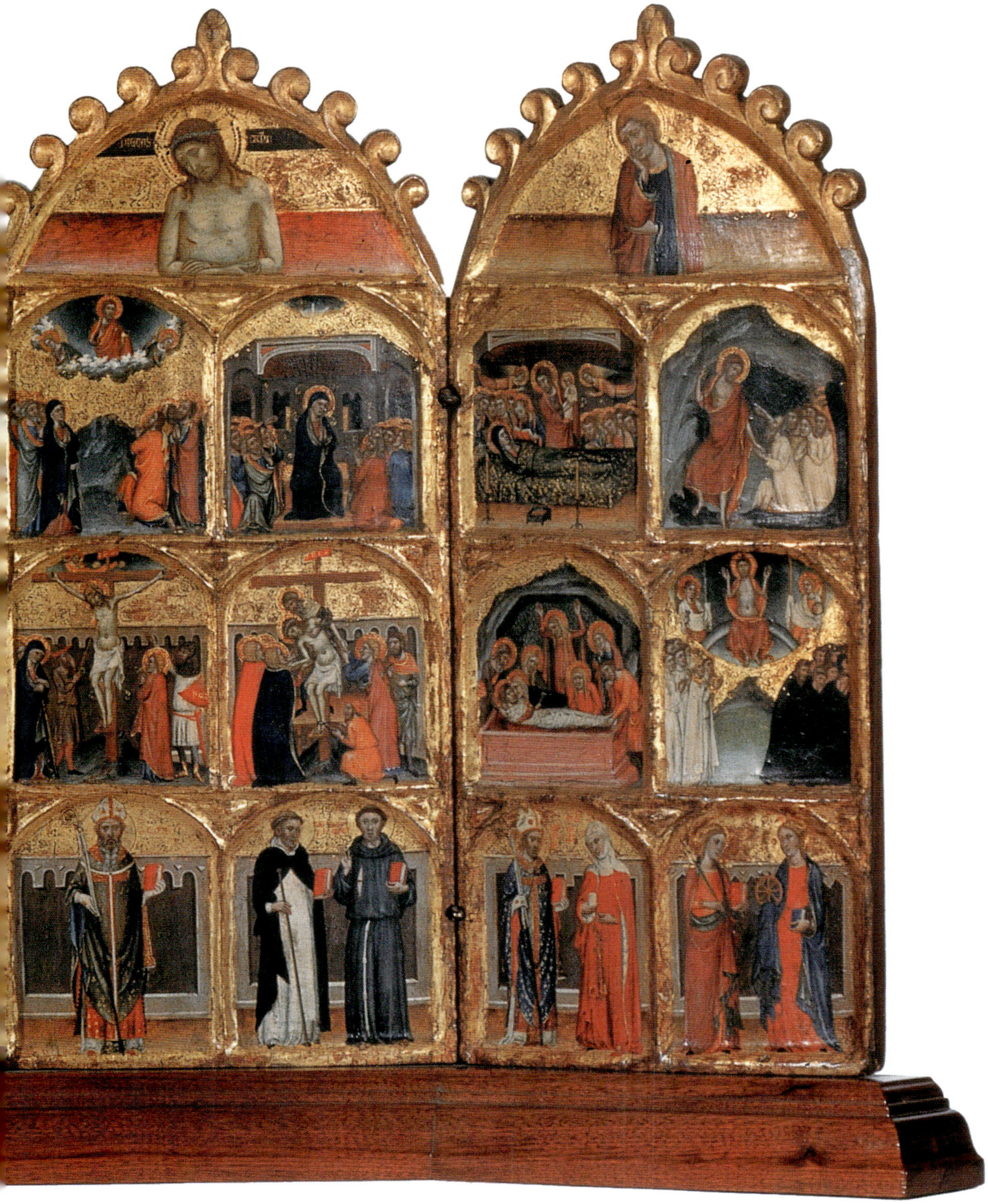

fragmentary late thirteenth-century altarpiece in The Cloisters (New York, Metropolitan Museum of Art, 55.62 a, b and 1977.94) and to similar *retablos* (figure 47). In these works, the scenes are set in architectural frames, often of deep red, above which are rubrics indicating the content of the scene (Latin on the altarpiece; Hebrew in the haggadah). The languages of these rubrics, assuming they served as instructions to the artists, indicate that both Jewish and Christian artists were active.[85] The action takes place below against blank backgrounds, with only the minimal props required by the narrative. Terracotta red and ochre are the dominant colors on both works, and they appear saturated rather than shaded. Throughout, the size of key figures such as Jesus or Moses and Aaron, or even the baker of *matzot* (the unleavened bread for Passover), is enlarged to indicate a subject's importance. Still, differences between the two works indicate that different artists were responsible for the haggadah and the *retablo*. Although the heads and hands of the figures of both works are outlined, rather than modeled, the painter of the Christian scenes often added a small circle of red paint to indicate a protruding cheek and furnished his figures with eyebrows, details absent on the haggadah figures. As is typical of the art of this period, figures are slim and drapery hides the body in both works, but the cloaks of the altarpiece figures are slightly more detailed, with a white highlight along the edge of the material. The haggadah and the *retablo* fragments in The Cloisters belong to a group of altarpieces whose style has been termed "linear Gothic," nearly all of them dated to the first half of the fourteenth century.[86]

The most lavish Passover manuscript of the period, the Golden Haggadah in the British Library (Add. 27210), can be dated to around 1320 on the basis of its figure style which is similar to that of the *Usatges de Paris* (Paris, Bibliothèque Nationale, ms. lat. 4670) and like the Latin work was produced in Barcelona or Lérida (figure 48). The iconography of the Creation scenes and other stylistic elements may be linked to similar scenes on a second *retablo* in The Cloisters, one dedicated to Saint Andrew (Metropolitan Museum, 25.120.257) (figure 49). Five scenes of the Creation story appear in the Golden Haggadah: Adam Naming the Animals in its own frame and the remaining four occupying a single frame of the four-frame scheme used on the miniature pages. The sequence reads chronologically from right to left, the direction in which Hebrew is read: Adam Naming the Animals (Gen. 2: 20), the Creation of Eve (Gen. 2:21–22), the Temptation of Eve (Gen. 3:1–5), the Man and his Wife with Loincloths (Gen. 3:7) and God (in the guise of an Angel) Reproaching Adam and Eve (Gen. 3:16–18). In the second, composite frame, the figure of Eve is shown tempted by the Serpent and simultaneously covering herself with a loincloth, while Adam both covers himself and raises his head as the angel reproaches him.[87] The rubric for the second frame refers only to the third episode: "Adam and his Wife were Naked." The *retablo* originally included seven Creation scenes, but the location of the last three is unknown. With one exception, each of the altarpiece scenes is given its own pictorial space: God Creates the Creatures of the Waters and the Birds (Day 5; Gen. 1:20–23), the Creation of Man (Day 6; Gen. 1:26–27), God Casts

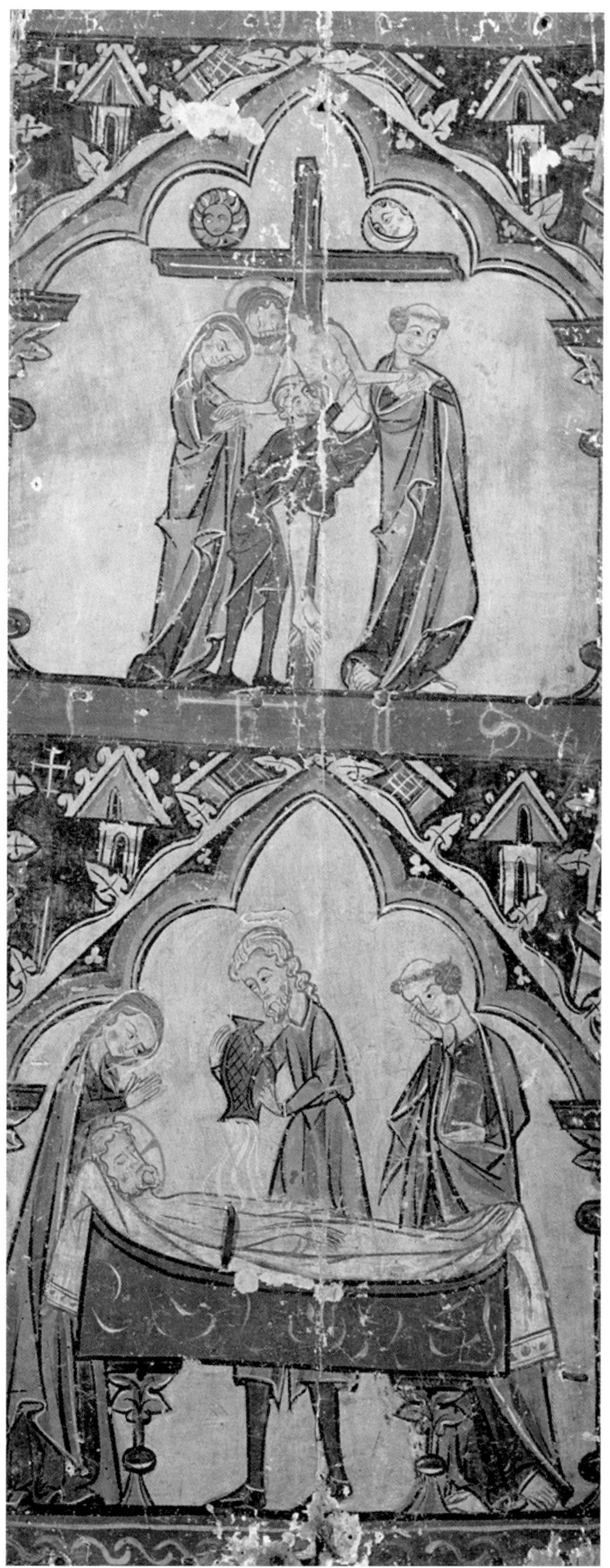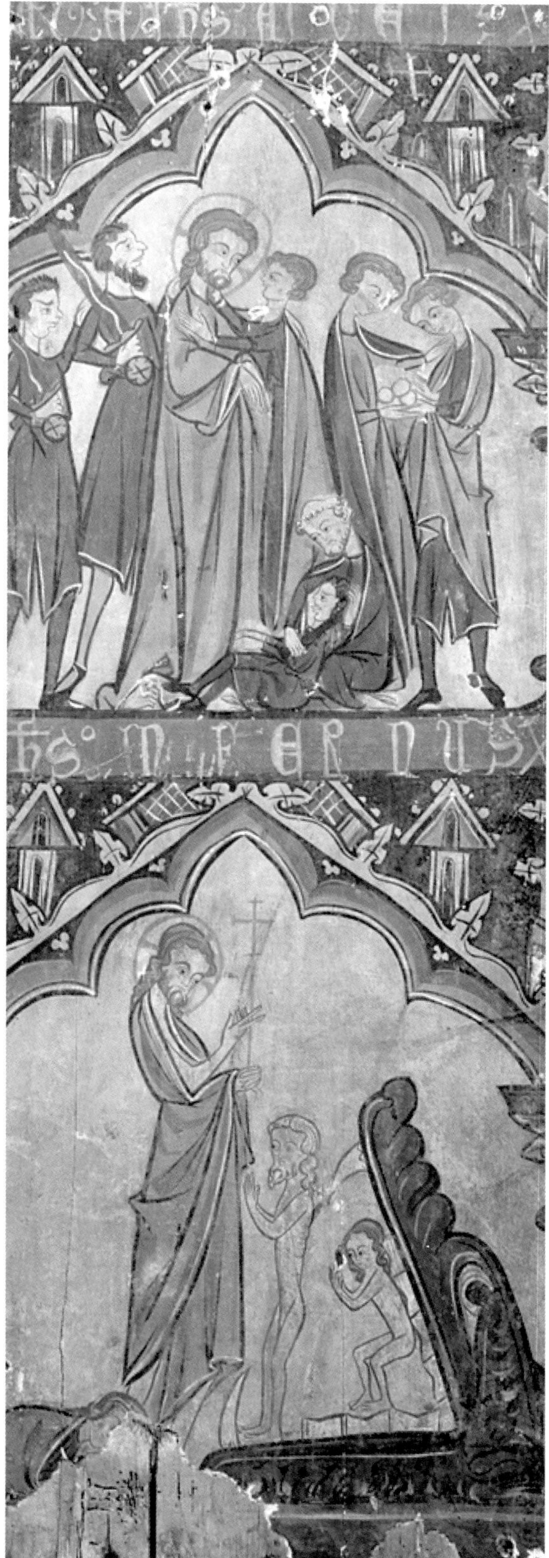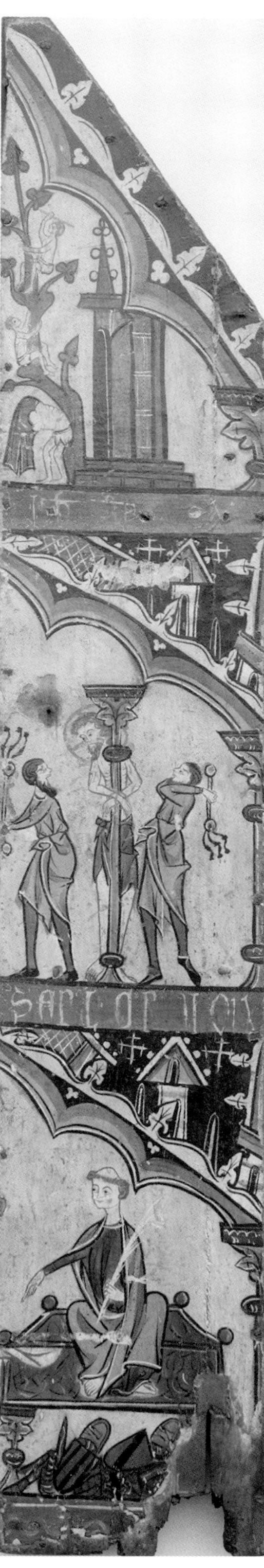

47. Anonymous
     Scenes from the Life of Christ
     Spanish, thirteenth century
     Tempera on wood
     (a) 42 × 15 × 1 in.
     (b) 42 × 17 × 1 in.
     (c) 59 × 10 ½ in.
     Metropolitan Museum of Art, The Cloisters Collection (55.62a,b) (1977.94)

a Deep Sleep on Adam (Gen. 2:21), God Presents Eve to Adam (Gen. 2:22), God Commands Adam and Eve not to Eat from the Tree of Knowledge (Gen. 2:16–17), the Temptation and Reproach (Gen. 3:1–6; 11), and the Expulsion (Gen. 3:24). All of these *retablo* and haggadah scenes are set against gold diapered backgrounds with the foregrounds made up of landscape elements: earth and stylized trees. The patches of earth on the *retablo* are composed of stylized forms stacked up against one another, while in the haggadah the landscape is a continuous, shaded mass. On the altarpiece, God dominates through his size or his appearance in a mandorla; in the haggadah scenes he is absent. Despite differences in the figure style between the haggadah and the altarpiece—the *retablo* figures are more linear—there are striking similarities between the two works, in particular their devotion of considerable space to the story of Creation and their emphasis on a few important figures in scenes set against a diapered gold background and anchored to a foreground of earth and stylized trees.

The Creation of Adam and Eve and the Fall was a popular theme in medieval Spanish art. In a Commentary on the Apocalypse of Beatus of Liébana dated 1000 is a Temptation with Eve at right and both figures covering their genitals with leaves.[88] Five scenes from the Creation of Adam through the Expulsion appear in silver-gilt reliefs on the reliquary shrine of Saint Isidoro dated 1063.[89] A much more extensive cycle appears on a cloister frieze of the cathedral of Girona dated before 1150: God Creating Adam, the Creation of Eve, God Warning Adam and Eve about the Tree of Knowledge, and a Temptation that repeats the iconography in the Beatus manuscript.[90] What is remarkable about this series is that God is an elderly bearded man, without a halo. Christian symbolism is lacking. The story of Adam and Eve was also painted on church walls and in manuscripts.[91] One mural in the Capilla de la Vera Cruz de Maderuelo (Segovia) from the third quarter of the twelfth century includes a composite Temptation/ Man and his Wife with Loincloths, the iconography of which is identical to that on the Saint Andrew *retablo* in The Cloisters.[92] An extensive biblical cycle was also painted in the chapter house of the convent of Sigena (Huesca) ca. 1230. The scenes included the Creation of Adam, the Creation of Eve, God Pointing to the Tree of Knowledge, the Temptation, and the Expulsion followed by later biblical subjects such as Moses Receiving the Tablets of the Law and the Anointing of David as King.

One image on the Saint Andrew altarpiece, a combination of the Creation of the Creatures of the Waters and the Birds on Day 5 with the Creation of the Beasts and Cattle on Day 6, may be related to the same scene in another haggadah manuscript, that found in Sarajevo.[93] In both images, the creatures of the water are seen swimming, while above them are birds, cattle, and wild animals. The role of God in the haggadah Creation scene is symbolized by a cone of gold rays that emanates from the heavens and falls on the earth. On the *retablo*, God is anthropomorphic and ensconced in heavenly clouds.[94] The image of the second day when the earth was separated from the firmament is shown in a similar way in the Sarajevo Haggadah (figure 13) and in the Harburg Pamplona Bible, a manuscript commissioned by King Sancho

48. Anonymous
The Golden Haggadah
Creation scenes
ca. 1320
Ink, gouache, and gilding on parchment
9 × 8 in.
British Library, London
Ms. Add. 27210, fol. 2v

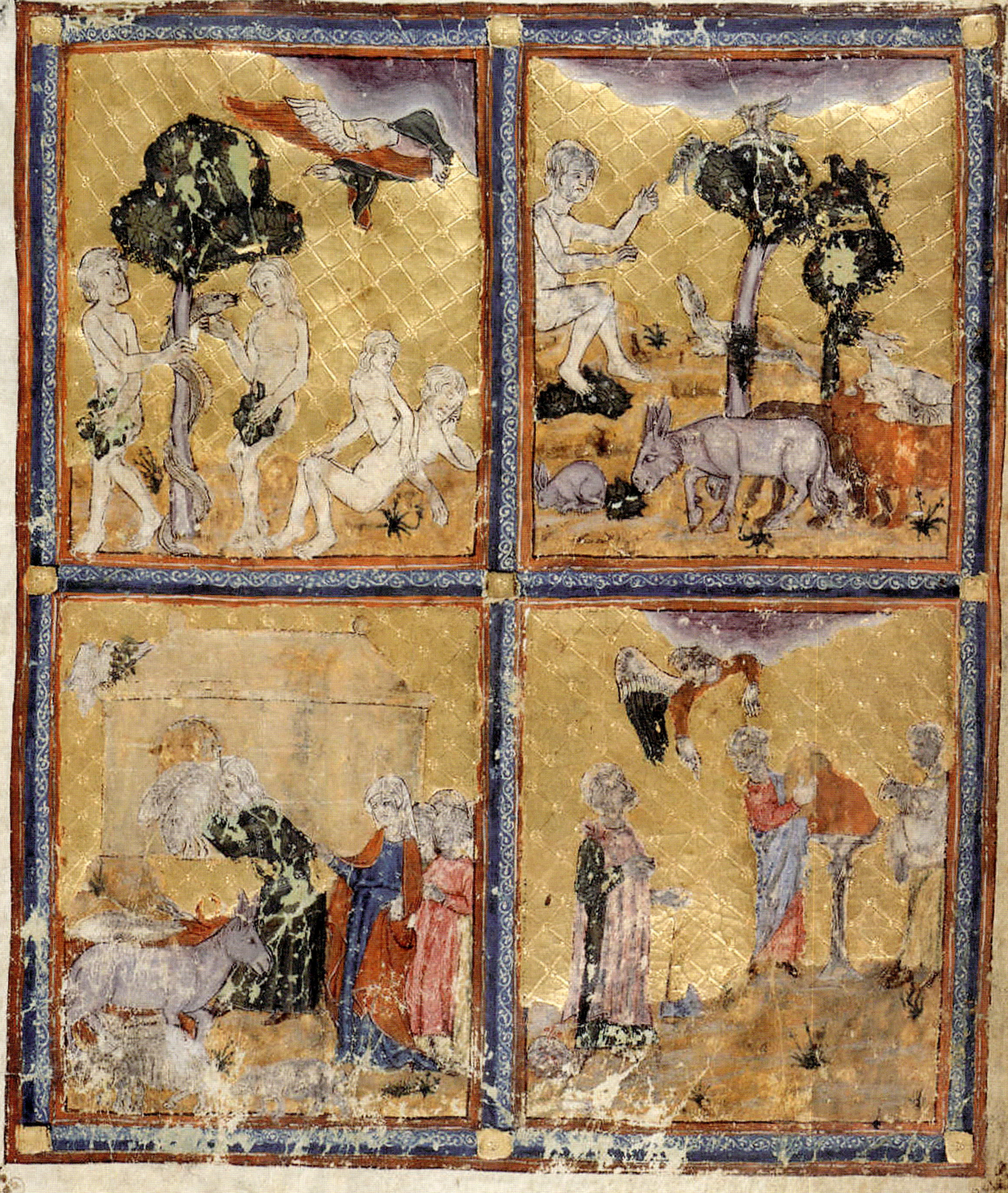

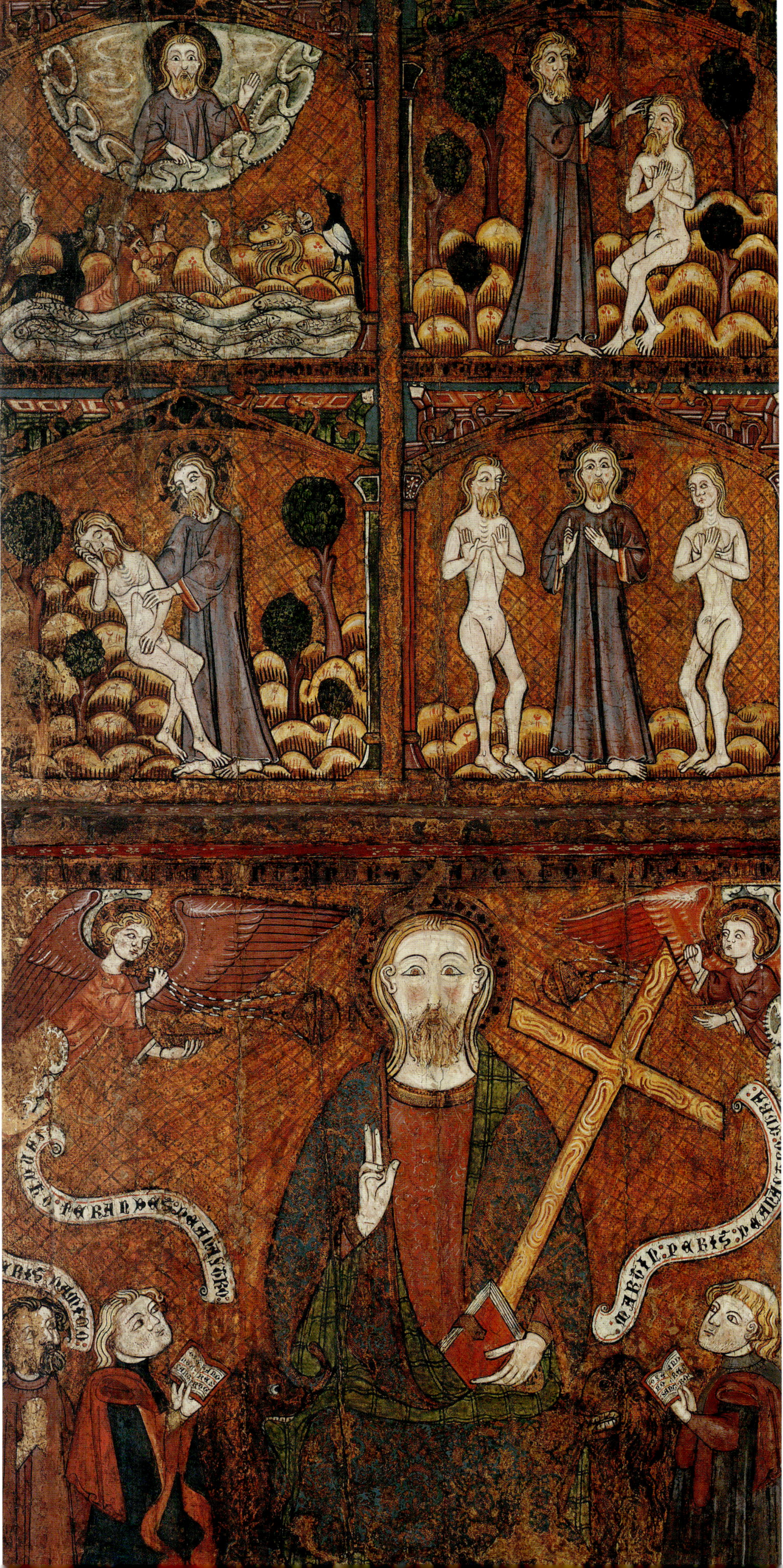

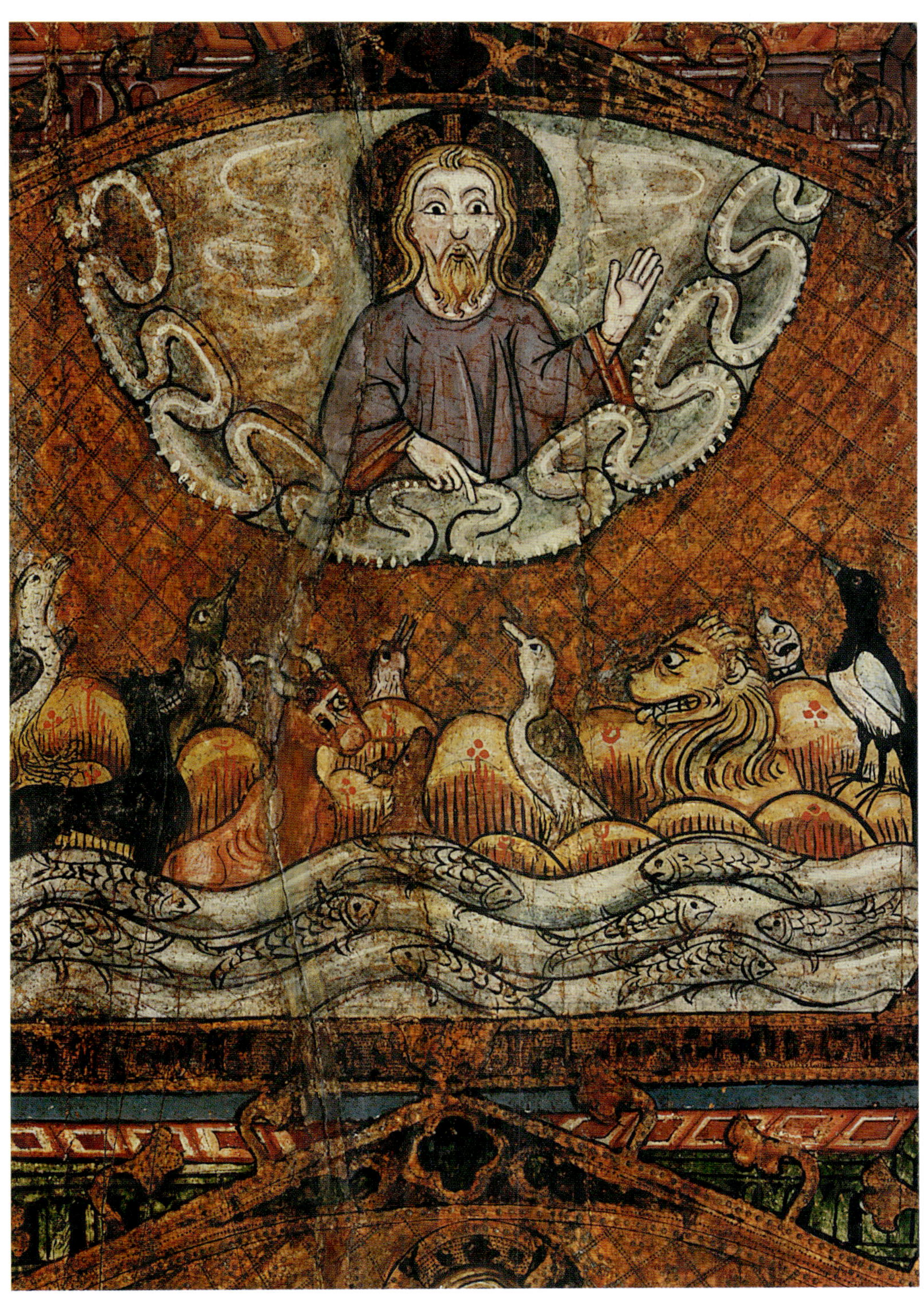

49. Anonymous
Altarpiece of Saint Andrew from Añastro
Late fourteenth century
Tempera on wood; punched and diapered; gold ground
78 ¼ × 39 ¾ in.
The Cloisters, Metropolitan Museum of Art, New York
MMA 25.120.257

the Strong of Navarre (1194–1234).[95] Another parallel between the Pamplona Bibles and the haggadot occurs in the scene of the Crossing of the Red Sea in which the water is depicted as a series of bands.[96] These interlocking relationships between art created under Christian auspices and the haggadot suggest an area of artistic interchange in addition to the work of Jewish artists for the Church and the depiction of Jews by Christian artists.

ART ON *CONVIVENCIA*

In this essay, we have examined the art of the fourteenth and fifteenth centuries in the Crown of Aragon as a means of understanding Jewish–Christian relations prior to the Expulsion. What has emerged is that the artists (and patrons) of the two religious groups had profound knowledge of each other's religious praxis, so much so that Christians represented Jewish life with fidelity and Jews produced art that was inspired by Christianity. In fact, Jews and Christians produced each other's art; Christian *retablos* were painted by Jews, church silver was made by Jewish silversmiths, and Hebrew manuscripts like Maimonides' *Guide to the Perplexed* were illuminated by Christians. In the practice of art, *convivencia* certainly reigned.

The profound knowledge of Jewish beliefs and customs evident in the altarpieces could have been the result of the employment of Jewish artists or *conversos* on a project, but it also could have been due to the small size of villages like Ejea whose parish churches commissioned *retablos* from major artists. In small towns and cities, the mingling of Jewish, Christian, and even Muslim residents was inevitable. At the time Blasco de Grañén painted its altarpiece, Ejea was home to some 250 Jews out of a total population of a thousand.[97] In addition, Jewish scholars became knowledgeable about Christian lore as a result their own interest or out of the need to counter the claims made by church spokesmen, often *conversos*, in disputations and conversionist sermons. They voluntarily attended sermons in churches and cathedrals,[98] where they could have been exposed to scenes from the Hebrew Bible on altarpieces and on sculpture. Christians attended sermons in synagogues out of their own curiosity, and their firsthand experience of Jewish houses of worship could serve as models for scenes on *retablos*. All the ways that Christians and Jews mixed in the fourteenth and fifteenth centuries, for business, as doctors attending patients, as workers and servants in each other's homes, as artists and artisans, and as colleagues exploring intellectual issues, allowed exposure to each other's way of life and art.

But, we must also ask: What was the effect of the art created during the fourteenth and fifteenth centuries on its viewers? Surviving Jewish art from Spain largely consists of manuscripts, although recent excavations have brought to light more ceremonial objects and visual culture.[99] Most of the illuminated manuscripts are Bibles and haggadot, although other genres such as philosophical and scientific treatises also exist. Ten of the haggadot have figurative compositions, but these manuscripts were an art form that was enjoyed privately in the Middle Ages.

The opposite is true of the Christian *retablos.* Altarpieces are definitely works of public art meant to teach, to inspire, and to invest the Church with grandeur.[100] The artists' practice of populating scenes from the Gospels and the Lives of the Saints with figures that appear to be modeled on local Jews, who are dressed in costumes visible in the course of daily life, and whose unkempt hair and beards were the result of royal edicts, must have had an effect on worshippers standing before large and impressive altarpieces. These depictions branded contemporary Jewry with the guilt of their ancestors who tormented Christ and the martyrs of the Church.[101] The portrayals were reminders of the Christian doctrine that the Jews of any age were equivalent to those alive during the early centuries of the Church. Jews were witnesses to the truth of Christianity and were, therefore, allowed to survive; still they embodied the guilt of their ancestors.

The negative message of historical scenes was compounded by representations of contemporary arenas of conflict between Jews and Christians. We have discussed representations of a disputation and of forced baptisms. The two altarpieces from the Cistercian monastery of Vallbona de les Monges painted in 1349–50 with their scenes of the Desecration of the Host were expressions of anti-Judaism linking the Black Death to Jewish transgressions.[102]

Another arena of conflict was the conversionist sermon that became a popular tactic of Christians seeking to convert Jews after 1242 when James I of Aragon and other secular rulers permitted the mendicant orders to preach in synagogues.[103] Scenes of conversionist sermons appear on altarpieces dedicated to Saint Stephen, who was known as a zealous preacher and died in Jerusalem ca. 35 C.E. A *retablo* by Jaume Serra (figure 50) of ca. 1385 shows Saint Stephen in a Gothic building that might be a church or a synagogue, flanked by Jewish men who are reacting to his sermon (figure 51). Interestingly, given the placement of the representation on an altarpiece, the Jews are shown reacting in diverse ways to what they have heard. An elderly man in the right foreground holds his Bible or prayer book up to the saint and appears to be arguing with Stephen. Behind him is a man who covers his ears in order not to hear blasphemy, and between the two is a man tearing up his Hebrew book having been convinced by the saint to abandon Judaism. The same actions are repeated by the Jews standing at left. Similar responses are depicted in a scene of Christ among the Doctors on a contemporaneous *retablo* by Lluís Borrassà.[104] Jews are known to have attended Christian sermons out of intellectual curiosity and the opposite was also true, Christians sometimes going to listen to sermons delivered in synagogues,[105] but in the scenes examined here the participants were not acting out of free will; rather they were participating in a compulsory event designed to convert them.

There are two unusual renderings of the Miracle of the Loaves and the Fishes that express a reconciliation between Jews and Christians, albeit in a Christian context. On

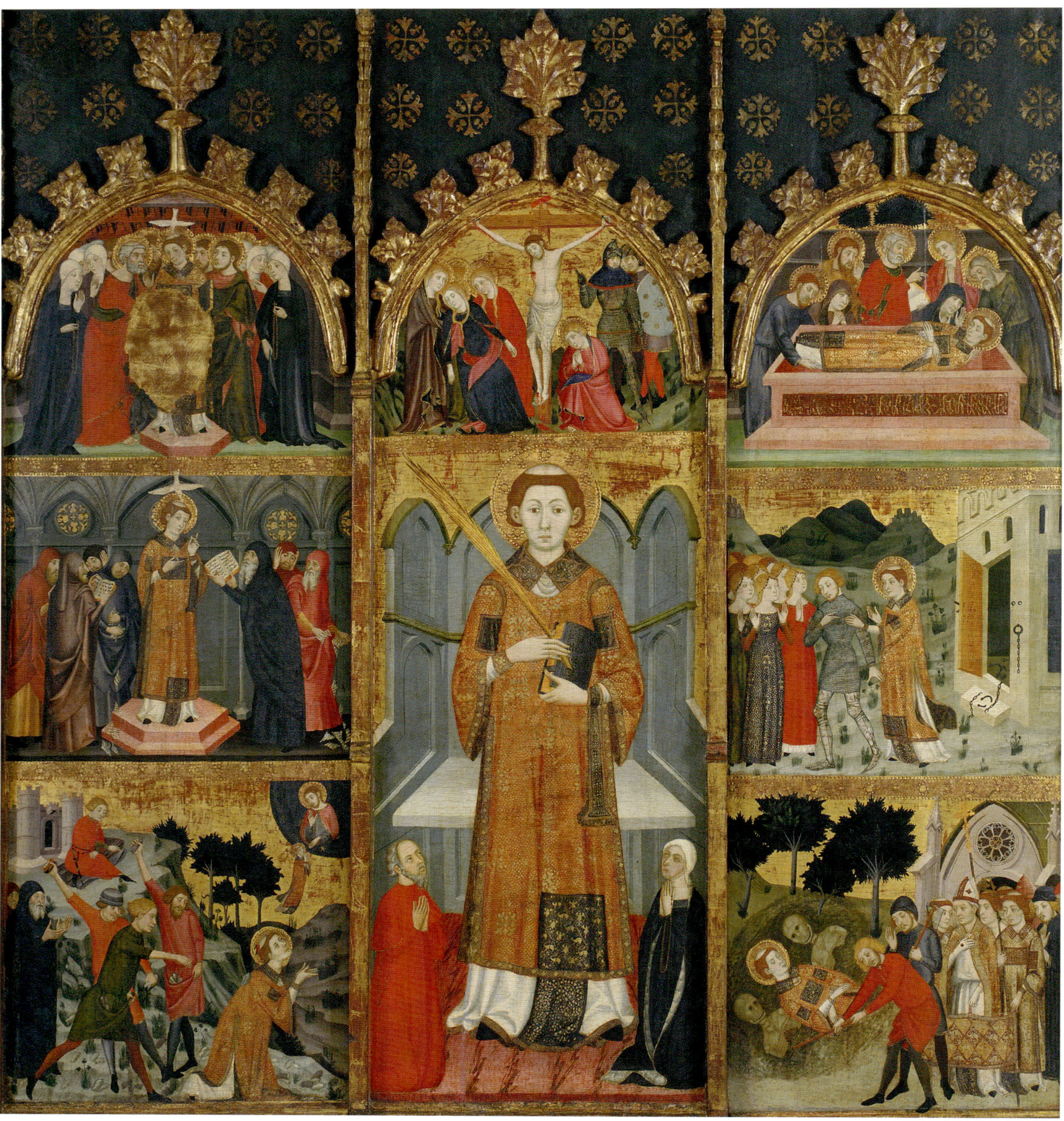

Fig. 50

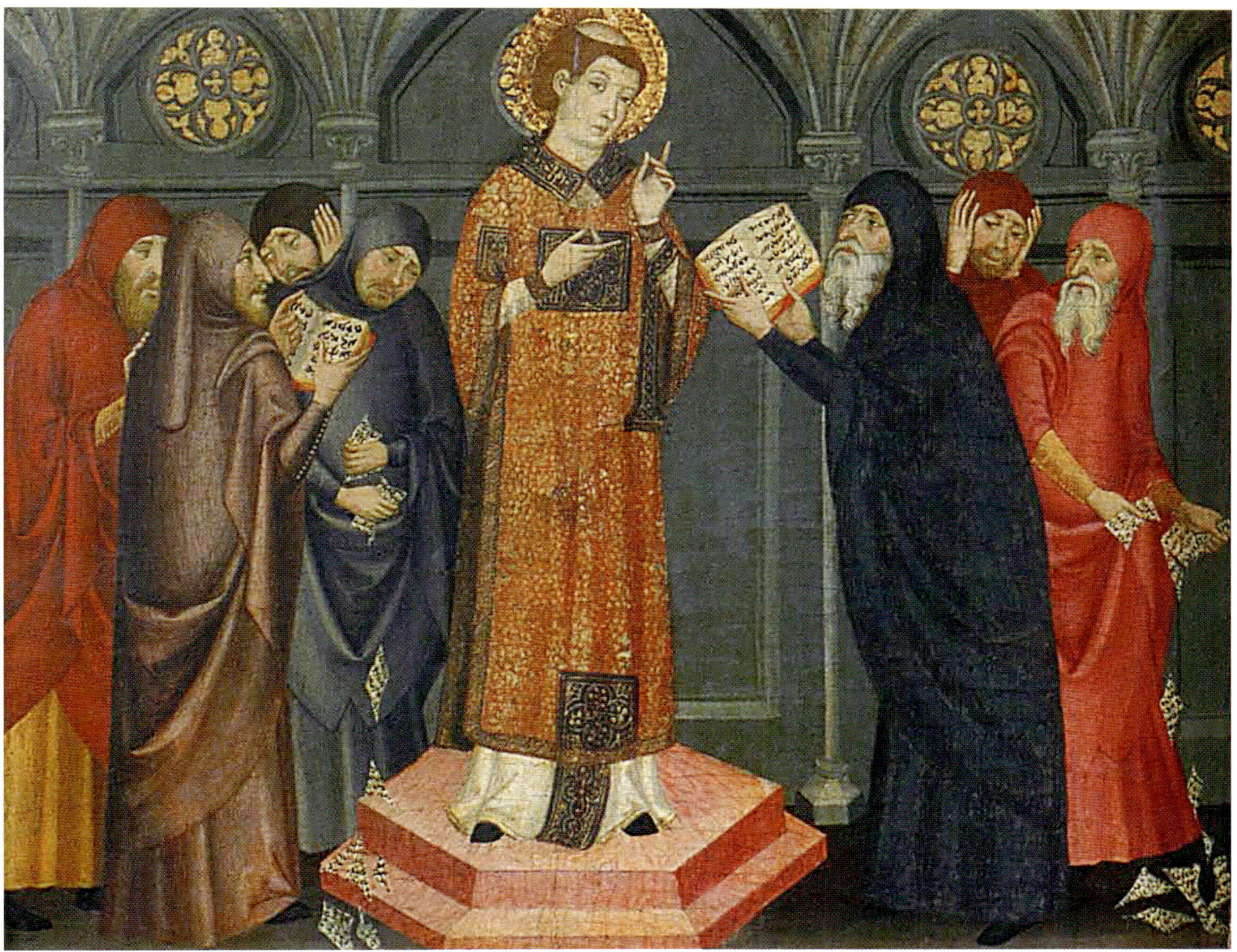

Fig. 51

the altarpiece of San Salvador in Ejea de los Caballeros painted by Blasco de Grañén and
Martín Soria between 1454 and 1476 (figure 52) and on the altarpiece of the Transfiguration
painted by Bernat Martorell between 1445 and 1452, the stream of people approaching Jesus
is made up of both Christians and Jews, the Jewish men identifiable by their dark cloaks and
untrimmed hair and beards. This treatment of the subject reflects the teachings of Abbot
Joachim of Fiore (ca. 1135–1202), who saw a future in which Jews and Christians would join
as one flock.[106] On another *retablo* painted by Martorell ca. 1435–45 on the theme of Saint
John the Baptist, two scenes on the right present Christians and Jews acting together.[107] Both

50. Jaume Serra
     Altarpiece of Saint Stephen from the church of Santa Maria de Gualter
     ca. 1385
     Tempera on panel
     Museu Nacional d' Art de Catalunya, Barcelona
     MNAC/MAC 9874

51. Jaume Serra
     Altarpiece of Saint Stephen from the church of Santa Maria de Gualter
     Saint Stephen Preaching in the Synagogue (detail)

Christian and Jewish women attend Anna in a scene of the birth of the saint. Below, Saint John preaches to a mixed group of Jews and Christians.

Joachim of Fiore was perhaps the first theorist of incremental progress ending in a "mutually beneficial union of Christians and Jews."[108] His ideas were disseminated throughout western Europe via the books of his followers, among whom were Arnold of Villanova, influential in Spain in the early years of the fourteenth century, and the Franciscan monk Francesc Eiximenis, born in Girona in 1327, who served Peter the Ceremonious of Aragon (1336–87) and other members of the royal family.[109] Eiximenis' writings that spread Joachite ideology throughout Spain were written in the last quarter of the fourteenth century. The Franciscan expanded Joachim's philosophy to include the concept that the "saints" of the Old Testament would be venerated along with those of the New: that is Saint Abraham, Saint David, Saint Isaiah and others.[110] The altarpiece scenes discussed above may be a reflection of this syncretist vision, as may the many portraits of Israelite kings and prophets on the *retablos*, although the prophets served a dual role as venerated holy figures and as predictors of the coming of Jesus as the messiah.

The record of Jewish life on the altarpieces of Aragon is a precious one. Manuscripts were the only art form Jews were allowed to take with them into exile in 1492 and the few genre scenes they contain yield only a partial glimpse of Jewish life. The figures that inhabit the miniatures showing the preparations and celebration of Passover in the haggadot are largely stereotypical. But the larger scale of the altarpieces and the superior skill of the artists afford us actual, particularized portraits of Jews living in the fourteenth and fifteenth centuries, as well as details of their dress and surroundings. Some of the paintings include Jewish figures as part of the daily life of medieval Aragon, like the shoemakers of the Manresa *retablo*, or the Jew on horseback depicted behind the Virgin Mary in a Pietà by Bartolomé de Cárdenas of 1490.[111] A similar rider is shown leaving a city on an altarpiece in Palma de Mallorca.[112] Their inclusion on the *retablos* exemplifies the social interaction that characterized Iberian society, and which has been termed *convivencia*.[113]

There is, however, another way to view the art we have been studying. Michael Camille has written that an innovation of Gothic artists was to see the past, the present and the future as unfolding in the present, with the present being the "real" time of the image.[114] Characters from the biblical past were shown as if existing in the present, just as the Jews in Spanish art represented their distant forebears, and synagogues were equated with the Jerusalem Temple. This approach was possible because medieval man did not see a gulf between himself and the time of Jesus and the saints. In fact popular religious texts encouraged people to visualize themselves as present at major events in Jesus' life, just as Jews are enjoined, to this day, to view themselves as participating in the Exodus from Egypt at the Passover Seder. This state of mind was an avenue for the integration of Jews into Christian life, which was sometimes beneficial, but too often detrimental.

52. Workshop of Blasco de Grañén and Martín Soria
Main altarpiece of Christ the Savior
Miracle of the Loaves and the Fishes (detail)
ca. 1441–87
Tempera on wood
61 ⁷⁄₁₆ × 34 ⅝ in.
San Salvador, Ejea de los Caballeros

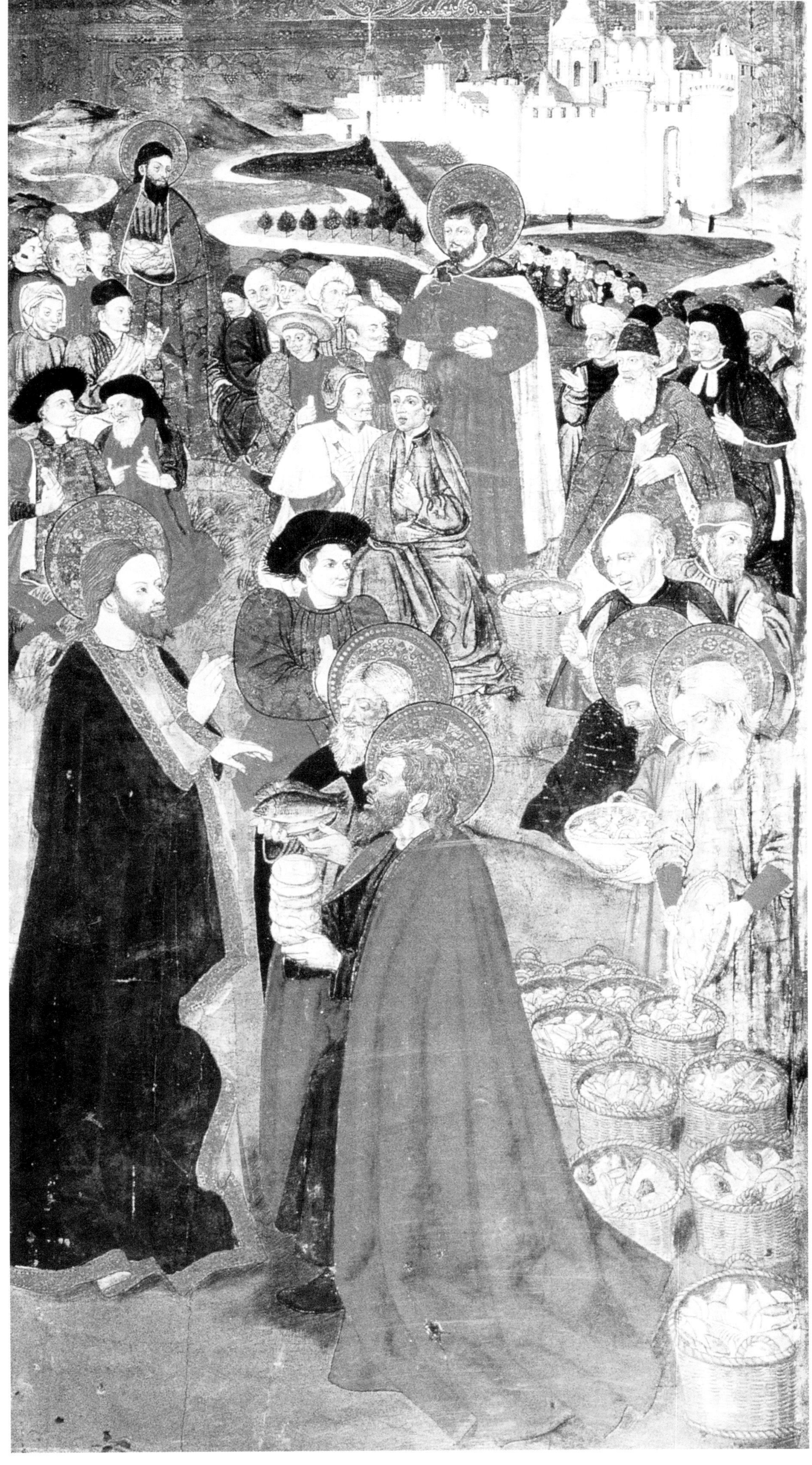

ENDNOTES

1   David Nirenberg, *Communities of Violence. Persecution of Minorities in the Middle Ages* (Princeton: Princeton University Press, 1996), 9.

2   On the traumatic events of 1391–1416, see Benjamin Gampel, "A Letter to a Wayward Teacher. The Transformations of Sephardi Culture in Christian Iberia," in *Culture of the Jews. A New History*, ed. David Biale (New York: Schocken Books, 2002), 230–38. For a discussion of continuities, see Jonathan Elukin, *Living Together. Living Apart. Rethinking Jewish-Christian Relations in the Middle Ages* (Princeton and Oxford: Princeton University Press, 2007), 112–14 and Mark D. Meyerson, *A Jewish Renaissance in Fifteenth-Century Spain* (Princeton and Oxford: Princeton University Press, 2004), 4–12.

3   Meyerson, *Jewish Renaissance*, 18–19.

4   Nirenberg, *Communities of Violence*, 20–45.

5   Thomas F. Glick, "An Introductory Note," in *Convivencia: Jews, Muslims and Christians in Medieval Spain*, ed. Vivian B. Mann, *et al.* (New York: The Jewish Museum and George Braziller, 1992), 1–9.

6   Elukin, *Living Together*, 135–38.

7   See, for example, a discussion of medieval Jews' knowledge of Christianity in Robert Chazan, *Fashioning Jewish Identity in Medieval Western Christendom* (Cambridge and New York: Cambridge University Press, 2005), 324–29. Chazan confines his discussion to the evidence of polemical literature. See also Ram Ben-Shalom, "Between Official and Private Dispute: The Case of Christian Spain and Provence in the Late Middle Ages," *AJS Review* 27:1 (2003), 23–72. Ben-Shalom discusses not only conversionist sermons and the well-known disputations at Barcelona and Tortosa, but also the various types of disputes which took place between Jews and Christians, some of them on a friendly plane.

8   Judith Berg Sobré, *Behind the Altar Table. The Development of the Painted Retable in Spain, 1300–1500* (Columbia: University of Missouri Press, 1989), 36–37.

9   An example of a similarly specific contract, written by leaders of the Jewish community of Arles some fifty years earlier, concerns a silver-gilt crown for the Torah scroll commissioned in March 1439 from the silversmith Robin Asard of Avignon. The Jewish patrons in Arles seem to have had no hesitation in hiring a Christian silversmith, despite the availability of numerous Jewish silversmiths in Aragon whose territory included Provence at the time of the commission. The contract reads in part:

> On March 24 1439, the Jews Massip, Durant, Bonsenhor de Argentieres, Bonjuhes de Beaucaire, and Moniac Bonfils, *baylons* of the synagogue of the Jews of Arles, ordered from Master Robin Asard, silversmith of Avignon, a crown for the Scroll of the Law…This one will have six towers with pillars at the angles, and a portal between the pillars, made like a masonry edifice. The upper border of the crown will be decorated above the portals with crenellations and loopholes, and the pillars and towers will likewise be decorated…On each of the pillars indicated above, there will be the head of a lion from which a silver chain will emerge. This chain will terminate into three tips, each furnished with a small round silver bell or *clochette*.

For the complete text see Vivian B. Mann, *Jewish Texts on the Visual Arts* (Cambridge: Cambridge University Press, 2000) 111–14.

10   Michael Baxandall, *Patterns of Intention. On the Historical Explanation of Pictures* (New Haven and London: Yale University Press, 1985), 107–8.

11   Richard Ettinghausen, Oleg Grabar, and Marilyn Jenkins-Madina, *Islamic Art and Architecture 650–1250* (New Haven and London: Yale University Press, 2001), 260.

12   Carmen Lacarra Ducay, "Estampas de la vida cotidiana durante el siglo XV a través se la pintura gótica bilbilitana," *VI Encuentros de Estudios Bilbilitanos*. Catalayud y Comarca (2000),382, 384–5.

13   On the altarpiece, see Carmen Lacarra Ducay, "Retablo de la Virgen con el Niño," in *Joyas de un Patrimonio* (Saragossa: Diputación de Zaragoza *et al.*, 1990), 97–119.

14   An unusual feature of the first encounter between Jesus and Anianus is the shoemaker's threatening gesture with his awl on the *retablo*. This aspect of the narrative may have migrated from another legendary encounter between Jesus and a shoemaker known as "The Wandering Jew," which first became popular in the early thirteenth century. (Jean-Claude Schmitt, 'La genèse médiévale de la légende et de l'iconographie du Juif errant," *Le Juif errant. Un témoin du temps* [Paris: Musée d'art et d'histoire du Judaïsme, 2001], 54–75.)

15   Another work commissioned by the Barcelona Guild of Shoemakers for the cathedral chapel of San Martín is today in the Louvre (R.F. 1967–6). It is an antependium with the Flagellation of Jesus. A single shoe in high relief appears on either side of the painting, echoing the shoes on the *retablo*.

16   Jews with red hair occur frequently on the fifteenth-century *retablos* of Mallorca and Palma de Mallorca. See Tina Sabater, *La pintura mallorquina del segle XV* (Edicions UIB, 2002), 149, fig. 3a; 153, fig. 4d; 203, fig. 37a. On the symbolism of red hair, see Ruth Mellinkoff, "Judas's Red Hair and the Jews," *Journal of Jewish Art* 9 (1982), 31–46.

17   Sara Lipton has noted a similar, but more limited transformation in the meaning of symbols depending on their historic context. A Scroll of the Law in the hands of God refers to the events at Sinai, but when scrolls are in the hands of contemporarily dressed Jewish figures, they may represent the Torah in the synagogue. (Sara Lipton, *Images of Intolerance. The Representation of Jews and Judaism in the* Bible Moralisée [Berkeley, Los Angeles, and London: University of California Press, 1999], 62.)

18   For an image of the scene see p 85.

19   For an account of the baptisms resulting from the pogroms of 1391 and the situation of *conversos*, see Meyerson, *Jewish Renaissance*, 22–24; 34–42.

20   A similar baptism scene appears on a fifteenth-century *retablo* in the Museo Diocesano in Huesca. (Miguel Angel Motis Dolader, *Aragón Sefarad* [Saragossa: Félix Arilla, 2005], 256).

21   On the history of the libel see Miri Rubin, *Gentile Tales. The Narrative Assault on Late Medieval Jews* (Philadelphia: University of Pennsylvania Press, 2004), 1 ff.

22   Marisa Melero Moneo, *La pintura sobre tabla del gótico lineal. Frontales, laterales de altar y retablos en el reino de Mallorca y los condados catalanes* [Memoria Artium 3]. (Barcelona: Edicions de la Universitat de Barcelona, 2005), 176–84; Alcoy i Pedrós, *L'art gòtic a Catalunya. Pintura I. De l'inici a l'italianisme* (Barcelona: Enciclopèdia Catalana, 2005) 127–29.

23 M. Rosa Manote i Clivilles *et al.*, *Gothic Art Guide* (Barcelona: Museu Nacional d'Art de Catalunya, 2000), 83–85; Alcoy i Pedrós, *L'art gòtic a Catalunya. Pintura I*, 213.

24 Elukin, *Living Together. Living Apart*, 68. A chronicle of the libel dated 1290 includes the incident depicted here. The man's wife and child view the assault on the host and promptly convert to Christianity. (Solomon Grayzel, *The Church and the Jews in the XIIIth Century. Vol. II, 1254–1314*, ed. Kenneth R. Stow [New York: Jewish Theological Seminary, and Detroit: Wayne State University Press, 1989], 198.)

25 Francesc Ruiz y Quesada, ed., *L'art gòtic a Catalunya. Pintura II. El corrent internacional* (Barcelona: Enciclopèdia Catalana, 2005), 44–45. The disputation scene is incorrectly labeled as a depiction of "Prophets."

26 Asunción Blasco Martínez, "Pintores y orfebres judíos en Zaragoza (siglo XIV)," *Aragón en la Edad Media* 8 (1989), 113–31.

27 See above, n. 7.

28 Blasco Martínez, "Pintores y orfebres judíos en Zaragoza," 120. The Jewish weavers' guild of Calatayud likewise had their own synagogue. (Mark Wischnitzer, *A History of Jewish Crafts and Guilds* [New York: Jonathan David, 1965], 109.)

29 Yom Tov Assis, ed., *The Jews in the Crown of Aragon. Regesta of the Cartas Reales in the Archivo de la Corona de Aragón. Part II: 1328–1493* (Jerusalem: Academon, 1995), vii. See Miguel Angel Motis Dolader, *Los judíos en Aragón en la Edad Media (siglos XIII–XV)* (Saragossa: Caja de Ahorros de la Inmaculada de Aragón, 1990), 152–60 for an analysis of Jewish artisanal trades and their integration into the Aragonese economy.

30 Núria de Dalmases i Balañà, "Aproximación a la orfebrería morellana," in *La memòria daurada. Obradors de Morella s. XIII–XVI* (n. p.: Pliego digital, 2000?), 120.

31 Meyerson, *Jewish Renaissance*, 110, 129–31.

32 Archivo Capitular de Tarazona, Protocolo de Làzaro de Larraz, 1380, fols. 22v.–23. For papal denunciations of pawning church vessels with Jews, see Grayzel, *The Church and the Jews*, 62–64.

33 For the evidence of the Levís' Jewish origins see José María Sanz Artibucilla, "Guillén y Juan de Leví pintores de retablos," *Sefarad* 4 (1944), 73–93. For a negative opinion, see Blasco Martínez, "Pintores y orfebres judíos," 119. *Retablo de Juan de Leví y su restauración. Capilla de los Pérez Calvillo. Catedral de Tarazona* (Saragossa: Felix Arilla, 1984), 30, n. 10.

34 *Retablo de Juan de Leví y su restauración*, 11.

35 *Retablo de Juan de Leví y su restauración*, 37.

36 On the depiction of Jews on medieval Spanish altarpieces, see Carmen Lacarra Ducay, "Representaciones de judíos en la pintura gótica aragonesa: siglos XIII al XV," *Boletín Museo e Instituto Camón Aznar* XCIX (2007), 235–58. On purple robes signifying potential penitents, see Laura Jacoby, Review of Anne Derbes and Mark Sandona, *The Usurer's Heart: Giotto, Enrico Scrovegni and the Arena Chapel in Padua* (University Park, University of Pennsylvania Press, 2008).

37 P. Fernando de Mendoza, "Con los judíos de Estelle," *Príncipe de Viana* 12 (1951), 244.

38 José María Azcárate, *Arte gotico en España* (Madrid: Ediciones Cátedra, 2007), 343; Berg Sobré, *Behind the Altar Table*, 18 *passim*. F. Olivan Bayle, *Bonanat y Nicolás Zahortiga y la pintura del siglo XV* (Saragossa: Ayuntimento de Zaragoza, Comisión de Cultura, 1978).

39 José González Luis, "Der 'Dialogus' des Petrus Alfonsi, ein polemisch-apologetischer Traktat," *Jewish Studies in a New Europe* (Copenhagen: C. A. Reitzel and the Kongelige Bibliotek, 1998), 302.

40 Chazan, *Fashioning Jewish Identity*, 331.

41 See Judith Berg-Sobré, *Bartolomé de Cárdenas "El Bermejo." Itinerant Painter in the Crown of Aragon* (San Francisco, London, and Bethesda: International Scholars Publications 1998), 74–77, fig. 16 for a discussion of the artist's use of Hebrew, which suggests *converso* origins.

42 Berg-Sobré, *Bartolomé de Cárdenas "El Bermejo,"* 70–79, fig. 16.

43 Alcoy i Pedrós, *L'art gòtic a Catalunya. Pintura I*, 275–77.

44 Joan Sureda i Pons, ed., *L'art gòtic a Catalunya. Pintura III. Darreres manifestacions*. (Barcelona: Enciclopèdia Catalana, 2006), 218–20.

45 Berg-Sobré, *Bartolomé de Cárdenas "El Bermejo,"* 226, fig. 19.

46 A facsimile of the Alba Bible has been published accompanied by essays on the manuscript: Moses of Arragel, trans., *La Biblia de Alba,* ed. Jeremy Schonfeld (Madrid: Fundación Amigos de Sefarad, 1992); see there the older bibliography. Also, Carl-Otto Nordström, *The Duke of Alba's Castilian Bible. A Study of the Rabbinical Features of the Miniatures* (Uppsala: Almquist and Wiksells, 1967) for a study of the iconography of the miniatures.

47 Chazan, *Fashioning Jewish Identity*, 65.

48 On the Ejea *retablo* see Carmen Lacarra Ducay, *Blasco de Grañén, pintor de retablos (1422–1459)* (Saragossa: Institución "Fernando el Católico," 2004), 44–90; eadem, "Retablo de San Salvador. Ejea de los Caballeros," in *Joyas de un Patrimonio* (Saragossa: Diputación de Zaragoza, *et al.*, 1990), 12–79. Some of the costs of the Ejea altarpiece were financed by a loan from Faym Baco, a Jew of Albalate de Cinca. (Achivio Parroquial de Ejea, Sección Pergaminos, s/n. Ejea, 19 de febrero de 1472; Lacarrra Ducay, *Blasco de Grañén*, 48–50.)

49 The purpose of the laws prescribing specific clothing was both to prevent sexual relations between Christians and Jews by clarifying the appearance of the latter and to assert royal control. For a discussion of clothing restrictions, see Jonathan Ray, *The Sephardic Frontier. The Reconquista and the Jewish Community in Medieval Iberia* (Ithaca and London: Cornell University Press, 2006), 156–64.

50 Lipton, *Images of Intolerance*, 86–87.

51 Solomon Alami, *Iggeret HaMusar [Treatise on Moral Behavior]*. The mention of deep mourning refers to the Jewish prohibition against shaving and haircutting while in mourning for a close relative.

52 Ann Rosalind Jones and Peter Stallybrass, *Renaissance Clothing and the Materials of Memory* (Cambridge: Cambridge University Press, 2002), 54–55.

53 Janina M. Safran, "Identity and Differentiation in Ninth-Century Al-Andalus," *Speculum* 76 (2001), 582.

54 Mark R. Cohen, *Under Crescent and Cross. The Jews in the Middle Ages* (Princeton: Princeton University Press, 1994), 62–64; Safran, "Identity and Differentiation," 582–83. In the mid-ninth century, the Abassid caliph al-Mutawakkil specified a *zunnar* made of rope or cord, as well as a hood (*taylasan*) and a conical cap (*qalansuwa*) as required dress for minorities. The caliph's stipulation that the *zunnar* be made of rope or cord marked a turning point in the meaning of the belt. Once a badge of honor, its material requirements transformed the *zunnar* into a sign of degradation, of second class status.

55 Jones and Stallybrass, *Renaissance Clothing*, 54–55.

56 Vivian B. Mann, "The Covered Gospels, the Torah Case and the Qur'an Box," in *Art and Ceremony in Jewish Life. Essays in the History of Jewish Art* (London: Pindar Press, 2005), 177–94.

57 D. Dimas Fernández-Galiano, ed., *Aragón. Reino y Corona* (Saragossa: Tipolínea, 2000), no. 71.

58 This altarpiece is unpublished.

59 Alcoy i Pedrós, *L'art gòtic a Catalunya. Pintura I*, 189, a scene of the Presentation of Jesus in the Temple on a *retablo* now in the Walters Art Museum.

60 Miguel Angel Espinosa Villegas, "La sinagoga," in *Lorca. Luces de Sefarad*, ed. Angel Iniesta Sanmartin *et al.* (Murcia: Industrias Gráficas Libecom, 2009), 48–77.

61 Juan García Sandoval, "El resplandor de las lámparas de vidrio de la sinagoga de Lorca. Estudio tipológico," in *Lorca. Luces de Sefarad*, 259–304.

62 Walter Cahn, "Solomonic Elements in Romanesque Art," in *The Temple of Solomon. Archaeological Fact and Medieval Tradition in Christian, Islamic and Jewish Art*, ed. Joseph Gutmann (Missoula, Mont.: Scholar's Press, 1976), 58.

63 For the Hebrew original, see Mann *et al.*, *Convivencia*, 216.

64 For a reproduction, see Juan José Martín González, ed., *Las edades del hombre. El arte en la iglesia de Castilla y Leon* (Salamanca: Europa Artes Gráficas, 1988), 97.

65 Robert Ousterhout, "Meaning and Architecture: A Medieval View," *Reflections* 2, 1 (1984), 37.

66 Françoise Piponnier and Perrine Mane, *Dress in the Middle Ages,* trans. Caroline Beamish (New Haven and London: Yale University Press, 2007), 16, 20.

67 Text from Alfred Ruben's, *A History of Jewish Costume* (London: Peter Owen Limited, 1973. pp.184-85). In 1456 the Jewish community of Morvedre passed sumptuary laws regulating Jewish women's dress and the amount of jewelry that could be worn in order to prevent ostentatious display that might lead to an increase in taxes. (Meyerson, *Jewish Renaissance*, 89.)

68 A singular exception is a twelfth-century mural in the cathedral of Tarazona showing a Jewish man and woman wearing cloaks emblazoned with the rotulus.

69 For an illustration see Bezalel Narkiss *et al.*, *Hebrew Illuminated Manuscripts in the British Isles. Volume One: The Spanish and Portuguese Manuscripts* (Oxford and Jerusalem, 1982), pl. LXXIII. For a reformulation of the law requiring Jews and Moors to wear long robes over their clothes enacted in 1412, see Rubens, *A History of Jewish Costume* 89–90.

70 Joan Molina i Figueras, "Al voltant de Jaume Huguet," in *L'art gòtic a Catalunya. Pintura III. Darreres manifestacions* (Barcelona: Enciclopèdia Catalana, 2006), 142–43.

71 For the composition on the Via Latina fresco, see Kurt Weitzmann, *The Age of Spirituality. Late Antique and Early Christian Art, Third to the Seventh Century* (New York: New York and Princeton: Metropolitan Museum of Art and Princeton University Press, 1979), fig. 43; on the mosaic in Sta. Maria Maggiore, see Wolfgang Fritz Volbach, *Early Christian Art* (New York: Harry N. Abrams, Inc., 1961), fig. 129.

72 Bonjuà Cabrit is cited in legal records as possessing a copy of Avicenna that was stolen from Meir of Figueras, the son of a deceased physician. (Robert I. Burns, *Jews in the Notarial Culture. Latinate Wills in Mediterranean Spain 1250–1350* (Berkeley, Los Angeles, and London: University of California Press, 1996), 64.

73 Her headdress is similar to that worn by the mistress of the household in the Seder scenes of the Sarajevo Haggadah and the Sister of the Golden Haggadah. See fig. 11 in Cecil Roth, *The Sarajevo Haggada* (Belgrade: Beogradski Izdavač-Grafički Zavod, 1975). Knowledge of this headdress had even spread to Germany by the beginning of the fifteenth century. In a scene of the Birth of Mary on the Buxtehuder Altar, Master Bertram painted the woman serving Elizabeth wearing a headdress with chin strap and circular element atop her head. (Jürgen Wittstock, ed., *Aus dem Alltag der mittelalterlichen Stadt. Hefte des Focke Museums*, no. 62 [1982], 165, fig. 7.)

74 J. M. Martí Bonet, *La catedral de Barcelona* (Barcelona: Editorial Escudo de Oro and Arxiu Diocesà de Barcelona, n.d.), 119.

75 Alfredo Romero Santamaría, ed., *Hebraica aragonalia. El legado judío en Aragón* (Saragossa: Palacio de Sastago–Diputación de Zaragoza, 2002), vol. 1, 155.

76 For the capital, see Elena Romero, ed., *La vida judía en Sefarad* (Toledo: Julio Soto Impresor, 1991), 60. Until early in the twentieth century, the Jewish women of Salonica wore headdresses whose constituent elements were similar to those depicted in Spanish art, but whose proportions were somewhat different. (Batsheva Goldman-Ida, "The Sephardic Woman's Head-Dress," in *From Iberia to Diaspora. Studies in Sephardic History and Culture,* ed. Yedida K. Stillman and Norman A. Stillman (Leiden, Boston, and Cologne: Brill, 1999), 525–30.

77 S. D. Goitein, *A Mediterranean Society. The Jewish Communities of the World as Portrayed in the Documents of the Cairo Geniza. Vol. 2: The Community* (Berkeley, Los Angeles, and London: University of California Press, 1999), 296; see also Cohen, *Under Crescent and Cross*, 95–96.

78 Goitein, *Mediterranean Society, Vol. 1: Economic Foundations*, 297.

79 Millard Meiss, "Italian Style in Catalonia and a Fourteenth-Century Catalan Workshop," *Journal of the Walters Art Gallery*, 4 (1941), 45–87.

80 Meiss saw a stylistic relationship between the Saint Mark altarpiece in the Morgan Library and the Saint Mark triptych in Manresa, but his conclusion was disputed by C. Post. Meiss, "Italian Style in Catalonia," 69 ; C. Post, *A History of Spanish Painting*, vol. IX, pt. 2 (Cambridge, Mass.: Harvard University Press, 1933), 243.

81 Francis Wormald, "Afterthoughts on the Stockholm Exhibition," *Konsthistorisk Tidskrift* (1953), 75–84. Others have attributed additional Hebrew manuscripts to the same atelier: Gabrielle Sed Rajna, "Hebrew Manuscripts of Fourteenth-Century Catalonia and the Workshop of the Master of Saint Mark," *Jewish Art*, 18 (1992), 117-28; Dalia-Ruth Halperin, "A Jew Among Us: The Catalan Micrography Maḥzor Artist and the Ferrer Bassa Atelier, " *Ars Jusaica*, 3(2007), 19-30.

82 Alcoy i Pedrós, *L'art gòtic a Catalunya. Pintura I*, 162.

83 Alcoy i Pedrós, *L'art gòtic a Catalunya. Pintura I*, 146–70. Recently, S. Shalev-Eyni published evidence that a Jewish scribe worked in a scriptorium on Lake Constance that produced both Hebrew and Latin manuscripts in the first decades of the fourteenth century (*Jews Among Christians. A Hebrew School of Illumination* [London: Harvey Miller Publishers, 2009]).

84 For a recent iconographic study of six of the manuscripts, see Katrin Kogman-Appel, *Illuminated Haggadot from Medieval Spain. Biblical Imagery and the Passover Holiday* (University Park: University of Pennsylvania Press, 2006).

85 That they were not titles for the finished miniatures is indicated by the discrepancies between the texts and the subjects depicted.

86 The architectural frame and drapery style of The Cloisters' *retablo* panels are particularly close to those of the *frontale* (altar frontal) of Santa Perpetua de Mogoda of the first or second quarter of the fourteenth century (Barcelona, Museo Diocesano, Inv. MDB/400). See Melero Moneo, *La pintura sobre tabla del gótico lineal*, 72–79.

87 This composition, Adam and Eve hiding their genitals with leaves and standing on either side of the Tree of Knowledge around which the serpent coils, is known as early as the fourth century and ca. 1000 in Spanish art. (See an engraved bowl in Jeffrey Spier *et al.*, *Picturing the Bible. The Earliest Christian Art* [New Haven and London: Yale University Press, 2007], fig. 4).

88 Metropolitan Museum of Art, *The Art of Medieval Spain: A.D. 500–1200* (New York: The Metropolitan Museum of Art, 1992), no. 81.

89 Pedro de Palol and Max Hirmer, *Early Medieval Art in Spain* (New York: Harry N. Abrams, Inc., 1966), pl. XX, and figs. 72–73.

90 For all the scenes, see Josep Calzada i Oliveras, *Die Kathedrale von Girona*, 2nd ed. (Barcelona: Escudo de Oro, 1988), 16. In the first decade of the twelfth century, a tapestry devoted to the theme of the Creation (museum of Girona cathedral) included two scenes of Adam and Eve: Adam Naming the Animals and the Creation of Eve. (Palol and Hirmer, *Early Medieval Art in Spain*, pl. XXXV.)

91 For example a Bible from the monastery of San Pedro de Cardeña in Burgos, ca. 1175 (Metropolitan Museum of Art, *Art of Medieval Spain*, no. 152).

92 Palol and Hirmer, *Early Medieval Art in Spain*, pls. XL and XLI. Adam and Eve also appear in frescoes from San Martín de Sescorts (Barcelona) and from Vic (Barcelona), both dating from the late eleventh to early twelfth century. (Palol and Hirmer, *Early Medieval Art in Spain*, pl. XXVI.)

93 Roth, *Sarajevo Haggada*.

94 In the early twelfth-century Creation Tapestry in Girona cathedral, the fifth day is similarly depicted: at bottom are the creatures of the water, above the birds craning their heads toward Jesus enthroned at center. Missing are the wild animals in the zone of the birds that appear in both the haggadah and the *retablo* scene.

95 François Boucher, *The Pamplona Bibles* (New Haven and London: Yale University Press, 1970), pl. 3. The two scenes of Adam and Eve in the manuscript are not comparable to those under discussion here.

96 Boucher, *Pamplona Bibles*, pl. 118; Narkiss *et al.*, *Hebrew Illuminated Manuscripts in the British Isles*, fig. 294.

97 Motis Dolader, *Los judíos en Aragón*, 52.

98 Ben-Shalom, "Between Official and Private Dispute".

99 For examples of newly excavated ceremonial art and visual culture, see Bango Torviso, *Memoria de Sefarad*, pp. 111–29 and *Lorca. Luces de Sefarad,* ed. Angel Iniesta Sanmartin *et al.*, pp. 372–85.

100 Baxandall, *Patterns of Intention*, 106.

101 Elukin, *Living Together. Living Apart*, 4.

102 Carmen Muñoz Párraga, "Los judíos en Aragón. Del mundo del Medievo al del Renacimiento," in *Encrucijada de Culturas* (Saragossa: Típolinea, 2008), 104.

103 Chazan, *Fashioning Jewish Identity*, 115.

104 Romero, *La vida judía en Sefarad*, 72.

105 Ben-Shalom, "Between Official and Private Dispute," 30, 35.

106 Robert E. Lerner, *The Feast of Saint Abraham. Medieval Millenar-ians and the Jews* (Philadelphia: University of Pennsylvania Press, 2001), 1.

107 For an illustration see Ruiz i Quesada, ed., *L'art gòtic a Catalunya. Pintura III*, 239.

108 Lerner, *Feast of Saint Abraham*, 19 and 24.

109 Marjorie Reeves, *The Influence of Prophecy in the Later Middle Ages. A Study in Joachimism* (Notre Dame, Ind. and London: University of Notre Dame Press, 1993), 221.

110 Lerner, *Feast of Saint Abraham*, 110.

111 Martí Bonet, *La catedral de Barcelona*, 111.

112 Montserrat Blanch, *El arte gotico en España* (Barcelona: Ediciones Poligrafa, 1972), 316.

113 Ray, *Sephardic Frontier*, 174.

114 Michael Camille, *Gothic Art. Glorious Visions* (Englewood Cliffs, N.J.: Prentice-Hall, 1996), 74, 82, 92.

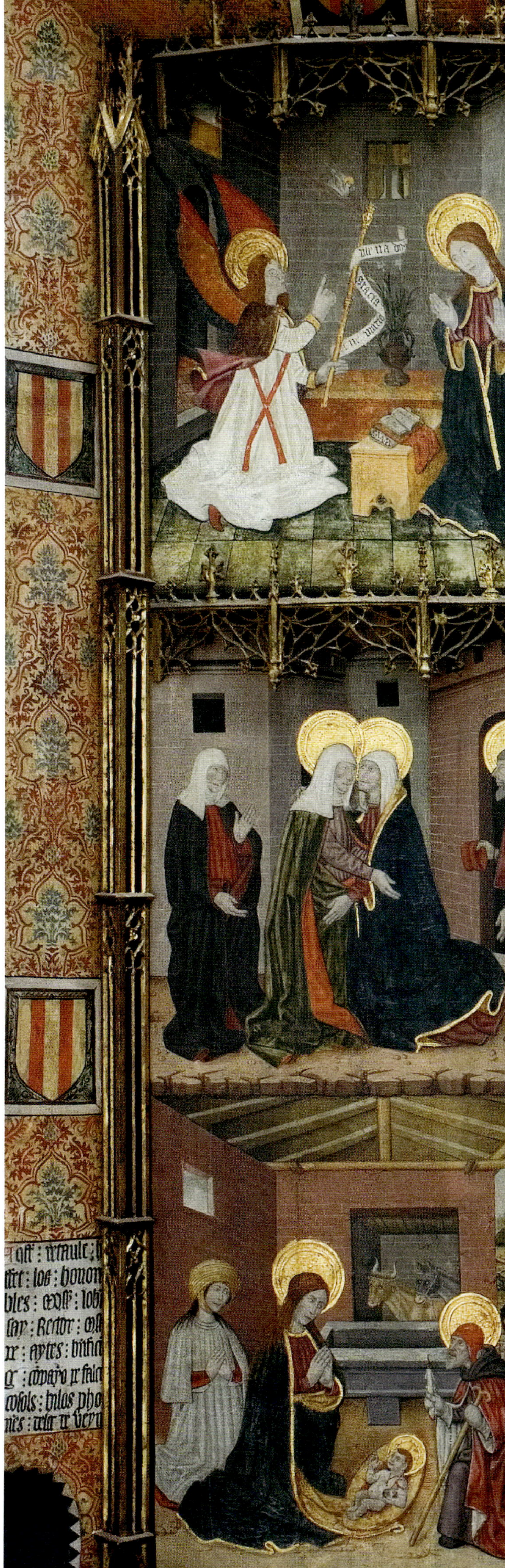

128

53. Pere Espalargues
   Altarpiece with Scenes from the Life of the
   Virgin from the Church of Enviny
   Catalonia, 1490
   Tempera on panel
   The Hispanic Society of America (A5)

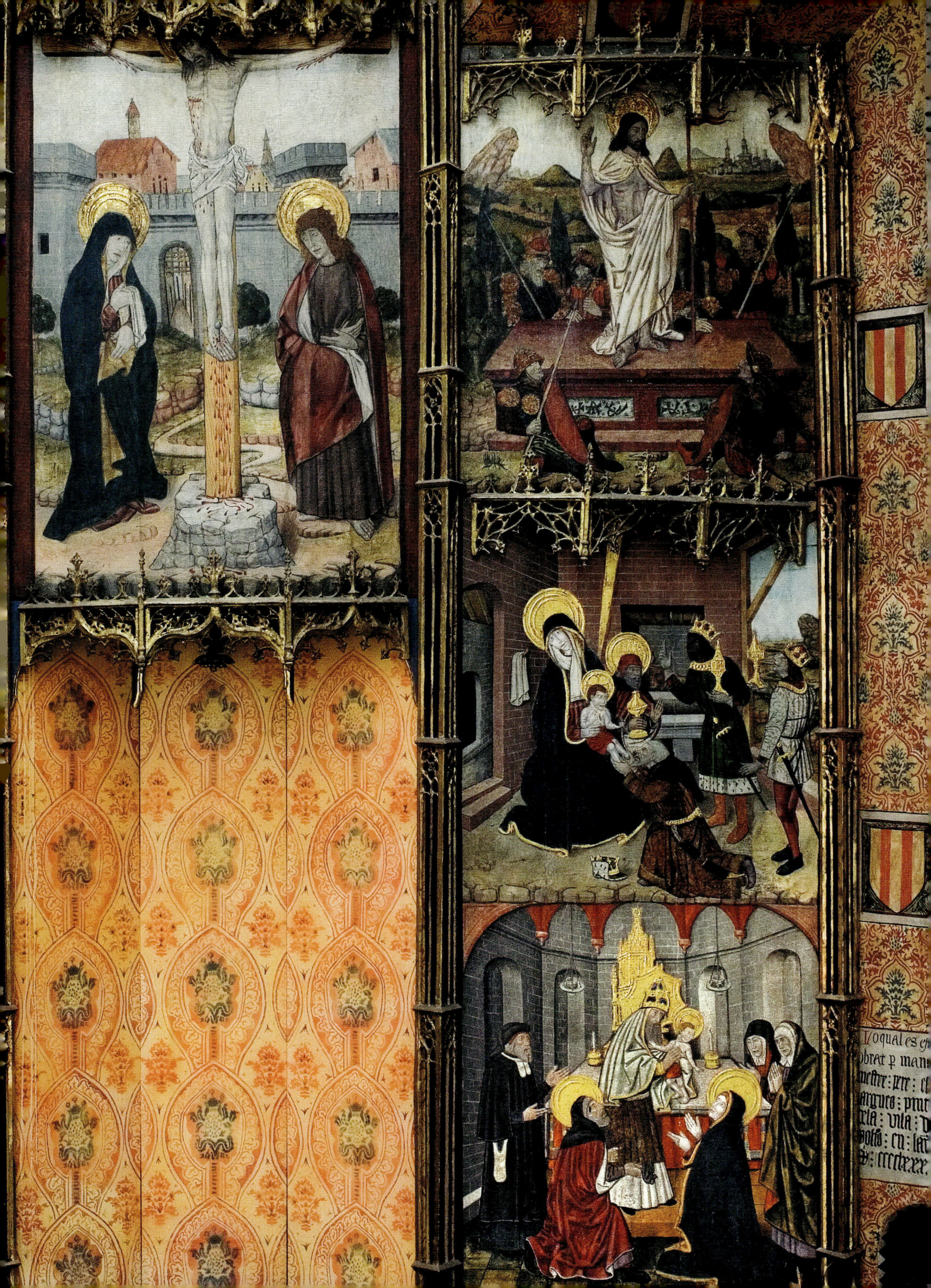
lo qual es g
obrat p man
nestar : xxx :
arguros : pmt
ria : vila :
goria : cn : lat
: ccccLxx.

A BRIEF SURVEY OF JEWISH STUDIES IN SPAIN

— Marcus B. Burke

The Jewish presence in medieval Iberia, whether in the Muslim or Christian areas of the Peninsula, has always been a well-known fact, so it is, in the strictly logical sense, surprising that the study of Jewish elements in medieval Spanish monumental painting was largely ignored until the past two decades.[1] As the current exhibition makes clear, the history of painting in the medieval Spanish kingdoms ought to be well endowed with the biographies of artists of Jewish descent, both practicing Jews or those converted to Catholicism (*conversos*), and any discussion of medieval iconography ought to take into account the numerous representations of contemporary Jewish life and ritual in narrative scenes, such as those of the Life of Christ. That this is not the case is in large part due to the curious nature of antisemitism in Spain, especially in the past 150 years.

All civil rights for adherents of Judaism ended in the kingdoms of Castile and Aragon when religious Jews were forced by the Edict of Expulsion of 1492 either to convert to Christianity or to leave Spain (figure 54). What may not be so universally understood is that the Expulsion was in fact the end product of decades of increasing antisemitic persecution. From the mid-1400s, racial or ethnic prejudice directed not so much against practicing Jews but rather against Christians of Jewish descent, especially families that had converted after the pogroms of 1391, was rampant and increasingly *de jure*. This special antisemitic prejudice would come to be enshrined in the new Spanish Inquisition, founded in 1478. As Benzion Netanyahu has forcefully demonstrated,[2] the racial antisemitism of the 1400s set the stage for the Expulsion of 1492 and established legal and social principles that would cause any hint of Jewish culture to be suppressed for nearly 400 years. Not only did the Inquisition investigate and harshly punish any return, real or imagined, to the tenets of Judaism on the part of Christians of Jewish

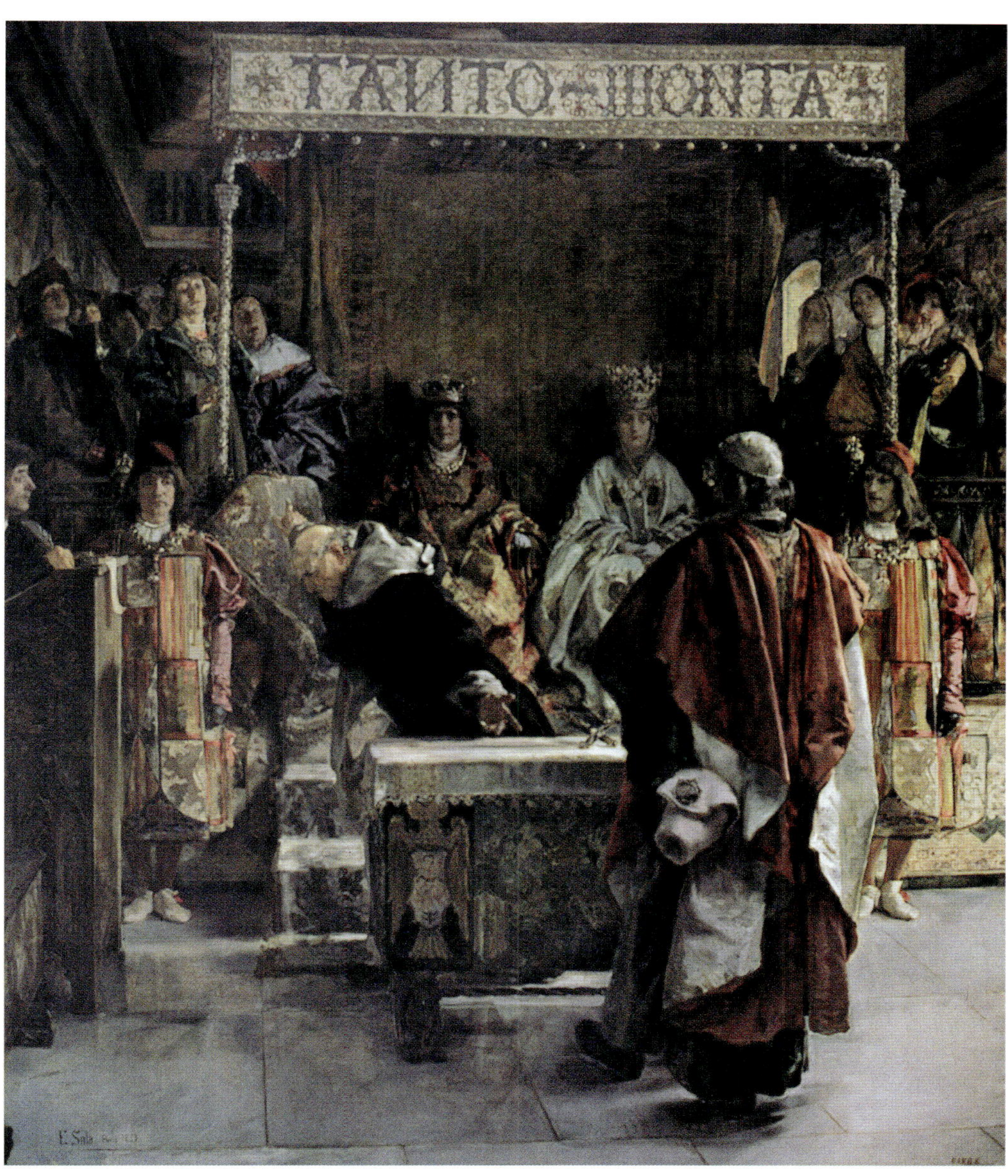

54. Emilio Sala Frances
The Expulsion of the Jews from Spain in 1492
1889
Oil on canvas
123 × 50 in.
Museo Nacional del Prado, Madrid

descent (called "New Christians" at the time), but it also became from the outset an instrument of ethnic persecution by which any "New Christian," no matter how pious, became suspect on account of his religious practice and fair game for exploitation and denunciation. In effect, the Inquisition became a permanent, institutionalized pogrom.

Moreover, from the mid-1400s, religious zeal justified the promulgation of laws of *limpieza de sangre*—or "clean blood"—by which even certifiably pious Christians could be deprived of advancement in society if they were proven to be descended from Jewish ancestors. The existence of these laws in a society whose upper bourgeoisie and nobility were often the product of ethnic intermarriages from the early Middle Ages onwards led to massive obfuscations of family history. Indeed, one need only look at King Ferdinand, the man who, with his wife Isabella the Catholic, founded the Inquisition and promulgated the Edict of Expulsion, to see an example of exalted rank who "had inherited Jewish blood," as the historian John H. Elliott has put it.[3] Recent genetic studies, although highly controversial, show some evidence of this Jewish heritage and have placed the ancient Palestinian component (including Israelite, Judaic, and Phoenician) of modern Spanish DNA at about twenty percent.[4] (How much of that component is medieval Sephardic, as opposed to other possible origins, is much discussed.)

A society hell-bent on silencing any whisper of Jewish origins was unlikely to celebrate the culture of the populations it expelled and suppressed, yet historical memory of the medieval Jewish inhabitants, especially in the context of Hispano-Islamic culture, was not entirely lost. For example, Sebastián de Covarrubias' 1612 dictionary could still comment on the Jewish and Muslim contributions to the Spanish language and cite medieval edicts concerning Jewish dress and social relations.[5] Nevertheless, by 1732, when the Spanish Royal Academy published its *Diccionario de autoridades*, the definition of the word *judío* had come to include its use as a serious insult.[6] As for religious toleration, that would have to wait nearly four centuries. In spite of the suspension of the Spanish Inquisition for a brief period during the Napoleonic invasion of Spain, and a liberal government installed at Cádiz in 1812, religious toleration was only legalized in Spain in 1855 and the 1492 Edict of Expulsion was not revoked until 1868. After that, a steady liberalizing trend led to religious freedom being included in the Constitution of 1869, with the Constitution of 1876 largely continuing the principles of 1869. It was not, however, until the Constitution of 1932, part of the upheaval of the Spanish Republic, that Church and State would be separated.

Alas, religious freedom in Spain was swept away, along with many other elements of liberal reform, by the victory of the fascist side in the Spanish Civil War, 1936–39. General Francisco Franco (1892–1975), leader of the fascist forces, restored Roman Catholicism as the unique religion of the country, and no public variation in faith, Protestant or Jewish, was allowed for Spanish nationals on the mainland—although citizens of Spain's Moroccan colonies were able to continue their Muslim and Jewish devotions.[7] At this point, the already bizarre nature of official Spanish antisemitism became surreal. As José Luis Rodríguez Jiménez and

Juan José Morales Ruiz have shown,[8] from the 1920s the rhetoric of right-wing political and militarist movements such as the Falange regularly included rants against a supposed "Judaeo-Masonic-Communist" conspiracy threatening the "greatness" of Spain. That there had been no native Spanish Jews practicing in Spain itself for over 400 years, and hardly any Masons since the days of Napoleon, was no impediment to the establishment of this myth.[9] For the fascist politicians, the "Judaeo-" component of this mantra was sufficient evidence of the decadence of communism—a case of guilt by association. (There were, of course, foreign socialists and communists of Jewish descent who came to Spain as volunteers to fight for the Republican side in the Spanish Civil War, but their Jewishness was clearly circumstantial to their presence—a point entirely lost on their antisemitic adversaries.) Combined with a program of national fascist propaganda that associated the Franco regime with the unifying efforts of the Catholic Monarchs—Ferdinand and Isabella, who had expelled the Jews from Spain—a distrust and even hatred of Jews became a hallmark of national policy.

How thoroughly this antisemitic fascist rhetoric was embraced by Spanish society as an article of faith may be illustrated by two anecdotes from the transitional era of the 1970s. The present author remembers, for example, a highly interesting man who was the owner of a *pensión* in Madrid across the Paseo from the Prado Museum. Taken to Argentina as a child in the 1930s, presumably by Republican refugees, he had served as an officer in the Argentinian navy before moving back to Spain and reclaiming his Spanish citizenship. A person of moderately liberal views—he lived in a common-law arrangement with an ex-nun, perhaps because of a previous marriage in Argentina—he was educated, cultured, and rather more modern than most Spaniards of his age. He and his companion, however, refused to use aerosol sprays as they cleaned the hostel. When asked why, he replied in all seriousness, "because they are produced by the international Jewish conspiracy." A second example, from the years just after Franco, is perhaps more instructive for the current purposes. At a *tertulia* (a type of intellectual cocktail party typical of Spain), a noblewoman was engaged in conversation about the genealogy of her illustrious family. A delicately worded question about whether she was aware of new investigations concerning possible *converso* elements in her family tree brought shocked incredulity. Just to ask such a question was an insult. A tremendous social *faux pas* had been committed, with apologies only being accepted because the transgressor was a stupid American whose Republican upbringing had obviously blinded him to the verities of aristocratic lineage. Now, there were in fact genealogists unearthing at that very moment documents proving the Jewish connection, but the noble lady could not even imagine that such an investigation could, in what she considered a sane world, take place. If the very idea of an investigation was unthinkable, there would be little chance for any discoveries that might illumine the true nature of late medieval society in her family. (Ironically, at the same gathering, a member of the younger generation of Spaniards, unrelated to the lady already mentioned, confided with some pride that she had discovered her family name implied Sephardic origins.)

Finally, one might mention a recent incident in Madrid, in which a Spanish driver, one of the most intelligent, creative, and prejudice-free persons known to the present author—and, it should be added, a dissident and exile under Franco—was cut off quite rudely in traffic by another driver. "Judío!" shouted the offended one. The transgressor was thus labeled no gentleman, devoid of any sense of Christian charity, and worthy of expulsion, if not from Spain, then at least from the national highway system. Now, it must be emphasized that the speaker had, in nearly thirty years of acquaintance, never once expressed any antisemitic or racist sentiments and had, on the contrary, often expressed respect and admiration for Jewish friends, colleagues, and supporters in Europe and the United States. Indeed, in the sense of any application to a real person, the term, "Jew," so used, would probably not have been recognized as antisemitic at all. It was used reflexively, without thinking, no doubt on the basis of long linguistic inculcation, beginning, say, on the boyhood soccer field when a schoolfellow was hogging the ball. Its use, however abstract, demonstrates the victory and social effect of the fascist myth of a "Judaeo-Masonic-Communist" conspiracy against Spanish "greatness"—even in the mouth of a one-time victim of Spanish fascism—and suggests how deeply entrenched antisemitic categories had become in the later twentieth century. That a word could be used in modern traffic in exactly the same way ("injurious and deprecatory") as documented in the 1732 dictionary definition also tells us something about the long-term endurance of social values in Spain.

At this point, the analysis that Gonzalo Álvarez Chillida has brought to modern Spanish antisemitism bears repeating. Álvarez identifies three aspects of prejudice against Jews: "popular antisemitism," based on legends, public rituals, and proverbs handed down for generations (as in the case from Madrid traffic); Roman Catholic theological antisemitism (particularly powerful in the Franco years); and the fascist political myth of a Jewish "conspiracy."[10] By the second half of the twentieth century, these three elements had developed into a tremendous impediment against social acceptance of Jewish topics.

Even under Franco, however, there was a slow trend towards increased tolerance. Promulgated in 1945, only six years after the end of the Spanish Civil War and, more importantly, in the year of the Allied triumph in the Second World War, a new constitutional document called the "Charter of the Spanish People" improved the conditions around religious freedom in Spain by allowing private non-Catholic devotions, but it continued (as had been the case in 1876) to suppress public expressions. In 1967, another promulgation protected public expressions of all faiths, as long as that expression did not contradict the primacy of Roman Catholicism. Finally, three years after Franco's death, the Constitution of 1978 once again separated Church and State, even while recognizing the important role of the Roman Catholic Church in education and public service. A more detailed law guaranteeing full religious freedom was passed in 1980. Today, there are an estimated 1.2 million Protestants resident in Spain, from 0.6 to 1 million Muslims, and from 40,000 to 50,000 Jews, many of whom are indeed Sephardim who have returned to Spain from Morocco and other Muslim countries.[11]

Scholarly interest in the Jewish contribution to Spanish culture parallels these historical developments. Henry Kamen, who has also depicted Spanish antisemitism in vivid terms throughout the centuries following 1492, has recounted how Spanish intellectuals in the later 1800s and early 1900s "tried to make up for four centuries of neglect and prejudice."[12] Kamen tells an interesting tale of pro-Jewish sentiments as they developed among philologists such as Adolfo de Castro (1823–1898) and Juan de Valera (1824–1905) in the mid-nineteenth century and Ramón Menéndez Pidal (1869–1968) in the twentieth, as they sought to revive interest in Sephardic culture. The first social history of Spanish Judaism ever published was Adolfo de Castro's 1847 *Historia de los judíos de España*, which detailed the high social and economic costs of the Expulsion of 1492. Its impact was greatly extended by translations into other languages, such as an English edition in 1853. Castro's lead was followed by historians such as José Amador de los Rios (1818–1878), Rafael Altamira (1866–1951), and, of particular importance for the United States, Américo Castro (1885–1972).[13]

That Américo Castro did his most important work on Spanish Jewish history in the United States is no accident. Kamen points out that there was "an unmistakable political agenda," usually (but not exclusively) associated with liberal causes, behind the new concern with Jewish history and Sephardic culture in the period 1840–1940—obviously the antithesis of the antisemitic polemics of right-wing apologists in the same period. The antithetical political agenda, that of the fascists, led to a general suppression of interest in Jewish studies, not to mention the emigration of many scholars of a liberal persuasion. Given the antisemitic rhetoric, it is not surprising to find, as Paloma Díaz Más has shown, that Jews are almost entirely absent from Spanish literature from 1936 to 1975.[14] There was, however, one important exception.

It is at this point that we come to a surprise in our survey. Although the great investigator of Sephardic poetry and songs in Ladino, Ramón Menéndez Pidal, had spent most of the Civil War years in exile and had, not long after his return to Spain in 1939, resigned as president of the Spanish National Academy, the interest in Sephardic culture which he had established was not entirely suppressed. (Menéndez Pidal would be re-elected as the academy's president in 1947 and continued to be a force of moderation in Spanish intellectual affairs.) In 1940, after the establishment of the Consejo Superior de Investigaciones Científicas (CSIC), the new Spanish national agency for scholarly and scientific research set up to sponsor (and politically control) research under the fascist regime, a new center for the study of Sephardic culture, now called the Instituto Arias Montano de Estudios Hebráicos, Sefardíes y de Oriente Próximo, was founded.[15] A publication sponsored by the center appeared in 1941, named *Sefarad* (figure 56). Devoted to Sephardic studies, the publication and the institutes that have supported it have kept Jewish topics an active part of Spanish scholarly discourse, although by necessity the subject matter has often concerned Jewish culture outside of Spain. What is more, the founding of *Sefarad* points to an astonishing facet of Franco's personality: an admiration for Sephardic culture. As Álvarez Chillida has demonstrated, Franco was not only less antisemitic than his

CONSEJO SUPERIOR DE INVESTIGACIONES CIENTIFICAS
INSTITUTO ARIAS MONTANO

SEFARAD

REVISTA DE LA ESCUELA DE ESTUDIOS HEBRAICOS

Año I.   MADRID 1941.   Núm. 1.

colleagues in the fascist movement, he had been, since his youth, pro-Sephardic (*filosefardí* in Spanish) and had demonstrated this in articles published about his experiences in Morocco.[16] Álvarez posits that Franco never abandoned his pro-Sephardic sentiments, which he sets in the context of late nineteenth-century pro-Sephardic studies. (We might add, in the light of Kamen's analysis of the related interest in bringing foreign Sephardic Jews back into the Spanish fold, that there was a type of cultural imperialism at work, at least on the subconscious level.) In any event, in spite of antisemitic legal persecution within Spain during the war years, some 20–30,000 Jews were allowed to cross the Pyrenees for transit through Spain (while others were prevented) and, again in spite of Spanish government resistance, another 2,000 Jews with Spanish passports resident in Axis-occupied countries were temporarily repatriated to Spain. Another 2,000 were not repatriated, and those who were saved were sent via Casablanca to other countries (which the international relief agencies of the time characterized as a second expulsion).[17] Individual Spanish diplomats and commercial agents throughout occupied Europe also took personal initiatives to save Jews by issuing passports on the basis of supposed Sephardic parentage, so that, for example, the Spanish diplomat and commercial agent Ángel Sanz Briz protected as many as 5,200 Jews in Hungary.[18]

To return to the issue at hand, we therefore find that, during the earlier Franco years, Sephardic studies were the one presence of a Jewish discipline in Spanish scholarship, and the Instituto Arias Montano was the location of much research that provided important precedents for the current interest in Jewish Spain.[19] In the period after the Second World War, these studies were also paralleled by investigations throughout the world of Jewish manuscripts and ritual objects from Spain (figure 55) and the Jewish element in medieval illumination, among which Carl-Otto Nordström's 1967 study of a fifteenth-century Castilian Bible, relating Christian illustration to Jewish art, now stands out as prophetic.[20] Again, the Instituto Arias Montano and *Sefarad* offered a forum and support for investigations and publications, funding for example the work of Leila Avrin and, particularly, Francisco Cantera Burgos.[21]

To this may be added, as the Franco years progressed and tourism began to be a dominating economic factor, increased interest in the Jewish presence

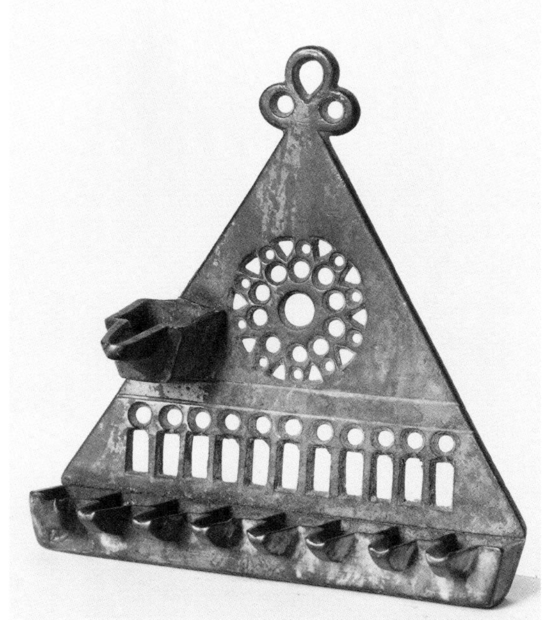

Fig. 55

55. Hanukkah lamp
Northern Aragon
Fourteenth Century
Bronze
Musée d'art et d'histoire du Judaïsme, Paris
Cl. 12248

56. *Sefarad*
1941
The Library of the Jewish Theological Seminary, New York

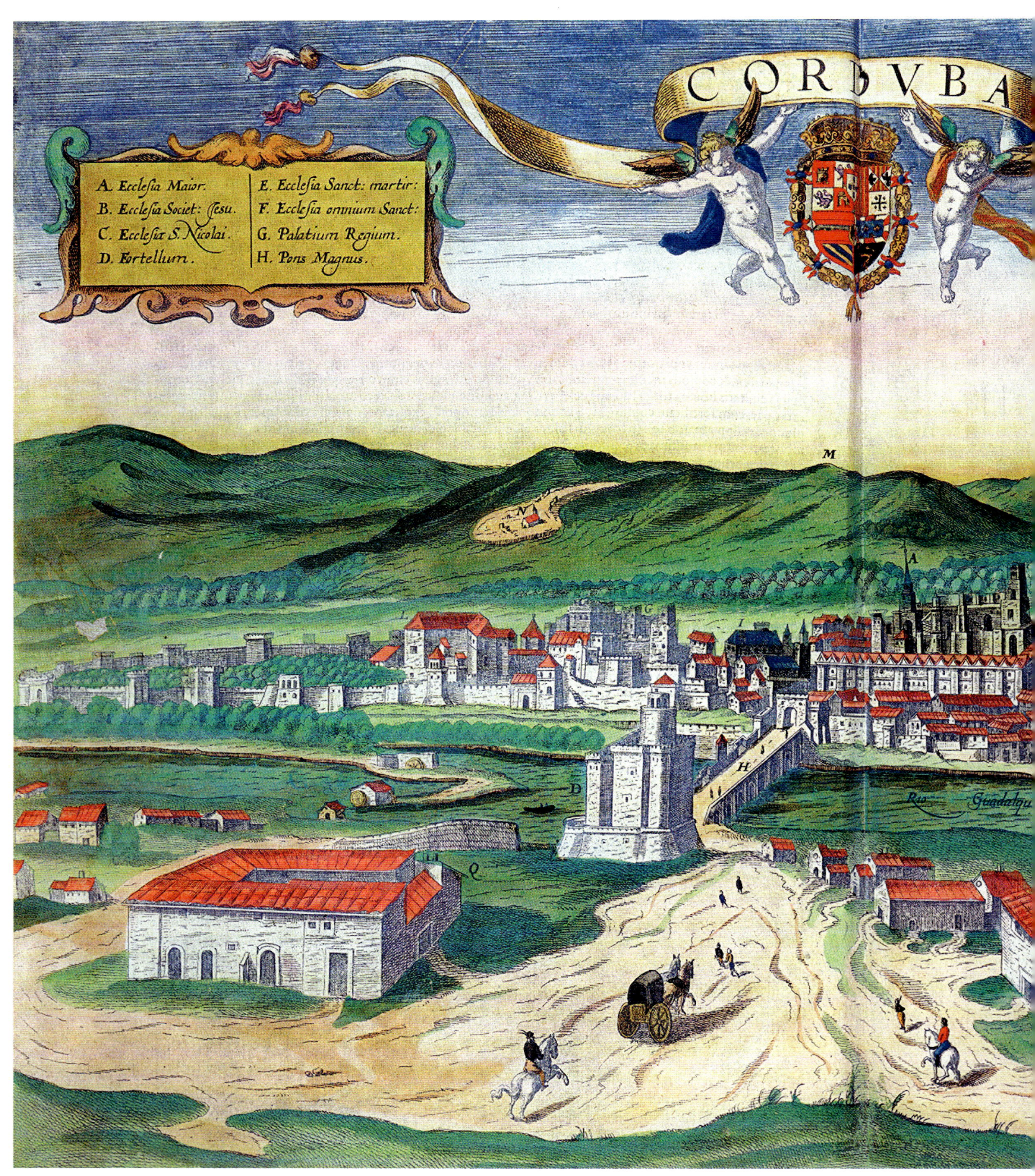

CORDVBA
A. Ecclesia Maior.
B. Ecclesia Societ: Iesu.
C. Ecclesia S. Nicolai.
D. Fortellum.
E. Ecclesia Sanct: martir:
F. Ecclesia omnium Sanct:
G. Palatium Regium.
H. Pons Magnus.
Rio Guadalqu

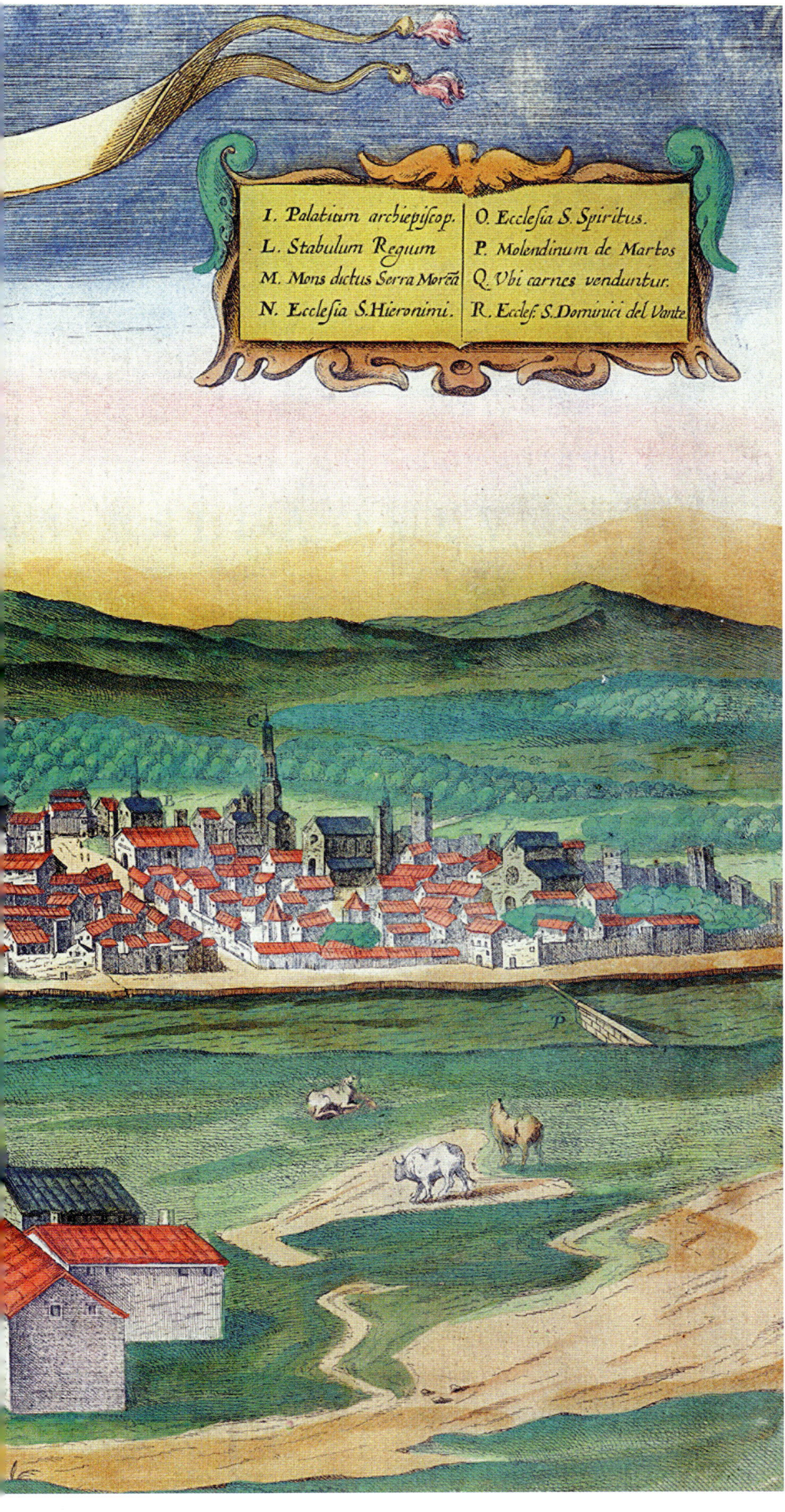

57. George Braun and Frans Hogenberg
Map of Cordoba from *Civitates Orbis Terrarum*
ca. 1572–1617
Colored engraving
Private Collection

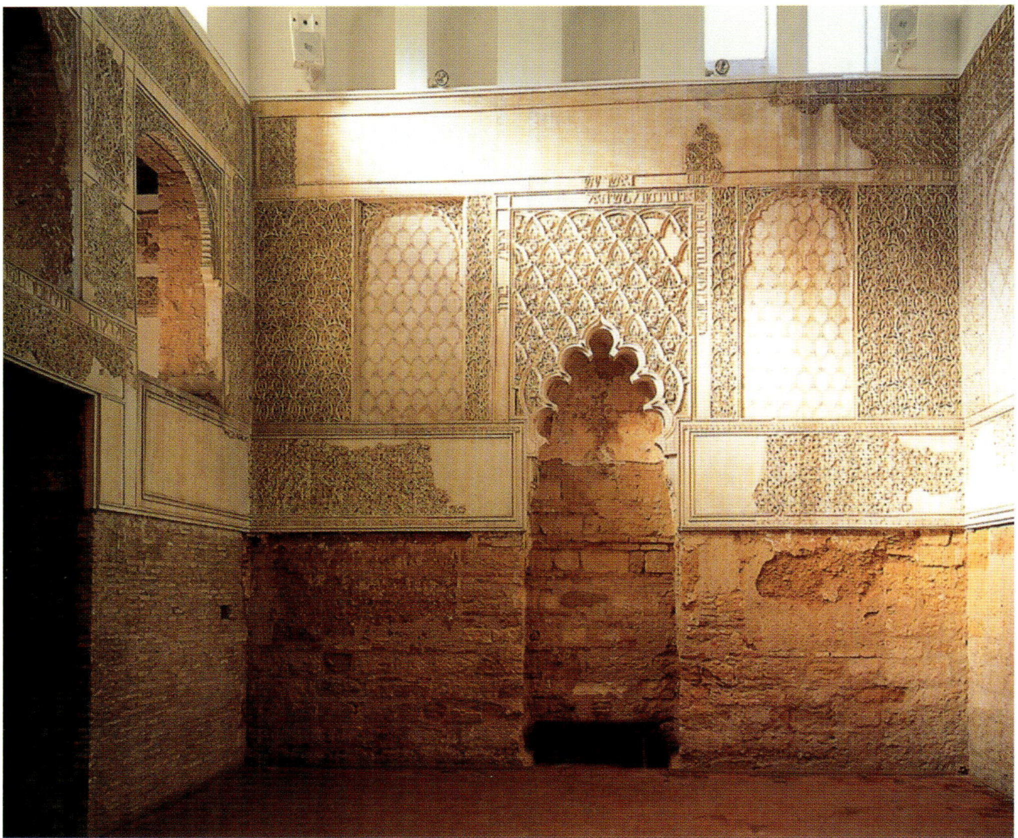

at Cordoba under the caliphs (900s–1000s) and in locales such as Toledo, where Jewish synagogues formed part of the architectural heritage of the subsequent Christian kingdoms (figure 58). (Indeed, the person who had organized the initial restoration of the synagogue of El Tránsito in Toledo, the marquis de la Vega Inclán, was royal commissioner of tourism from 1911 to 1928 and the man responsible for establishing the Paradores chain of quality tourist hotels in restored Spanish landmarks.[22]) In the case of both Cordoba and medieval Toledo, however, the moments of Jewish–Muslim and Jewish–Christian rapprochement were safely contained in a world that no longer existed—even the name of the monument in Toledo, which reflects its transformation into the church of El Tránsito after the Expulsion, certifies its status as something that existed "then," not "now" (figures 59-60, 61-62). Still, the economic value of these monuments, along with the presence of medieval Jewish intellectuals such as Maimonides in Muslim Cordoba, led to the study of the Jewish context in the caliphate and *taifas* (Muslim-ruled principalities), an interest which has continued to the present in the works of historians such as Luis Suárez Fernández (since 1980) and Antonio Antelo Iglesias, who has spoken of the late caliphate and *taifa* periods as a "golden age" for Iberian Jews.[23] In general, however,

58. Cordoba synagogue (interior)
    Cordoba, Spain

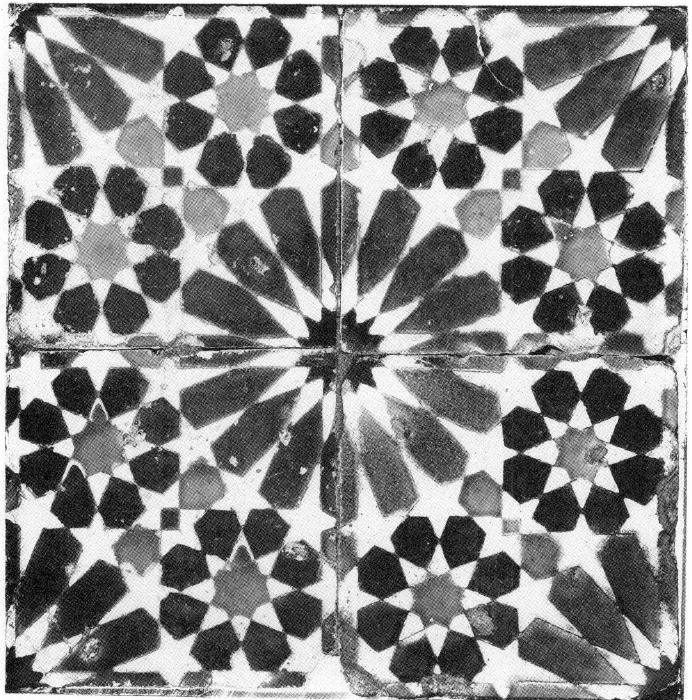

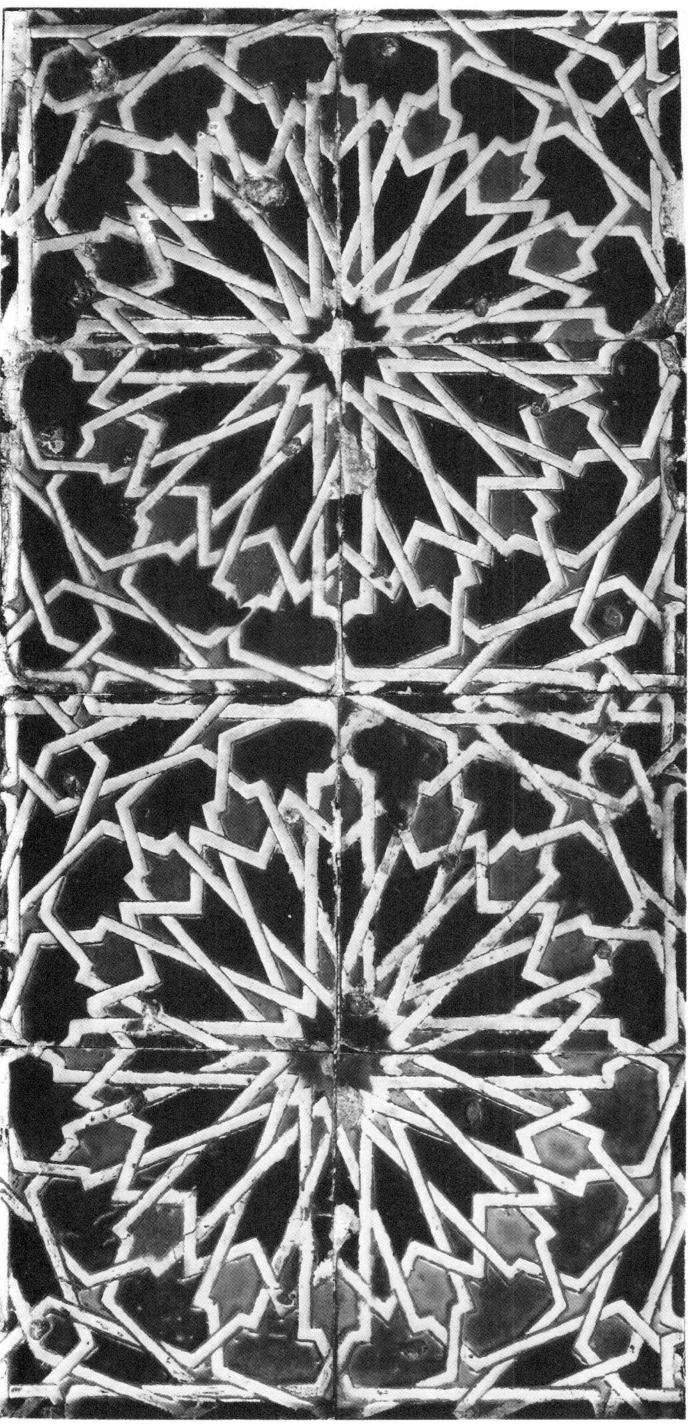

59. Tile
El Tránsito Synagogue, Toledo
ca. 1360
Tin-glazed earthenware
The Hispanic Society of America, New York
E1324

60. Tile
El Tránsito Synagogue, Toledo
ca. 1360
Tin-glazed earthenware
The Hispanic Society of America, New York
E1326

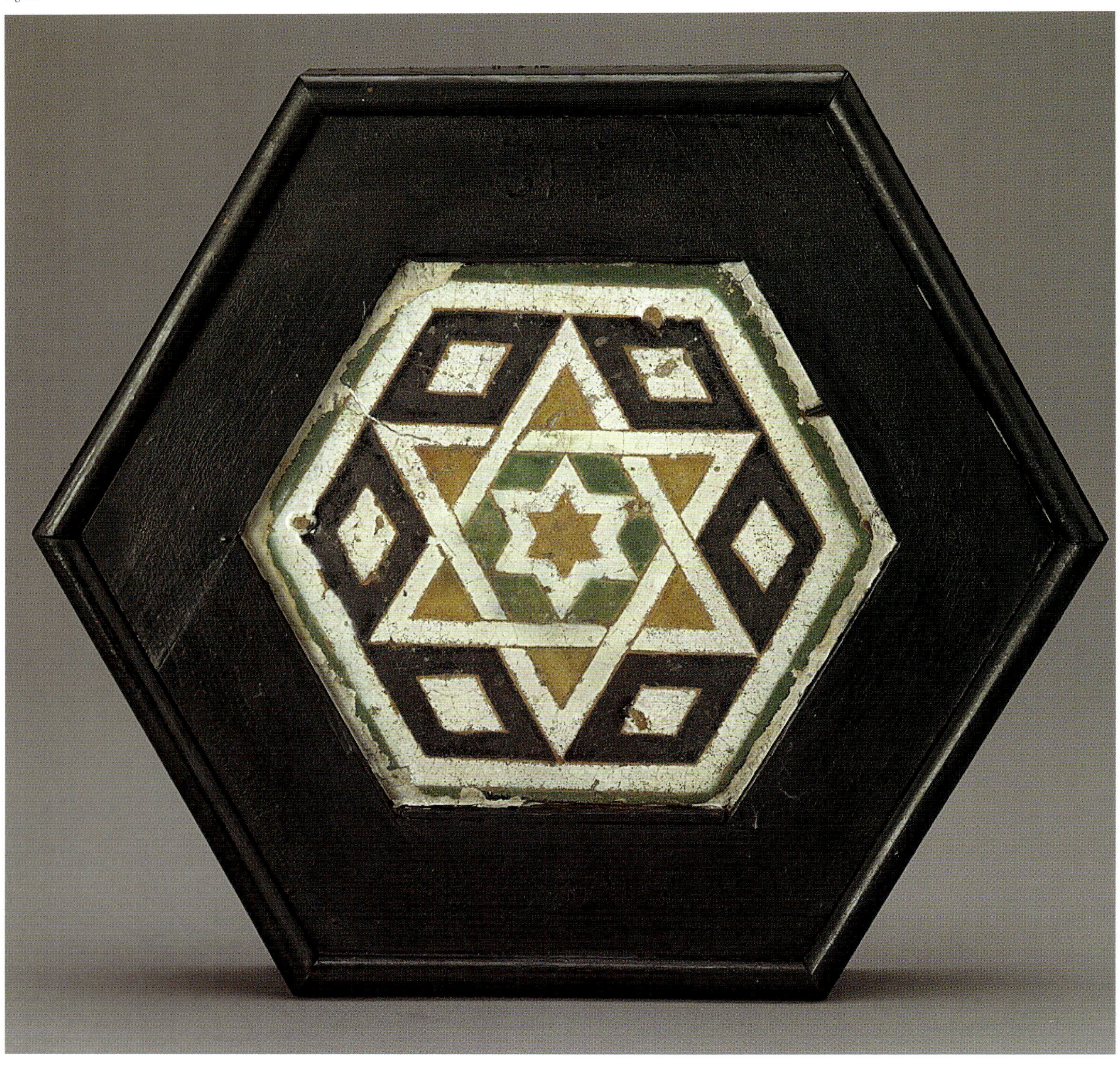

61. Tile
    El Tránsito Synagogue , Toledo
    ca. 1360
    5 ½ × 5 in.
    The Hispanic Society of America, New York (E1326)

62. El Tránsito Synagogue (exterior)
    Toledo, Spain

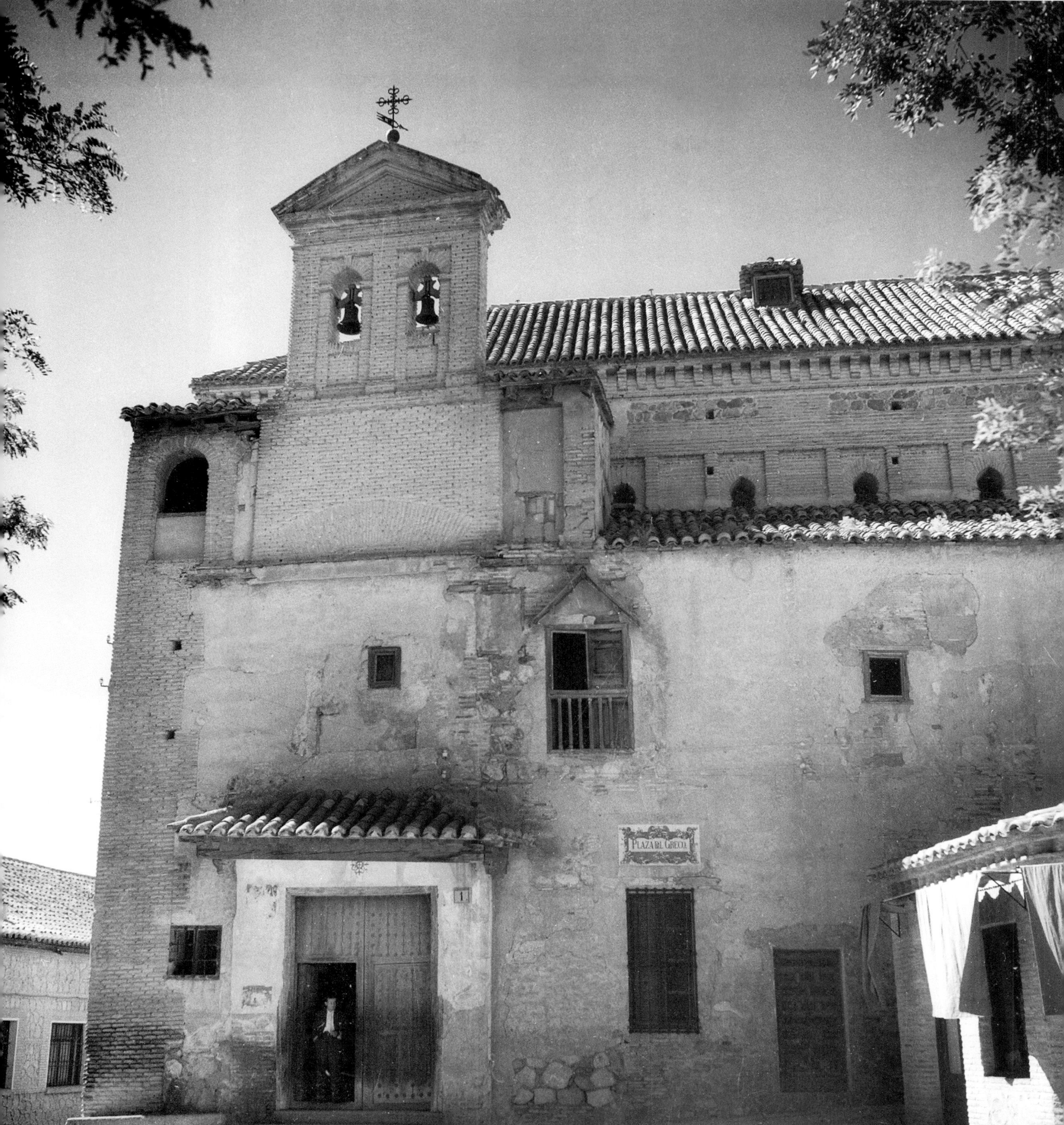

Fig. 62

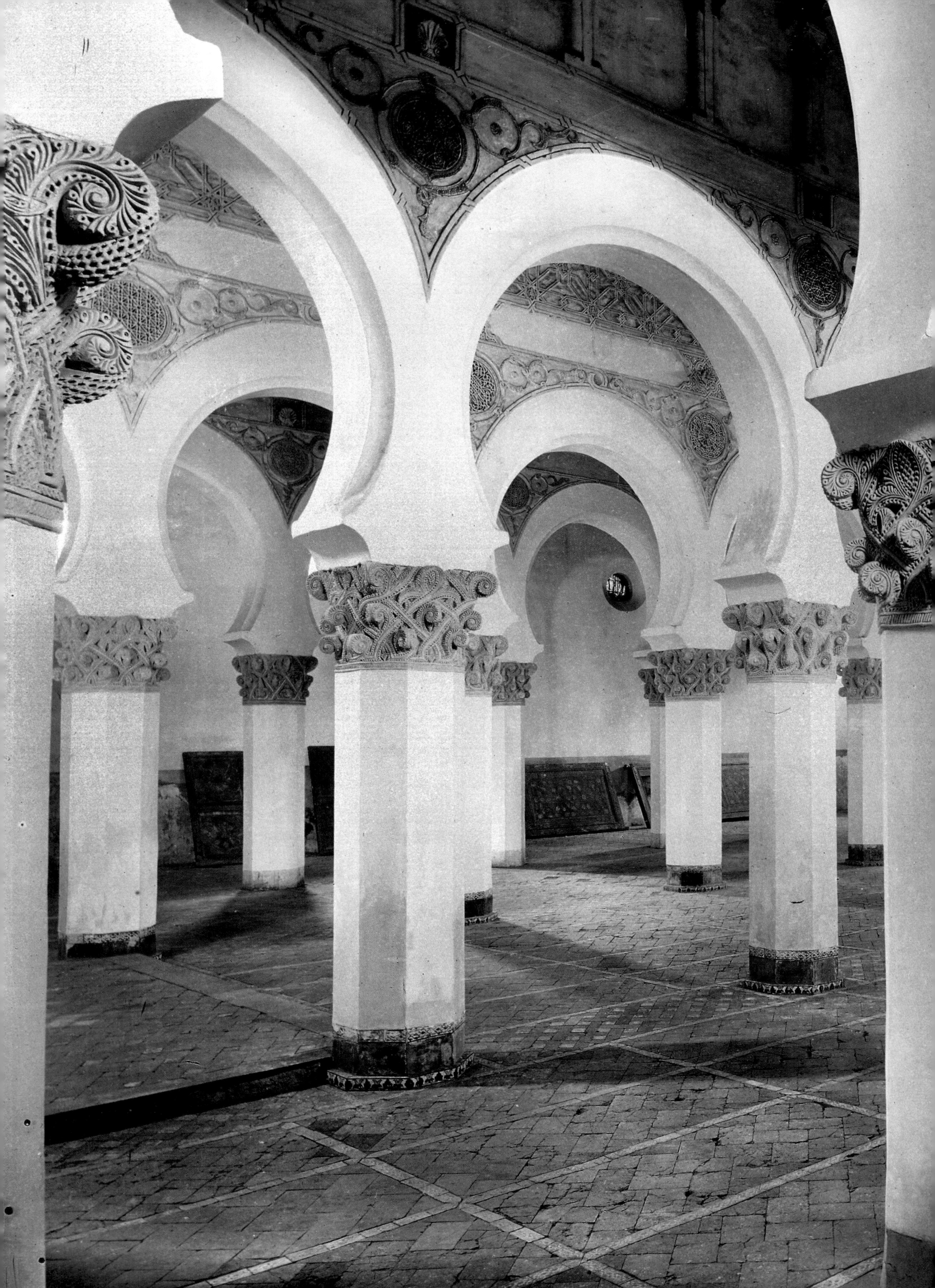

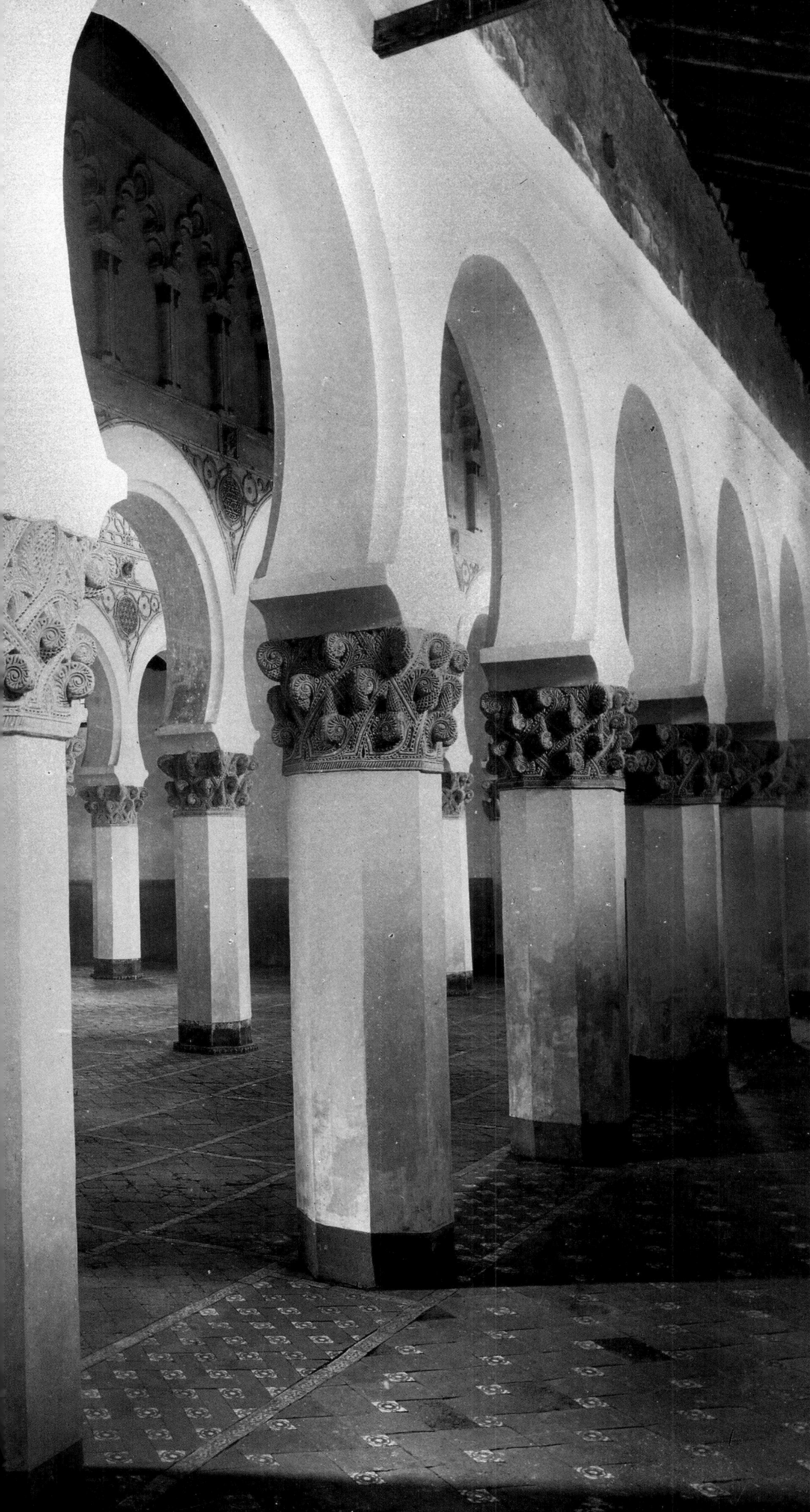

63. Santa Maria la Blanca
ca. 1300
Toledo, Spain

Sephardic studies, at least within Spain, have existed in a type of intellectual ghetto. Nordström's attempts to show cross-ethnic artistic response were not the norm.

Turning from general cultural studies to art history proper and aesthetics, we find that the absence of interest in Jewish topics, especially after 1936, becomes a gaping void. José Ortega y Gasset, the conservative Republican phenomenologist philosopher and aesthetician (who opposed both Primo de Rivera and the Franco regime), is almost silent on Jewish issues. Chandler Rathfon Post, the American scholar who wrote the standard history of medieval Spanish painting in the 1930s, approaches his subject almost exclusively from the point of view of connoisseurship.[24] For example, the author's obsession with Lluís Borrassà stretching over seven volumes of the series never touches on potential Jewish connections, although his discussion of Juan de Leví does speculate on the family's *converso* origins, since "converted Jews of the name of Leví were very numerous."[25] (Post's source of information on the Leví atelier, Manuel Serrano y Sanz, originally published documents linked to Guillén and Juan de Leví without commenting on their possible ethnic identities.[26]) Otherwise, to the extent it can be determined, Post was unconcerned with the work of Spanish Jewish artists. Similarly, the medieval volumes of the standard Spanish-language art historical series, *Ars Hispaniae*, which began appearing in the late 1940s, do not even include the word *judío* in their indices. José Gudiol Ricart, who worked closely with both Post and with another American scholar, Walter W. S. Cook, published the volume on Gothic painting in this series. While according Juan de Leví the honor of having been "the first exponent of the International [Gothic] Style in the Aragonese School," he makes no mention of the painter's origins, following the formalist approach he shared with Post.[27] His discussion of Borrassà and his school is similarly formalist.[28] José María Azcárate's useful and informative text, *Arte gótico en España*, of 1990, published as part of the prestigious *Manuales Arte Cátedra* series, continues Post's and Gudiol's formalist approach based on objects extant in Spain, although Azcárate follows Gudiol's lead by setting his connoisseurship-based analyses into their proper art-historical contexts. Again, the word *judío* does not feature in the index and only appears in the text as part of iconographical descriptions. The two synagogues in Toledo, whose patrons and bibliography are duly cited, are discussed under the heading of "islamicized Christian architecture (mudéjar)".[29] The synagogues are properly examined in this context, but in keeping with his formalist approach overall, almost no social history beyond the offices of the patrons is included. There was also a meta-historical aspect—an art-historical attitude—not in itself antisemitic but a function of the circumstances prevailing in Spain since 1492. This was the assumption, especially with regard to the period after 1391, that there was no Jewish visual culture *per se* in medieval Spain, even though Azcárate's work followed the publication of Ana María López Álvarez's publications on medieval Jewish art and architecture in the 1980s.[30] In the previous generation, Leopoldo Torres Balbas had stated unequivocally that "the Israelites of Christian Spain lacked their own art."[31] (How Torres Balbas, on whose descriptions Azcárate's text is based at many points, thought he could describe the three extant Mudéjar synagogues of Spain in one laconic entry, again devoid of context except for mention of the patrons and a note that the balcony in Cordoba "was destined for women," will pass without comment.[32]) One of the few weak points of Azcárate's book is the extraordinarily brief discussion of manuscript illumination, only mentioning in passing a "judeo-catalán" haggadah in the British Museum.[33] The term "judeo-catalán," is instructive, as it might be taken to imply that "Jewish" and "Catalan" are distinct ethnic categories. The extended discussion of Lluís Borrassà, including notice of his manumitted slave of the same name who became a master painter in Mallorca, gives no hint of any Jewish connections,[34] and, as in Gudiol, the mention of the Leví family omits Post's speculation of a possible Jewish or *converso* origin.[35] None of this is to imply an antisemitic program on the part of Post, Gudiol, or Azcárate—the information is simply not there, may not have been obvious in their sources and, in any event, was not part of the art-historical discourse of the time.

For the decorative arts, Cristina Sigüenza Pelarda's study of costumes depicted in Aragonese Gothic painting, published in 2000, offers an interesting case study in the advances that have been made in Jewish studies and the importance of regional patronage for scholarship as it has affected cultural history writing in Spain itself. Thus, she points to ethnic stereotypes in the depiction of Jews, discusses technological trade secrets of certain Jewish cloth manufacturers, mentions Jewish female hair fashions among many influences on hair design—although without describing the Jewish designs themselves—and cites restrictions on colors worn and the use of identifying badges for Jews.[36] Her main discussion of Jewish fashions occurs under the category of "The Marginalized Groups: Jews, Prostitutes, and Vagabonds"; relatively brief, it provides extremely useful documentation from contemporary sources.[37] Oddly, her mention elsewhere of costumes in a work by Juan de Leví does not pick up on the artist's obvious Jewish connections.[38]

Nearly half a century separated the researches of Post and those of Judith Berg Sobré, whose indispensible study of Spanish medieval *retablos* (altar ensembles) appeared in 1989. Berg Sobré, like Azcárate, incorporated connoisseurship and formalist analysis into larger art-historical schema, but was also concerned to explain to her non-Spanish audience the construction, spatial relationships, technical properties, painterly aspects, and stylistic innovations at each major center of production, to which she added in-depth documentary studies of patronage and contracts between artists themselves. Two artists whom she often cites are Lluís Borrassà and Juan de Leví. Leví, for example, is shown collaborating with other artists, providing an early example of a full altar ensemble, being responsible for innovative *retablo* design, and expressing a classic sense of the International Gothic style (figure 64).[39] Nowhere, however, is there a discussion of how Leví's ethnic origins or religion might have affected his imagery, or even a repetition of Post's comment about his having been a *converso*. Where Berg Sobré does discuss Jews is in her explication of iconography, seeing them principally as an audience for proselytizing images.[40] When she considers images in which Jews appear, she assumes

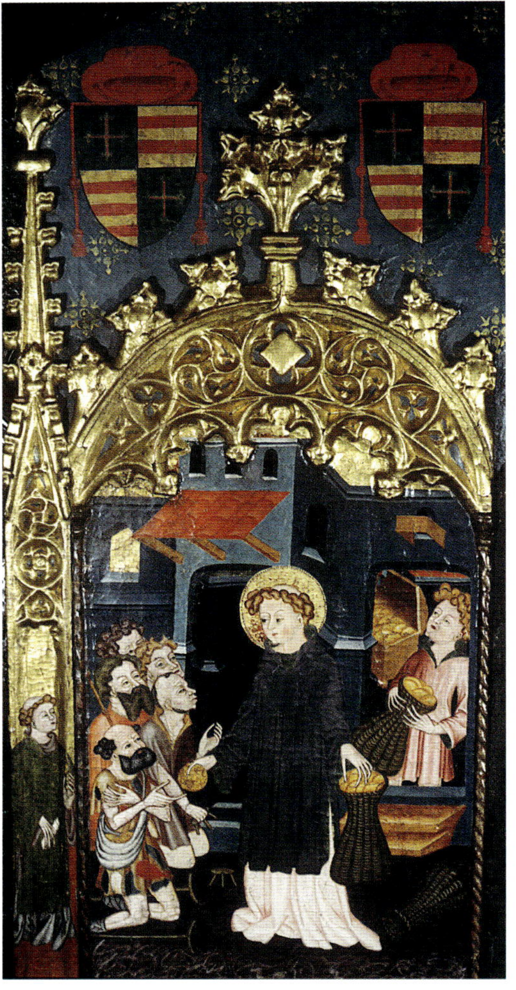

that their presence is a negative one, as in the scene of Christ among the Doctors, although she points out the probable accuracy of the depiction of synagogue interiors.[41] She does suggest that there is "some figural art of Jewish origin in manuscript illuminations" but, noting the regional variations in style among the extant examples, doubts there was any common Jewish artistic factor.[42] In sum, she accepts the conventional wisdom that Jewish Spain was in total disarray after 1391 and feels that "the Jews seem to have had little influence on Christian painting."[43]

That Berg Sobré, who in subsequent contexts has shown considerable interest and sensitivity to the subject at hand, and who certainly cannot be accused of harboring an antisemitic agenda, should have missed evidence that the present exhibition makes manifest is no criticism of her exemplary scholarship. Rather, it indicates the extent to which the issue of Jewish contributions simply did not exist, either as a body of information or as any aspect of the discourse of Spanish art history, at the time she was doing her primary research, namely the 1970s and early 1980s. It would take new data, and a different array of information, before art historians within Spain and without would be free to examine the topic in ways that might produce new results.

In English-language studies, one can cite the work of architectural historians such as Don A. Halperin and cultural historians such as R. D. Barnett in preparing the ground for interest in Sephardic studies,[44] but the sea change that would open the subject of the Jewish contribution to medieval Hispanic culture to a wider audience was the exhibition *Convivencia*, mounted in 1992 at the New York Historical Society by the Jewish Museum and curated by Vivian B. Mann and Jerrilynn D. Dodds, in collaboration with Thomas F. Glick.[45] The pioneering nature of this effort, and the astonishing effect it had on its American audience, cannot be overstated, although oddly, critical response was slow to develop at the time. The concept of *convivencia*, the "living together" of the Muslim, Christian, and Jewish communities in medi-

64. Juan de Leví
Altarpiece in the Pérez Calvillo chapel
The Charity of Saint Lawrence (detail)
1408
Tempera and gilding on wood
Cathedral of Tarazona, Tarazona

eval Iberia, and their concomitant sharing of culture has come to dominate the point of view of historical and cultural studies ever since. So, for example, María Elena Díez Jorge's recent study of Mudéjar art is subtitled *Expresión estética de una convivencia* (The Aesthetic Expression of *Convivencia*), and one of her chapters is entitled "Cosmic visions of Peace in the three religions of the book."[46] Conferences on medieval Spanish art now regularly feature papers on Jewish topics, as for example in the 2006 conference on the subject at Princeton, in which Pamela Patton gave a presentation involving Muslim connections for Iberian Jews.[47]

Parallel to this new English-language interest was a tremendous upsurge in regional studies within Spain itself, driven by the new federal structure of the Spanish republic after 1978, which gave a great deal of autonomy to the Spanish regions (roughly equivalent to the state governments in the U.S. federal system). This made it possible for scholars in regions such as Aragon to find funding for their researches into the *convivencia* of the medieval period. To this was added regional interest in developing new culturally significant tourist attractions and augmented budgets for local archeological excavations and architectural restoration. To continue with the example of Aragon, Saragossa became a center of the new Jewish studies, under the leadership of scholars such as Carmen Lacarra Ducay,[48] whose advice and intervention have been of such importance for the current project. In Madrid, at the Instituto Arias Montano and in centers such as Toledo, the work of Ana María López Álvarez and her colleagues has similarly opened many new fields of inquiry. Furthermore, the investigations in Spain have truly taken the spirit of *convivencia* to heart, encompassing not only archeological discoveries and manuscript studies, but also topics such as iconography and cross-ethnic contributions.

How do you describe an absence? How do you define a lack? The explosion of scholarly interest in the art of medieval Spanish Jewry internationally since 1980 can be documented and measured; the accompanying bibliography is intended to allow the reader to do this for him- or herself. Not only is a new scholarly interest now "on the map," but also a body of data, with its documents, archives, objects, buildings—a whole field of material culture and history formerly overlooked but now recognized as being both fascinating and central to the story of a multi-ethnic, multi-religious society. Against this newfound reality, the relative silence of the preceding half century fairly screams, not so much in condemnation as in lament for opportunities missed.

65. Nicolás and Martín Zahortiga
Altarpiece from the collegiate church of Santa
María de Borja
The Marriage of Mary and Joseph (detail)
ca. 1460
Oil on panel
51 × 39 in.
Museo de Borja, Borja

66. Nicolás and Martín Zahortiga
Altarpiece from the collegiate church of Santa
María de Borja
The Circumcision of Christ (detail)
ca. 1460
Oil on panel
51 × 39 in.
Museo de Borja, Borja

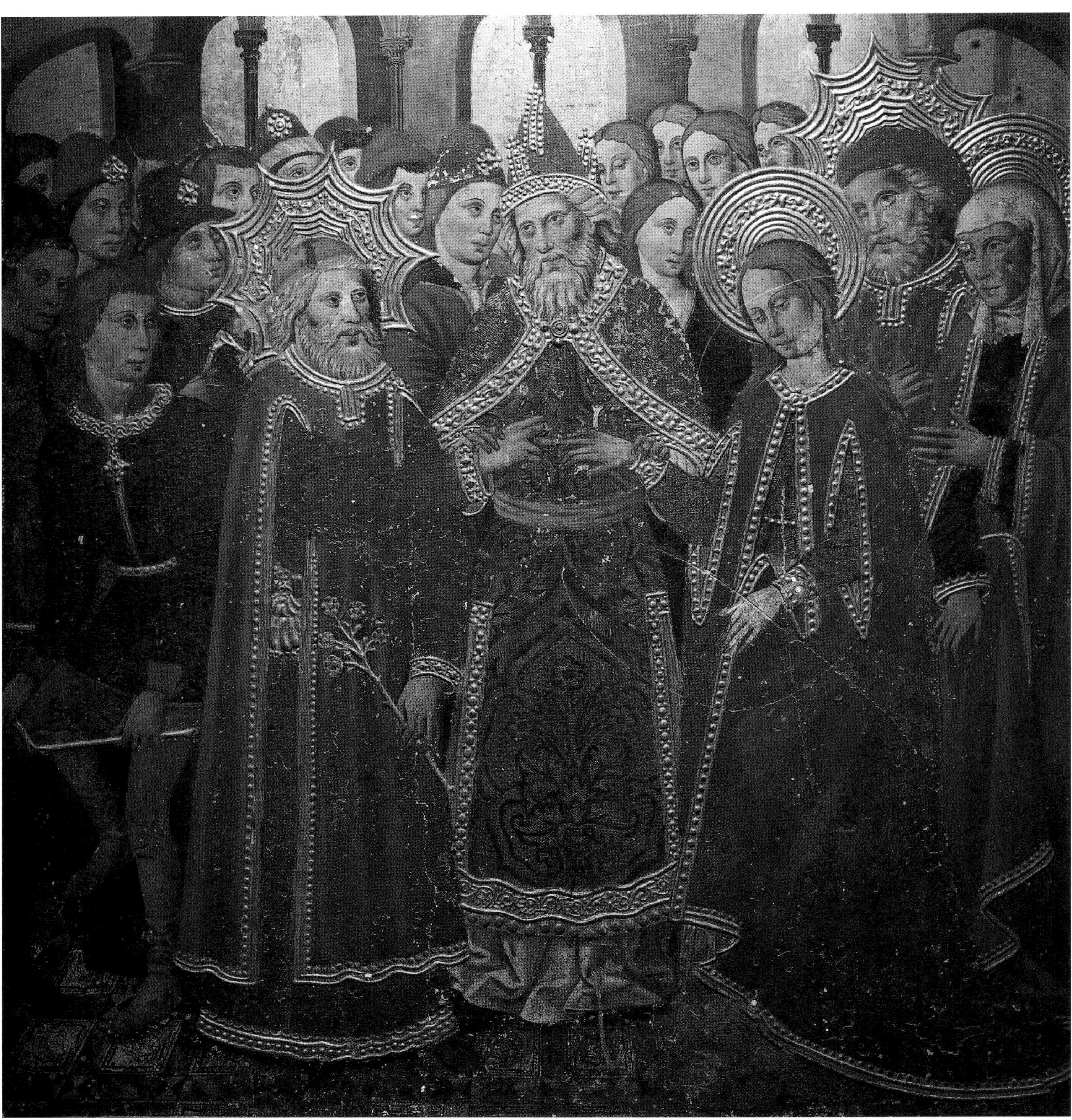

Fig. 65

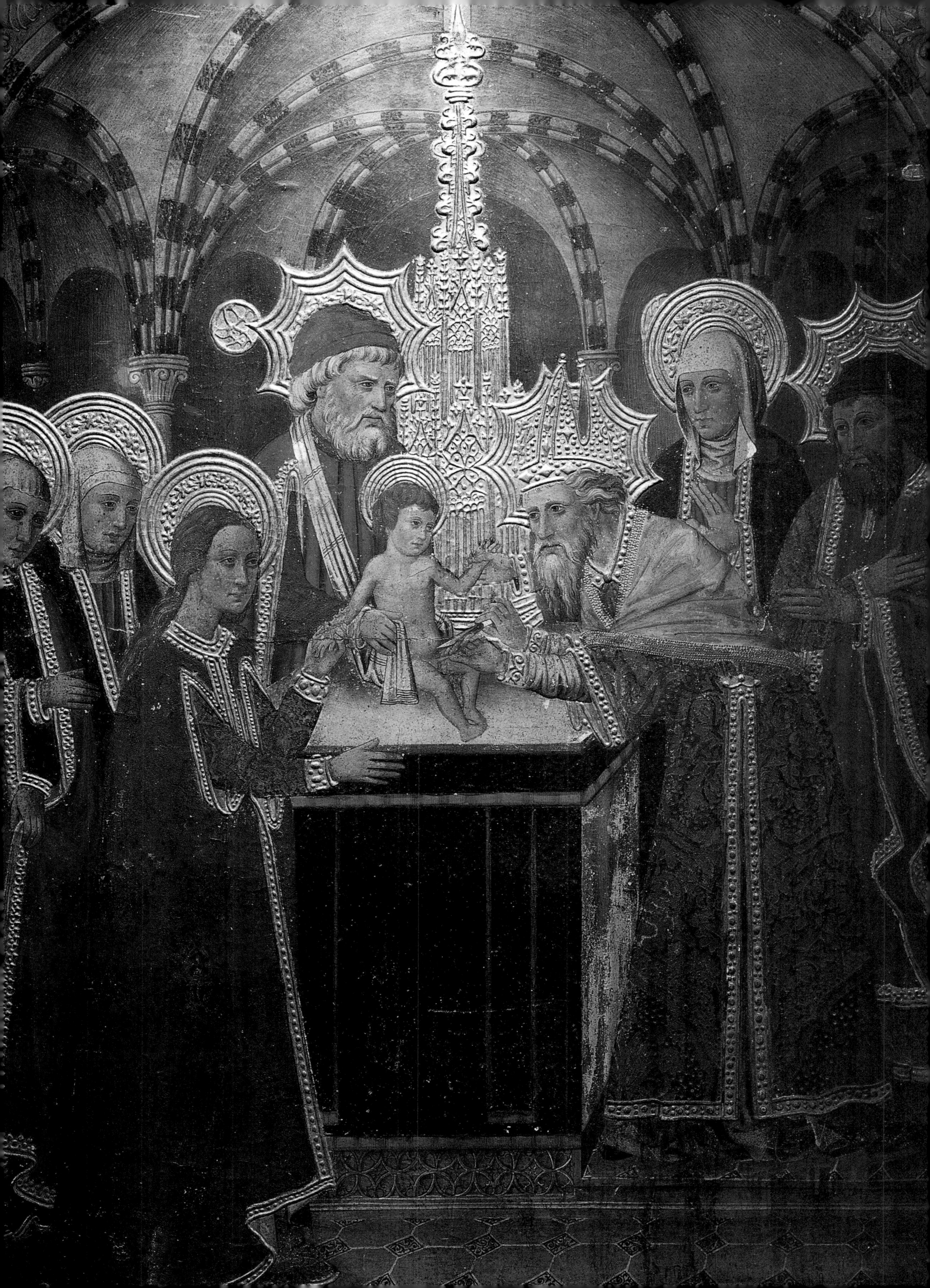

ENDNOTES

1   I am indebted to Andrea Ortuño for assistance in researching this topic.

2   Benzion Netanyahu, *The Origins of the Inquisition in Fifteenth-Century Spain* (New York: Random House, 1995), *passim*, esp. 938ff.

3   John H. Elliott, *Imperial Spain, 1469–1716* (London: Penguin Books, 1970), 21.

4   See Susan M. Adams, et al., "The Genetic Legacy of Religious Diversity and Intolerance: Paternal Lineages of Christians, Jews, and Muslims in the Iberian Peninsula," *The American Journal of Human Genetics* 83 (6), December 4, 2008, 725–36; also retrievable from http://www.cell.com/AJHG/abstract/S0002-9297(08)00592-2. Cf. Pierre A. Zalloua, *et al.*, "Identifying Genetic Traces of Historical Expansions: Phoenician Footprints in the Mediterranean." *The American Journal of Human Genetics* 83 (5), October 30, 2008, 633–42; also retrievable from http://www.cell.com/AJHG/abstract/S0002-9297(08)00547-8; see http://www.nytimes.com/2008/12/05/science/05genes.html?_r=1&ref=science.

5   Sebastián Covarrubias Orozco, *Tesoro de la lengua castellana, o española* (Madrid: Luis Sánchez, 1611), 492v.

6   Academia Real Española (1726–1737), *Diccionario de la lengua castellana* ["*Diccionario de autoridades*"], (Madrid: Francisco de Hierro, 1732), vol. 3, 325.

7   J. D. Hughey, *Ebb Tide of Religious Liberty in Spain* (Chicago: University of Chicago Press, 1955), 488–90; also retrievable from http://www.archive.org/stream/religiousfreedom013524mbp/religiousfreedom013524mbp_djvu.txt.
Compare the situation in Morocco in 1860, when the Spanish were attempting to conquer the country, as related in Henry Kamen, *The Disinherited: Exile and the Making of Spanish Culture, 1492–1975* (New York: Harper Collins, 2007), 42.

8   Juan José Morales Ruiz, "La obsesión antimasónica de Franco: Masones y judíos en el discurso represivo del franquismo"; and José Luis Rodríguez Jiménez, "El discurso antisemita en el fascism español," in Javier Tusell Gómez and José Antonio Ferrer Benimeli, eds., *Los judíos en la historia de España* [Actas del curso celebrado en la UNED de Calatayud en mayo de 2002] (Saragossa: Diputación Provincial, and Calatayud: Universidad Nacional de Educación a Distancia, 2003), 131–60 and 89–130, respectively. The subject has been treated at greater length by Haim Avni, *España, Franco y los judios* (Madrid: Altalena, 1982); and by Antonio Marquina Barrio and Gloria Ospina, *España y los judíos en el siglo XX* (Madrid: Espasa-Calpe, 1987).

9   On the central role of myth-making in Spanish culture and self-identity, see Henry Kamen, *Imagining Spain: Historical Myth and National Identity* (New Haven and London: Yale University Press, 2008).

10 Gonzalo Álvarez Chillida, "Franco y los judíos en la Segunda Guerra Mundial," in Tusell and Ferrer, eds., *Los judíos*, 2003, 162ff.

11 United States Department of State (2005) [Statistics on world nations]: retrieved May 9, 2009 from http://www.state.gov/g/drl/rls/irf/2005/51582.htm; see Pedro C. Moreno, ed., *Handbook on Religious Liberty Around the World* (Charlottesville, V.A.: The Rutherford Institute, 2009): retrieved May 9, 2009 from http://religiousfreedom.lib.virginia.edu/rihand/Spain.html; and J. D. Hughey, "Church, State, and Religious Liberty in Spain," *Journal of Church and State* 23 (3), Autumn 1991, 486–90.

12 Kamen, *The Disinherited*, 39–52.

13 See Américo Castro, *España en su historia: Cristianos, moros y judíos* (Buenos Aires: Editorial Losada, 1948); idem (Edmund L. King, trans.), *The Structure of Spanish History* (Princeton: Princeton University Press, 1954).
See also José Amador de los Ríos, *Estudios históricos, políticos y literarios sobre los judíos de España* (Madrid: D. M. Diaz, 1848); idem, *Historia social, política y religiosa de los judíos de España y Portugal*, 3 vols. (Madrid: T. Fortanet, 1875–76); Adolfo de Castro, *Historia de los judíos en España*, Cádiz, 1847 and its English translation (Edward Kirwan, trans.), *The History of the Jews in Spain, from the Time of their Settlement in that Country till the Commencement of the Present Century* (Westport, Conn.: Greenwood Press, 1972). See Santiago Palomero Plaza, "'Historia de los judíos de España', por D. Adolfo de Castro (Cádiz, 1847)," in Elena Romero Castelló, ed., *Judaísmo hispano: Estudios en memoria de José Luis Lacave Riaño* (Madrid: Consejo Superior de Investigaciones Científicas, 2003), vol. 2, 819–26.

14 Paloma Díaz Más, "Judíos y conversos en la literatura española contemporánea," in Yedida K. and Norman A. Stillman, *From Iberia to Diaspora: Studies in Sephardic History and Culture* [Brill's Series in Jewish Studies, 19] (Leiden and Boston: Brill, 1999), 347–48. For a broader study, see Ángel Pulido, ed. Jacobo Israel Garzón, *El sefardismo en España: La Academia de la Lengua Española y los sefardíes* (Madrid: Hebraica Ediciones, 2006).

15 Díaz Más, "Judíos y conversos," *passim*; Álvarez Chillida, "Franco y los judíos," 172. See also Avni, *España, Franco y los judíos* and Lués 1987, *passim*.

16 Álvarez Chillida, "Franco y los judíos," 172–73.

17 Álvarez Chillida, "Franco y los judíos," 178–79.

18 Álvarez Chillida, "Franco y los judíos," 179; Arminda Rosales [Review of Diego Carcedo, *Un español frente al Holocausto* (Madrid: Temas de Hoy, 2000)], in *Sefarad*, online edition, 2001; retrieved April 21, 2009 from http://sefarad.rediris.es/textos/osanzbriz.htm.

19 Díaz Más, "Judíos y conversos," *passim*.

20 Carl-Otto Nordström, *The Duke of Alba's Castilian Bible: A Study of the Rabbinical Features of the Miniatures* [Figura: Uppsala Studies in the History of Art, new ser., 5], (Uppsala: Acta Universitatis Upsaliensis [Almqvist & Wiksells], 1967). See also the review by Joseph Gutmann in *Speculum* 43 (3), July 1968, 527–29. Also retrievable from http://www.jstor.org/stable/2855862.

21 Leila Avrin, "The Spanish Passover Plate in the Israel Museum," *Sefarad* 39, 1979, 27–46; Francisco Cantera Burgos, *Sinagogas de Toledo, Segovia, y Córdoba* (Madrid: <publisher?>, 1973); idem, *Las juderías medievales en la provincia de Guadalajara* (Madrid, 1975); idem, *Sinagogas españolas, con especial estudio de la de Córdoba y la Toledana de El Tránsito* (Madrid: Instituto Benito Arias Montano, 1984); Cantera Burgos and J. M. Villas Vallicrosa, *Las inscripciones hebraicas de España* (Madrid, 1956).

22 María Luisa Menéndez Robles, *El marqués de la Vega Inclán y los orígenes del turismo en España* (Madrid: Ministerio de Industria, Turismo y Comercio, 2006).

23 Antonio Antelo Iglesias, *Judíos españoles de la Edad de Oro (siglos XI–XII): Semblanzas, antología y glosario* (Madrid: Fundación Amigos de Sefarad: Universidad Nacional de Educación a Distancia, 1991). Luis Suárez Fernández, *Judíos españoles en la Edad Media*

(Madrid: Rialp, 1980).

24 Chandler Rathfon Post, *A History of Spanish Painting* (Cambridge, Mass.: Harvard University Press, 1930–66), esp. vols. 3 (1930), 4 (1933), 6 (1935), 7 (1938), and 8 (1941).

25 Post, *Spanish Painting* vol. 3, 168.

26 M. Serrano y Sanz, "Juan de Leví y Pedro Rupert," *Revista de Archivos, Bibliotecas y Museos*, 3rd series, 35, 1916, 415–16.

27 José Gudiol Ricart, *Pintura gótica* [Ars Hispaniae 9] (Madrid: Editorial Plus-Ultra, 1955), 158–63.

28 Ricart, *Pintura gótica* 91 ff.

29 José María Azcárate, *Arte gótico en España* [Manuales Arte Cátedra] (Madrid: Ediciones Cátedra, 1990), 80–83.

30 Ana María López Álvarez, *Catálogo del Museo Sefardí, Toledo* (Madrid: Ministerio de Cultura, 1986); eadem, "La galería de las mujeres de la sinagoga de El Tránsito: nuevos hallazgos," *Sefarad* 47, 1987, 301–14.

31 Leopoldo Torres Balbas, *Arte Almohade – Arte Nazarí – Arte Mudéjar* [Ars Hispaniae 4] (Madrid: Editorial Plus-Ultra, 1949), 308.

32 Torres Balbas, *Arte Almohade*, 308–9.

33 Azcárate, *Arte gótico*, 294. Cf. Joaquín Yarza Luaces, *Introducción al arte español: Baja Edad Media, los siglos del gótico* ([Madrid:] Sílex, 1992. Yarza devotes more space (and assigns more importance) to manuscripts, but omits mention of Jewish works.

34 Azcárate, *Arte gótico*, 326–30.

35 Azcárate, *Arte gótico*, 341–43.

36 Cristina Sigüenza Pelarda, *La moda en el vestir en la pintura gótica aragonesa* (Saragossa: Institución "Fernando el Católico," 2000), 17, 24, 45, 64–67, respectively.

37 Sigüenza Pelarda, *La moda*, 119–24.

38 Sigüenza Pelarda, *La moda*, 164.

39 Judith Berg Sobré, *Behind the Altar Table: The Development of the Painted Retable in Spain, 1350–1500* (Columbia: University of Missouri Press, 1989), 21, 93, 94, 211, respectively.

40 Judith Berg Sobré, *Behind the Altar Table: The Development of the Painted Retable in Spain, 1350–1500*, 170–72.

41 Judith Berg Sobré, *Behind the Altar Table: The Development of the Painted Retable in Spain, 1350–1500*, 171.

42 Judith Berg Sobré, *Behind the Altar Table: The Development of the Painted Retable in Spain, 1350–1500*, 263.

43 Judith Berg Sobré, *Behind the Altar Table: The Development of the Painted Retable in Spain, 1350–1500*, 170f., 263.

44 Richard David Barnett, ed., *The Sephardic Heritage: Essays on the History and Cultural Contribution of the Jews in Spain and Portugal, vol. 1: The Jews in Spain and Portugal Before and After the Expulsion of 1492* (New York: Ktav, 1971). Don A. Halperin, *The Ancient Synagogues of the Iberian Peninsula* (Gainesville: University of Florida Press, 1969).

45 Vivian B. Mann, Thomas F. Glick, and Jerrilynn D. Dodds, *Convivencia: Jews, Muslims, and Christians in Medieval Spain* (New York: The Jewish Museum and George Braziller, 1992). Cf. Holland Cotter, "Review/Art; Coexistence in Medieval Spain, at Least Until 1492," *The New York Times*, November 13, 1992, section C, 29.

46 María Elena Díez Jorge, *El arte mudéjar: Expresión estética de una convivencia* (Granada: Universidad de Granada, Instituto de la Paz y los Conflictos, 2001), 70ff.

47 Pamela Patton, "An Islamic Envelope Flap Binding in the Cloister of Tudela: Another Muslim Connection for Iberian Jews?", in Colum Hourihane, ed., *Spanish Medieval Art: Recent Studies* (Tempe and Princeton: Arizona Center for Medieval and Renaissance Studies and Princeton University Index of Christian Art, 2007), 65–88.

48 For example, see Carmen Lacarra Ducay, "Representaciones de judíos en la pintura gótica aragonesa, siglos XIII al XV," *Boletín [del] Museo e Instituto "Camón Aznar"* 99, 2007, 235–58.s

GLOSSARY

atelier an artist's workshop

banco lowest register of panels on a *retablo* (equivalent of predella)

confraternity a lay brotherhood. In medieval Spain, members often pursued the same profession.

converso a Jew who had converted to Christianity

convivencia lit. living together; the mingling of Christian, Jewish, and Muslim cultures in medieval Spain

Crown of Aragon at its height in the fourteenth century, the kingdom consisted of Aragon, Catalonia, Valencia, Mallorca, Provence, Sardinia, Sicily, and other territories

de jure by right

Disputation a dialogue between members of different faiths that attempts to prove the superiority and validity of one faith over another, or that seeks to defend a faith against the criticism of adherents of another religion. During the High Middle Ages, disputations were used to challenge Jewish beliefs.

exilarch a lay ruler of the Jewish community in Babylonia from the second century C.E. through the thirteenth century. The exilarchs claimed Davidic descent.

gaon the head of a Torah academy who was an intellectual and religious leader of Babylonian Jewry

haggadah (pl. haggadot) book for the Seder or service held in the home on the first two nights of Passover. (In Israel, the Seder is held only on the first night of the holiday.)

halakhah the body of Jewish law comprising biblical law, the oral law transmitted in the Mishnah and the Talmud, and subsequent legal codes (adj. halakhic)

iconography the subject matter or symbolic meanings attached to images; the analysis of subject matter and its meaning

Inquisition A Church tribunal for the investigation and punishment of heresy

judería Jewish quarter of a town or city in medieval Spain

judío Spanish for Jew

parochial church parish church

pogrom an organized, often officially encouraged massacre or persecution of a minority group, especially one conducted against Jews

polychromy the art of employing many colors, as in painting or architecture.

predella see *banco*

qehilah a congregation of Jews, a Jewish community

retablo an altarpiece composed of multiple panels set at the back of the altar table (lit. behind the table). *Retablos* are often set in elaborate sculpted frames.

sacristy the room in a church where vestments and sacred objects are stored and where the priests don their vestments

Sepharad Hebrew for Spain (adj. Sephardic, Spanish-Jewish)

Sephardi(m) a Jew (or Jews) who traces his/her lineage to medieval Spain

sumptuary laws regulations pertaining to expenditures for clothing, celebrations and the like

Talmud commentary on Jewish Law formulated in Babylonia and Palestine between the third and the sixth centuries (adj. talmudic)

Transubstantiation the moment during the Mass when the wafer and the wine are believed to be transformed into the body and blood of Christ

EXHIBITION CHECKLIST

Petrus Roselli
Portolan chart
Mallorca, 1468
23 × 34 in.
The Hispanic Society of America,
New York (K35)

Tiles from the synagogue of El Tránsito,
Toledo
Toledo, ca. 1360
Tin-glazed earthenware
The Hispanic Society of America,
New York (E1324, E1326, E1359)

Pere Espalargues
Altarpiece with scenes from the
Life of the Virgin
Enviny, 1490
Tempera on panel
129 × 128 in.
The Hispanic Society of America,
New York (A5)

Anonymous
Altarpiece of the Virgin and Child:
The Circumcision of Christ
Castile, 1450–99
Tempera on panel
37 × 41 in.
The Hispanic Society of America,
New York (A1/6)

Anonymous
Altarpiece of the Virgin and Child: The
Nativity and the Adoration of the Magi
Castile, 1450–99
Tempera on panel
75 × 29 in.
The Hispanic Society of America,
New York (A1/2)

Anonymous
Scenes from the Life of Saint Martin:
The Mass of Saint Martin
Castile, ca. 1401–99
Tempera on panel
45 × 37 in.
The Hispanic Society of America,
New York (A9/1)

Pere Lembrí
Catalan *retablo*: David, Saint Agnes,
The Annunciation
Catalonia, ca. 1301–99
Tempera on panel
88 × 28 in.
The Hispanic Society of America,
New York (A3/1)

Pere Lembrí
Catalan *retablo*: Isaiah, Saint Peter Walking
on the Water, Saint Peter Martyr
Catalonia, ca. 1301–99
Tempera on panel
89 × 28 in.
The Hispanic Society of America,
New York (A3/2)

Pere Lembrí
Catalan *retablo*: Ezekiel, An Archangel,
Christ the Judge of the World
Catalonia, ca. 1301–99
Tempera on panel
89 × 27 in.
The Hispanic Society of America,
New York (A3/4)

Pere Lembrí
Catalan *retablo*: A Prophet, A Saint (Scho-
lastica?), The Founding of a Monastery,
Saint Bernard of Clairvaux
Tempera on panel
Catalonia, ca. 1301–99
89 × 37 in.
The Hispanic Society of America,
New York (A3/3)

Pere Lembrí
Catalan *retablo*: Moses, The Pentecost,
A Saint (Petronilla?)
Catalonia, ca. 1301–99
Tempera on panel
89 × 27 in.
The Hispanic Society of America,
New York (A3/5)

Pere Lembrí
Catalan *retablo*: Daniel, Saint Gertrude of
Nivelles, The Crucifixion, Saint Agatha
Catalonia, ca. 1301–99
Tempera on panel
89 × 37 in.
The Hispanic Society of America,
New York (A3/6)

Anonymous
Panels with scenes from the Life of Christ
Spanish, thirteenth century
Tempera on wood
59 × 10 in.
Metropolitan Museum of Art,
The Cloisters Collection (1977.94)
Bequest of Carl Otto von Kienbusch

Anonymous
Panels with scenes from the Life of Christ
Spanish, thirteenth century
Tempera on wood
(a) 42 × 15 × 1 in., (b) 42 × 17 × 1 in.
Metropolitan Museum of Art,
The Cloisters Collection (55.62a,b)

Anonymous
Christ among the Doctors
Catalonia, early fifteenth century
Tempera and gold on wood
44 × 30 in.
Metropolitan Museum of Art,
The Friedsam Collection (32.100.123)
Bequest of Michael Friedsam, 1931

Domingo Ram
Altarpiece of Saint John the Baptist:
Annunciation to Zacharias
1480
Tempera on wood, gold ground
37 × 27 in.
Metropolitan Museum of Art,
The Cloisters Collection (25.120.929)

Domingo Ram
Altarpiece of Saint John the Baptist: Saint
John Preaching in a Field and Saint John
Preaching in a Synagogue
1480
Tempera on wood, gold ground
60 × 28 in.
Metropolitan Museum of Art,
The Cloisters Collection (251. 120. 669)

Anonymous
Altarpiece of Saint Andrew:
Scenes of the Creation, with scenes from
the Life of Saint Andrew on the reverse
Añastro, Castile, late fourteenth century
Tempera on wood
78 × 38 in.
Metropolitan Museum of Art,
The Cloisters Collection, 1925 (25.120.257)

Michael Lupi de Çandiu (illuminator)
Vidal Mayor of James I, Initial A:
Two Jews in Conversation
Aragon, second half of the thirteenth century
Tempera colors and gold leaf on parchment
14 × 9 in.
J. Paul Getty Museum, Los Angeles
(83.MQ.165.243v)

Anonymous
Moreh Nevukhim (*Guide to the Perplexed*)
by Maimonides
Barcelona, 1348
Ink, gold and gouache on vellum
8 × 5 in.
Det Kongelige Bibliotek, Copenhagen
(Cod. Heb. 37, fol. 114a)

Hispano-Moresque haggadah
Castile, late thirteenth century
6 × 5 in.
British Library, London
(Ms. Or. 2737, fol. 85r)

Miguel Jiménez and Martín Bernat
Altarpiece of the True Cross: Saint Helena
Meeting with the Jews
Saragossa, 1485–87
Oil on panel
61 × 45 in. (with frame),
51 × 36 in. (without frame)
Museo de Zaragoza, Saragossa

Miguel Jiménez and Martín Bernat
Altarpiece of the True Cross:
Saint Helena Interrogating Judas
Saragossa, 1485–87
77 × 45 × 5 in. (with frame), 67 × 37 in.
(without frame)
Museo de Zaragoza, Saragossa

Miguel Jiménez and Martín Bernat
Altarpiece of the True Cross:
The Prophets Malachi,
Daniel, and Ezekiel Saragossa,
1485–87
Oil on panel
25 × 60 in. (with frame),
18 × 56 in. (without frame)
Museo de Zaragoza, Saragossa

*Ceremonial de consagración y de la coro-
nación de los Reyes de Aragon*
(*Ceremony of the Consecration and
Coronation of the Kings of Aragon*)
Saragossa, fourteenth century
Ink, gouache, gold leaf on parchment
Museo Lázaro Galdiano, Madrid
(Ms. Reg. 14425)

Seder plate
Teruel, fifteenth century
Ceramic: tin, copper, and magnese glaze
Diameter: 13 in.
Museu de Ceràmica, Barcelona

Hanukkah lamp
Teruel, fifteenth century
Ceramic
19 × 3 × 2 in.
Museo de Teruel, Teruel

Plate
Teruel, mid-fourteenth century
Ceramic
5 × 18 in.
Museo de Teruel, Teruel

Workshop of Arnau Bassa
Disputation of Saint Stephen with the Jews
1345–49
Tempera on panel
Museo Nacional d'Art de Catalunya,
Barcelona

Nicolás and Martín Zahortiga
Altarpiece from the collegiate church
of Santa María de Borja
The Expulsion of Joachim and Anna from
the Temple
Borja, ca. 1460
Museo de Borja, Borja

Nicolás and Martín Zahortiga
Altarpiece from the collegiate church
of Santa María de Borja
The Presentation of Jesus in the Temple
(The Circumcision)
Borja, ca. 1460
Museo de Borja, Borja

Nicolás and Martín Zahortiga
Altarpiece from the collegiate church
of Santa María de Borja
Jesus and the Doctors
Borja, ca. 1460
Museo de Borja, Borja

ABOUT THE CONTRIBUTORS

Thomas F. Glick is Professor of History at Boston University. A historian of medieval science and technology, he has specialized in the impact of Muslim culture on Christian Spain. His books include *Islamic and Christian Spain in the Early Middle Ages* (2nd ed., 2005) and *From Muslim Fortress to Christian Castle* (1995). He is co-editor of *Medieval Science, Technology and Medicine: An Encyclopedia* (2005).

Carmen Lacarra Ducay is Professor of Ancient and Medieval Art History at the University of Saragossa, where she specializes in medieval art from Aragon and Romanesque and Gothic art from Navarre (from the twelfth to the fifteenth centuries). She has served as consultant to numerous exhibitions, including *The Splendor of the Renaissance in Aragon* (2009–10); *The Journey of Cosimo III de' Medici to Santiago de Compostela* (2004–5); and *Hispano-Flemish Gothic Painting: Bartolomé Bermejo and his Time* (2003).

Vivian B. Mann is Director of the Master's Program in Jewish Art at the Graduate School of the Jewish Theological Seminary, and Curator Emerita of the Jewish Museum. Her latest book, *Art and Ceremony in Jewish Life: Essays in Jewish Art History*, was published in 2005. In 1999 Mann received the Jewish Cultural Achievement Award in Jewish Thought from the National Foundation for Jewish Culture. She is one of the senior editors of *Images: A Journal of Jewish Art and Visual Culture*.

Marcus B. Burke is Curator of Paintings, Drawings, and Metalwork at The Hispanic Society of America, New York. He has taught at Yale University, SUNY Purchase, and the University of Texas. Dr. Burke co-curated the 1990 exhibition *Mexico: Splendors of Thirty Centuries* at the Metropolitan Museum of Art. He has been a guest curator at the Art Museum of South Texas, the Davenport Museum of Art, Iowa, and the Heckscher Museum of Art, Huntington, New York.

SELECTED BIBLIOGRAPHY

Compiled by Marcus B. Burke and Andrea Ortuño

Adams, Susan M., *et al.* "The Genetic Legacy of Religious Diversity and Intolerance: Paternal Lineages of Christians, Jews, and Muslims in the Iberian Peninsula," *The American Journal of Human Genetics* 83 (6), December 4, 2008, 725–36.

Alcoy i Pedrós, Rosa. "La ricezione della pittura giottesca in Spagna, dai Bassa a Starnina," in *Giotto e il Trecento*, ed. Alessandro Tomei. Geneva and Milan: Skira, 2009, 321–34.

__________. *L'art gòtic a Catalunya. Pintura I. De l'inici a l'italianisme*. Barcelona: Enciclopèdia Catalana, 2005.

Alberch i Fugueras, Ramón (trans. Christopher Short). *The Jews in Girona*. Girona: Diputació de Girona, Caixa de Girona, Patronat Municipal "Call de Girona", 1994.

Álvarez Chillida, Gonzalo. "Franco y los judíos en la Segunda Guerra Mundial," in Tusell and Ferrer, eds., *Los judíos*, 161–81.

Amador de los Ríos, José. *Estudios históricos, políticos y literarios sobre los judíos de España*. Madrid: D. M. Diaz, 1848.

__________. *Historia social, política y religiosa de los judíos de España y Portugal*. 3 vols. Madrid: T. Fortanet, 1875–76.

Assis, Yom Tov. *The Jews in the Crown of Aragon. Regesta of the Cartas Reales in the Archivo de la Corona de Aragón. Part II: 1328–1493*. Jerusalem: Academon, 1995.

__________. *The Golden Age of Aragonese Jewry: Community and Society in the Crown of Aragon, 1213–1327*. London: Littman Library of Jewish Civilization, 1997.

__________. *Jewish Economy in the Medieval Crown of Aragon, 1213–1327: Money and Power*. Leiden: E. J. Brill, 1997.

Avni, Haim. *España, Franco y los judíos*. Madrid: Altalena, 1982.

Avrin, Leila. "The Mocatta Haggadah and Other Works by the Master of the Catalan Mahzor," in *Hebrew Studies: Papers Presented at a Colloquium on Resources for Hebraica in Europe, Held at the School of Oriental and African Studies, University of London, 11–13 September 1989*. London: British Library, 1991, 139–48.

Azcárate, José María. *Arte gótico en España* [Manuales Arte Cátedra]. Madrid: Ediciones Cátedra, 2006.

Baer, Yitzhak. *A History of the Jews in Christian Spain*. 2 vols. Philadelphia: Jewish Publication Society, 1961–66.

Bango Torviso, Isidro Gonzalo. *Memoria de Sefarad*. Madrid: Sociedad Estatal para la Acción Cultural Exterior, 2002.

__________. *Remembering Sepharad: Jewish Culture in Medieval Spain*. Madrid: Sociedad Estatal para la Acción Cultural Exterior, 2003.

Bayle, F. Olivan. *Bonanat y Nicolás Zahortiga y la pintura del siglo XV*. Saragossa: Ayuntimento de Zaragoza, Comisión de Cultura, 1978.

Beckwith, B. Rachel. "Haverford College's Thirteenth-Century Hebrew Bible: A Case Study in Manuscript Attribution," *Manuscripta*, vol. 42, no. 1, March 1998, 30–52.

Beinart, Haim. *Expulsion of the Jews from Spain*. Jerusalem: The Magnes Press, Hebrew University, [5] 755 [1994].

Ben-Dov, Me'ir. *Batei-keneset bi-Sefarad u-morashtam*. Tel Aviv: Devir, 1989.

Ben-Shalom, Ram. "Between Official and Private Dispute: The Case of Christian Spain and Provence in the Late Middle Ages," *AJS Review* 27:1 (2003), 23–72.

Benito Ruano, Eloy. *Los orígenes del problema converso*. Madrid: Real Academia de la Lengua, 2001.

Berg-Sobré, Judith. *Behind the Altar Table. The Development of the Painted Retable in Spain, 1300–1500*. Columbia: University of Missouri Press, 1989.

——————. *Bartolomé de Cárdenas "El Bermejo." Itinerant Painter in the Crown of Aragon*. San Francisco, London, and Bethesda: International Scholars Publications, 1998.

Blasco Martínez, Asunción. *La judería de Zaragoza en el siglo XIV*. Saragossa: Institución "Fernando el Católico," 1988.

——————. "Pintores y orfebres judíos en Zaragoza (siglo XIV)," *Aragon en la Edad Media* 8 (1989), 113–31.

Blázquez Miguel, Juan. *Toledot: Historia del Toledo judío*. Toledo: Editorial Arcano, [1989].

Calzada i Oliveras, Josep. *Die Kathedrale von Girona*, 2nd edn. Barcelona: Escudo de Oro, 1988.

Campanys, Mariona, ed. *La Cataluña judía*. Girona: Ajuntament, Departament de Cultura, 2002.

Cantera Burgos, Francisco. *Sinagogas de Toledo, Segovia, y Córdoba*. Madrid: Consejo Superior de Investigaciones Científicas, Instituto B. Arias Montano, 1973.

——————. *Las juderías medievales en la provincia de Guadalajara*. Madrid, 1975.

Cantera Montenegro, Enrique. *Los judíos en la Edad Media hispana*. Madrid: A-Z, 1986.

Carcedo, Diego. *Un español frente al Holocausto*. Madrid: Temas de Hoy, 2000.

Cardaillac, Louis, ed. *Tolède, XIIe–XIIIe: musulmans, chrétiens et juifs: le savoir et la tolérance*. Paris: Editions Autrement, 1991.

Carrasco, Juan, Fermín Miranda García, and Eloísa Ramírez Vaquero, *Los judíos del Reino de Navarra*. 4 vols. Navarra: Gobierno de Navarra, Depatamento de Educación y Cultura, 1994.

Carrete Parrondo, Carlos, ed. *Fontes Iudaeorum Regni Castellae*. Salamanca: Universidad Pontificia de Salamanca, and Granada: Universidad de Granada, 1981–[1997].

Casanovas, Jordi. "Aspectes poc coneguts de la collecció epigràfica hebraica Barcelonina / Aspects peu connus de la collection épigraphique hébraïque de Barcelone," in *Miscellània en homenatge a Joan Ainaud de Lasarte*. Barcelona: Publicacions de l'Abadia de Montserrat, MNAC, 1998, vol. 1, 367–74.

Chabàs, Josep. "L'activitat astronòmica a l'época del rei Pere (segle XIV)," in Vernet and Parés, eds., *Ciència*, 483–514.

Chazan, Robert. *Barcelona and Beyond: The Disputation of 1263 and its Aftermath*. Berkeley: University of California Press, 1992.

——————. *Fashioning Jewish Identity in Medieval Western Christendom*. Cambridge and New York: Cambridge University Press, 2005.

Cohen, Evelyn M. "The Sister Haggadah and its 'Poor Relation'," in *Proceedings of the Eleventh World Congress of Jewish Studies, Jerusalem*. Jerusalem: World Union of Jewish Studies, and Magnes Press, Hebrew University, 1994, 17–24.

Cohen, Mark R. *Under Crescent and Cross. The Jews in the Middle Ages*. Princeton: Princeton University Press, 1994.

Comes, Mercè. "La cartografia a Mallorca i a Barcelona," in Vernet and Parés, eds., *Cièn-*

cia, 515–73.

Conde y Delgado de Molina, Rafael, ed. *La expulsión de los judíos de la Corona de Aragón: Documentos para su estudio.* Saragossa: Institución "Fernando el Católico," 1991.

Cooperman, Bernard Dov, ed. *In Iberia and Beyond: Hispanic Jews between Cultures: Proceedings of a Symposium to mark the 500th Anniversary of the Expulsion of Spanish Jewry.* Newark: University of Delaware Press, 1998.

Cortés Cortés, Gabriel. *Historia de los judíos mallorquines y de sus descendientes cristianos.* Palma de Mallorca: M. Font, 1985.

Dahan, Gilbert. *The Christian Polemic against the Jews in the Middle Ages.* Notre Dame, Ind.: University of Notre Dame Press, 1998.

Díez Jorge, María Elena. "Algunas percepciones cristianas de la alteridad artística en el medioevo peninsular," *Cuadernos de arte de la Universidad de Granada*, vol. 30, 1999, 29–47.

________. *El arte mudéjar: Expresión estética de una convivencia.* Granada: Universidad de Granada, Instituto de la Paz y los Conflictos, 2001.

Dimas Fernández-Galiano, D., ed. *Aragón. Reino y Corona.* Saragossa: Tipolínea, 2000.

Dodds, Jerrilyn D. *Architecture and Ideology in Early Medieval Spain.* University Park and London: University of Pennsylvania Press, 1990.

________. "Mudejar Tradition and the Synagogues of Medieval Spain: Cultural Identity and Cultural Hegemony," in Mann *et al.*, *Convivencia*, 113–32.

Dodds, Jerrilyn D., María Rosa Menocal, and Abigail Krasner Balbale, *The Arts of Intimacy: Christians, Jews, and Muslims in the Making of Castilian Culture.* New Haven: Yale University Press, 2008. [Reviewed by Cynthia Robinson in *The Art Bulletin*, 91 (3), 2009, 369–373.]

Durán Gudiol, Antonio. *La judería de Huesca.* Saragossa: Guara, [1984?].

Edmunds, Sheila. "The Kennicott Bible and the Use of Prints in Hebrew Manuscripts," in *Le stampe e la diffusione delle immagini e degli stili* (*Atti del XXIV Congresso Internazionale di Storia dell'Arte 1979*, vol. VIII), ed. Henri Zerner. Bologna: CLUEB, 1983, 23–29.

Elukin, Jonathan. *Living Together. Living Apart. Rethinking Jewish–Christian Relations in the Middle Ages.* Princeton and Oxford: Princeton University Press, 2007.

Enciclopedia judaica castellana. El pueblo judío en el pasado y el presente: su historia, su religión, sus costumbres, su literatura, su arte, sus hombres, su situación en el mundo. Mexico City: Editorial Enciclopedia Judaica Castellana, 1948–51.

Encuentros Judaicos de Tudela. *Luces y sombras de la judería europea (siglos XI–XVII): Primeros Encuentros Judaicos de Tudela.* [Pamplona]: Gobierno de Navarra, ca. 1996.

Espinosa Villegas, Miguel Angel. "Los conceptos estéticos y la arquitectura de los judíos," *Cuadernos de arte de la Universidad de Granada*, vol. 26, 1995, 475–87.

________. "Anotaciones para una revisión de casa entre los judíos españoles," *Cuadernos de arte de la Universidad de Granada*, vol. 29, 1998, 7–15.

________. "El modelo arquitectónico sefardí: Entre Oriente y Occidente," in *Arte e identidades culturales. Actas del XII Congreso Nacional del Comité Español de Historia del Arte: Homenaje a D. Carlos Cid Priego.* Oviedo: Universidad de Oviedo, Vicerrectorado de Extensión Univestaria, 1998, 97–103.

________. *Judaísmo, estética y arquitectura:*

La sinagoga sefardí. Granada: Universidad de Granada, 2002.

Fishof, Iris. "A Legacy on Parchment: The Sassoon Spanish Haggadah," *Israel Museum Journal* 10 (spring 1992), 9–14.

Gampel, Benjamin R. *The Last Jews on Iberian Soil. Navarrese Jewry 1479-98*. Berkely, Los Angeles, and London: University of California Press, 1999.

________. "A Letter to a Wayward Teacher. The Transformations of Sephardi Culture in Christian Iberia," in *Culture of the Jews. A New History*, ed. David Biale. New York: Schocken Books, 2002.

________, ed. *Crisis and Creativity in the Sephardic World, 1391–1648*. New York: Columbia University Press, 1997.

García-Arenal, Mercedes, and Béatrice Leroy. *Moros y judíos en Navarra en la baja Edad Media*. Madrid: Hiperión, 1984.

Garel, Michel. "The Foa Bible," *Journal of Jewish Art* 6 (1979), 78–85.

________. "Le mobilier du sanctuaire: un folio détaché," *Journal of Jewish Art* 9 (1982), 105–7.

Gerber, Jane S. *The Jews of Spain: A History of the Sephardic Experience*. New York: Free Press, 1992.

Gitay, Zefira. "The Image of Moses in the Spanish Haggadot," in Stillman and Stillman, eds., *From Iberia to Diaspora*, 515–24.

Glick, Thomas. "'Thin Hegemony' and Consensual Communities in the Medieval Crown of Aragon," in *El feudalisme comptat i debatut: Formació i expansió del feudalisme català*, eds. M. Barceló *et al.* Valencia: Universitat de València, 2003, 523–38.

________. "'My Master, The Jew': Observations on Interfaith Scholarly Interaction in the Middle Ages," in Hames, ed., *Jews, Muslims and Christians*, 157–82.

Goitein, S. D. *A Mediterranean Society. The Jewish Comunities of the World as Portrayed in the Documents of the Cairo Geniza. vol 2. The Community*. Berkeley, Los Angeles, and London: University of California Press, 1999.

Gonzalo Maeso, David. *Garnata al-yahud: Granada en la historia del judaísmo español* ("Estudio preliminar por Ma. Encarnación Varela Moreno"). Granada: Universidad de Granada, 1990.

González, Juan José Martín, ed. *Las edades del hombre. El arte en la iglesia de Castilla y Leon*. Salamanca: Europa Artes Gráficas, 1988.

González, José Luis, "Der 'Dialogus' des Petrus Alfonsi, ein polemisch-apologetischer Traktat," in *Jewish Studies in a New Europe*. Copenhagen: C. A. Reitzel and Det Kongelige Bibliotek, 1998, 302.

Grayzel, Solomon. *The Church and the Jews in the XIIIth Century. Vol. II. 1254–1314*, ed. Kenneth R. Stow. New York: Jewish Theological Seminary of America, and Detroit: Wayne State University Press, 1989.

Gudiol Ricart, José. *Pintura gótica* [Ars Hispaniae 9]. Madrid: Editorial Plus-Ultra, 1955.

Gutmann, Joseph. Review of Nordström, *Duke of Alba's Castilian Bible*, in *Speculum*, July 43 (3), 1968, 527–29. Also retrievable from http://www.jstor.org/stable/2855862.

________. "On Medieval Hanukkah Lamps," *Artibus et Historiae*, no. 40 (XX), 1999, 187–90.

Gutwirth, Eleazar. "Widows, Artisans and the *Issues of Life*: Hispano-Jewish Bourgeois Ideology", in Cooperman, ed., *In Iberia and Beyond*, 143–74.

Halperin, Don A. *The Ancient Synagogues of the Iberian Peninsula*. Gainesville: University of Florida Press, 1969.

Hames, Harvey J. *The Art of Conversion:*

Christianity and Kabbalah in the Thirteenth Century. Leiden: E. J. Brill, 2000.

__________, ed. *Jews, Muslims and Christians In and Around the Crown of Aragon.* Leiden: E. J. Brill, 2004.

Harris, Julie A. "Good Jews, Bad Jews and No Jews at all: Ritual Imagery and Social Standards in the Catalan Haggadot," in *Church, State, Vellum, and Stone: Essays on Medieval Spain in Honor of John Williams*, ed. Therese Martin. Leiden: Brill, 2005, 275–96.

Hillgarth, J. N. *The Spanish Kingdoms, 1250–1516.* New York: Clarendon Press, 1976.

Hourihane, Colum. *Spanish Medieval Art: Recent Studies.* Tempe and Princeton: Arizona Center for Medieval and Renaissance Studies and Princeton University Index of Christian Art, 2007.

Iniesta Sanmartin, Angel, *et al. Lorca. Luces de Sefarad.* Murcia: Industrias Gráficas Libecom, 2009.

Isaacs, Abraham Lionel. *Els jueus de Mallorca.* Mallorca: M. Font, 1986.

Jacobs, Joseph. *An Inquiry into the Sources of the History of the Jews in Spain.* London: David Nutt, 1894. [Reviewed by Meyer Kayserling in the *Jewish Quarterly Review* 8 (April 1896), 486–99. Available on JSTOR.]

Jornades d'Història dels Jueus a Catalunya. Aactes: Girona, abril 1987. [Girona]: Ajuntament de Girona, [1990].

Kalmar, Ivan Davidson. "Moorish Style: Orientalism, the Jews, and Synagogue Architecture," *Jewish Social Studies* 7 (Spring–Summer 2001), 68–100.

Kaufmann, D. "Art in the Synagogue," *Jewish Quarterly Review* 9 (January 1897), 254–69.

Klagsbald, Victor. "Sceau de Salomon Bar Ephraïm Ben Al Hadad et du symbolisme du croissant de lune et de l'étoile," *Revue des études juives*, vol. 150, nos. 3–4, July–December 1991, 547–56.

Klein, Elka. *Jews, Christian Society, and Royal Power in Mediaeval Barcelona.* Ann Arbor: University of Michigan Press, 2006.

Lacarra Ducay, Carmen. "Nuevas noticias sobre Martín de Soria, pintor de *retablos* (1449–1487)," *Artigrama* 2 (1985), 23–446.

__________. "Juan de Leví, pintor al servicio de los Pérez Calvillo en su capilla de la Seo de Tarazona (1403–1408)," in *Retablo de Juan de Leví y su restauración. Capilla de los Pérez Calvillo, Catedral de Tarazona.* Saragossa: Diputación General de Aragón, Departamento de Cultura y Educación, 1990, 29–45 and 57–63.

__________. "Retablo de la Virgen con el Niño," in *Joyas de un Patrimonio.* Saragossa: Diputación de Zaragoza *et al.*, 1990.

__________. *Arte gótico en el Museo de Saragossa.* Saragossa: Gobierno de Aragón, Departamento de Cultura y Turismo, 2003.

__________. *Blasco de Grañén pintor de retablos (1422–1459).* Saragossa: Institución "Fernando el Católico", Excma. Diputación de Saragossa, 2004.

__________. "Representaciones de judíos en la pintura gótica aragonesa: siglos XIII al XV," *Boletín [del] Museo e Instituto "Camón Aznar,"* 99, 2007, 235–58.

Lazar, Moshe, ed. *The Sephardic Tradition: Ladino and Spanish Jewish Literature.* New York: Norton, 1972.

Lerner, Robert E. *The Feast of Saint Abraham. Medieval Millenarians and the Jews.* Philadelphia: University of Pennsylvania Press, 2001.

Lipton, Sara. *Images of Intolerance. The Representation of Jews and Judaism in the* Bible Moralisée. Berkeley, Los Angeles, and London: University of California Press, 1999.

Lomba Fuentes, Joaquín. *La raíz semítica de lo europeo. Islam y judaísmo medievales*. Madrid: Akal, 1997.

López Alvarez, Ana María, and María Luisa Menéndez Robles. "Palacios y mansiones de la España judía," *Espacio, tiempo y forma. Serie 7, Historia del arte*, vol. 6, 1993, 97–116.

__________. "La galería de las mujeres de la sinagoga de El Tránsito: Nuevos hallazgos," *Sefarad* 47 (1987), 301–14.

López-Ibor, Marta. *Los judíos en España*. Madrid: Anaya, 1990.

Maccoby, Haim, ed. *Judaism on Trial*. Rutherford, N.J.: Farleigh Dickinson University Press, 1982.

Majada Neila, J. *Tras la estela de los judíos en Málaga*. Málaga: Diputación Provincial de Málaga, 1992.

Mann, Vivian B., Thomas F. Glick, and Jerrilynn Dodds, *Convivencia: Jews, Muslims and Christians in Medieval Spain*. New York: The Jewish Museum and George Braziller, 1992. [Reviewed in *Minerva*, vol. 3, no. 6, November–December 1992, 16–17.]

Manote i Clivilles, M. Rosa, *et al. Gothic Art Guide*. Barcelona: Museu Nacional d'Art de Catalunya, 2000.

Martí Bonet, J. M. *La catedral de Barcelona*. Barcelona: Editorial Escudo de Oro and Arxiu Diocesà de Barcelona, n.d.

Mas Arrondo, Carlos, and Joaquín Fernández Cacho. *Los judíos: Una minoría religiosa en el Aragón medieval. Guía didáctica*. Saragossa: Diputación and Ibercaja, 2002.

Meruéndano Arias, Leopoldo. *Los judíos de Ribadavia: Origen de las 4 parroquias*. Lugo: Alvarellos, 1981.

McVaugh, Michael R. *Medicine before the Plague: Practitioners and their Patients in the Crown of Aragon, 1285–1345*. Cambridge: Cambridge University Press, 1993.

Meiss, Millard. "Italian Style in Catalonia and a Fourteenth-Century Catalan Workshop," *Journal of the Walters Art Gallery* 4 (1941), 45–87.

Melero Moneo, Marisa. *La pintura sobre tabla del gótico lineal. Frontales, laterales de altar y retablos en el reino de Mallorca y los condados catalanes* [Memoria Artium 3]. Barcelona: Edicions de la Universitat de Barcelona, 2005, 176–84.

Mellinkoff, Ruth. "Judas's Red Hair and the Jews," *Journal of Jewish Art* 9 (1982), 31–46.

Metropolitan Museum of Art. *The Art of Medieval Spain A.D. 500–1200*. New York: The Metropolitan Museum of Art, 1992.

Meyerson, Mark. *The Muslims of Valencia in the Age of Fernando and Isabel: Between Coexistence and Crusade*. Berkeley: University of California Press, 1991.

__________. "Defending their Jewish Subjects: Elionor of Sicily, Maria de Luna, and the Jews of Morvedre," in *Queenship and Political Power in Medieval and Early Modern Spain*, ed. Theresa Eremite. Aldershot, England: Ashgate, 2005, 55–77.

Mitre Fernández. *Judaísmo y cristianismo: Raíces de un gran conflicto histórico*. Madrid: ISTMO, [1980?].

Molina i Figueras, Joan. "Al voltant de Jaume Huguet," in Sureda i Pons, ed., *L'art gòtic a Catalunya. Pintura III*, 142–43.

Morales Ruiz, Juan José. "La obsesión antimasónica de Franco: Masones y judíos en el discurso represivo del franquismo," in Tusell and Ferrer, eds., *Los judíos*, 131–60.

Morte García, Carmen. "Del Gótico al Renacimiento en los *retablos* de pintura aragonesa durante el reinado de Fernando el Católico," in *La pintura gótica durante el siglo XV en tierras de Aragón y en otros territorios peninsulares*. Saragossa: Institución "Fernando el Católico", Excma. Diputación de Saragossa, 2007, 335–72.

Motis Dolader, Miguel Angel. *Los judíos en Aragón en la Edad Media (siglos XIII–XV)*. Saragossa: Caja de Ahorros de la Inmaculada de Aragón, 1990.

__________, ed. *Hebraica aragonalia: El legado judío en Aragón*. Saragossa: Diputación and Ibercaja, 2002.

Muñoz Párraga, María del Carmen. "Los judíos en Aragón. Del mundo del Medievo al del Renacimiento," in *Encrucijada de Culturas*. Saragossa: Típolinea, 2008, 104.

Muñoz Párraga, María del Carmen, and Isidro Bango Torviso, eds. *Memoria de Sefarad*. Madrid: Sociedad Estatal para la Acción Cultural Exterior, 2002.

Narkiss, Bezalel, *et al. Hebrew Illuminated Manuscripts in the British Isles. Volume One: The Spanish and Portuguese Manuscripts*. Oxford and New York: Oxford University Press for the Israel Academy of Sciences and Humanities and the British Academy, 1982.

Netanyahu, Benzion. *The Origins of the Inquisition in Fifteenth-Century Spain*. New York: Random House, 1995.

Nirenberg, David. *Communities of Violence: Persecution of Minorities in the Middle Ages*. Princeton: Princeton University Press, 1996.

Nordström, Carl-Otto. *The Duke of Alba's Castilian Bible: A Study of the Rabbinical Features of the Miniatures* [Figura: Uppsala Studies in the History of Art, new ser., 5]. Uppsala: Acta Universitatis Upsaliensis [Almqvist & Wiksells], 1967.

Pacios López, Antonio. *La Disputa de Tortosa*. 2 vols. Madrid: C.S.I.C., 1957.

Palomero Plaza. *Historia de la Sinagoga de Samuel Ha Leví y del Museo Sefardí*. Madrid: Ministero de la Cultura, 2007.

Palol, Pedro de, and Max Hirmer. *Early Medieval Art in Spain*. New York: Harry N. Abrams, 1966.

Pérez, Joseph. *Historia de una tragedia: La expulsión de los judíos de España*. Barcelona: Crítica (Grupo Grijalbo-Mondadori), 1993.

Pfandtner, Karl-Georg. "Dated Medieval Illuminated Hebrew Manuscripts: An Under-Exploited Resource for Western Manuscript Studies," *Manuscripta*, vols. 47–48, 2003–4, 107–34, pls. 12–14.

Post, Chandler Rathfon. *A History of Spanish Painting*. Cambridge, Mass.: Harvard University Press, 1930–66.

Ray, Jonathan. *The Sephardic Frontier. The* Reconquista *and the Jewish Community in Medieval Iberia*. Ithaca and London: Cornell University Press, 2006.

Rodríguez Jiménez, José Luis. "El discurso antisemita en el fascism español," in Tusell and Ferrer, *Los judíos*, 89–130.

Romano, David. *Judíos al servicio de Pedro el Grande de Aragón (1276–1285)*. Barcelona: Universidad de Barcelona, Facultad de Filología, 1983.

__________. *De historia judía hispánica*. Barcelona: Universitat de Barcelona, 1991.

Romero, Elena, ed., *La vida judía en Sefarad*. Toledo: Julio Soto Impresor, 1991.

Roth, Cecil. *A History of the Marranos*. New York: Hermon Press, 1974.

__________. *The Sarajevo Haggadah*. Belgrade: Beogradski Izdavač-Grafički Zavod, 1975.

Rubin, Miri. *Gentile Tales: The Narrative Assault on Late Medieval Jews*. Philadelphia: University of Pennsylvania Press, 1999.

Ruiz y Queseda, Francesco, ed. *L'art gòtic a Catalunya. Pintura II. El corrent internacional.* Barcelona: Enciclopèdia Catalana, 2005.

Sabater, Tina. *La pintura mallorquina del segle XV.* Palma: Edicions UIB, 2002.

Sáenz-Badillos, Angel, ed. *Judíos entre árabes y cristianos: Luces y sombras de una convivencia.* Cordoba: Ediciones El Almendro, [2000?].

Safran, Janina M. "Identity and Differentiation in Ninth-Century Al-Andalus," *Speculum* 76 (2001), 582.

Salgado, Felipe Maíllo, ed. *España, al-Andalus, Sefarad: Síntesis y nuevas perspectivas.* Salamanca: Universidad de Salamanca, 1988.

Samsó, Julio. "Traduccions i obres científiques originals elaborades en medis jueus. El desenvolupament de l'hebreu com a llengua científica," in Vernet and Parés, eds., *Ciència,* 297–325.

Schmauser, Caroline, and Monika Walter. *Bon compaño, jura di: El encuentro de moros, judíos y cristianos en la obra cervantina.* Frankfurt am Main: Vervuert, and Madrid: Iberoamericana, 1998.

Schmitt, Jean-Claude. "La genèse médiévale de la légende et de l'iconographie du Juif errant," *Le Juif errant. Un témoin du temps.* Paris: Musée d'art et d'histoire du Judaïsme, 2001, 54–75.

Sed-Rajna, Gabrielle. "Hebrew Manuscripts of Fourteenth-Century Catalonia and the Workshop of the Master of St. Mark," *Jewish Art* 18 (1992), 117–28.

__________. "Le rôle de l'Espagne dans la transmission de l'iconographie biblique," *Espacio, tiempo y forma. Serie 7, Historia del arte,* vol. 6, 1993, 81–95.

__________. "The Image as Exegetical Tool: Paintings in Medieval Hebrew Manuscripts of the Bible," in *The Bible as Book: The Manuscript Tradition.* New Castle, Del.: Oak Knoll Press, in association with The Scriptorium, Center for Christian Antiquities, 1998, 215–21, pls. 30–38.

Serrano y Sanz, M. "Juan de Leví y Pedro Rupert," *Revista de Archivos, Bibliotecas y Museos,* 3rd series, 35, 1916, 415–16.

Signos: Arte y cultura en el Alto Aragón medieval (exhibition catalogue). Saragossa: Gobierno de Aragón, 1993.

Sigüenza Pelarda, Cristina. *La moda en el vestir en la pintura gótica aragonesa.* Saragossa: Institución "Fernando el Católico," 2000.

Sobré, Judith Berg. *Behind the Altar Table: The Development of the Painted Retable in Spain, 1350–1500.* Columbia: University of Missouri Press, 1989.

Solà-Solé, Josep M., Samuel G. Armistead, and Joseph H. Silverman, eds. *Hispania Judaica: Studies on the History, Language, and Literature of the Jews in the Hispanic World.* 3 vols. Barcelona: Puvill, [1980–84].

Suárez Fernández, Luis. *Judíos españoles en la Edad Media.* Madrid: Rialp, 1980.

Sureda i Pons, Joan, ed. *L'art gòtic a Catalunya. Pintura III. Darreres manifestacions.* Barcelona: Enciclopèdia Catalana, 2006.

Torroba Bernaldo de Quirós, Felipe. *Historia de los Sefarditas.* Buenos Aires: Editorial Universitaria, 1968.

Tusell Gómez, Javier and José Antonio Ferrer Benimeli, eds. *Los judíos en la historia de España* [Actas del curso celebrado en la UNED de Calatayud en mayo de 2002], Saragossa: Diputación Provincial, and Calatayud: Universidad Nacional de Educación a Distancia, 2003.

Van Der Horst, P. W. Review of Noy, *Jewish Inscriptions,* in *Journal of Theological Studies,* vol. 45, no. 2, October 1994, 701–4.

Wischnitzer, Mark. *A History of Jewish Crafts
    and Guilds.* New York: Jonathan David, 1965.
Wolff, Philippe, "The 1391 Pogrom in Spain:
    Social Crisis or Not?," *Past & Present*, no. 50,
    February 1971, 4–18.
Yarza Luaces. *Introducción al arte español: Baja
    Edad Media, los siglos del gótico.* [Madrid:]
    Sílex, 1992.

*****

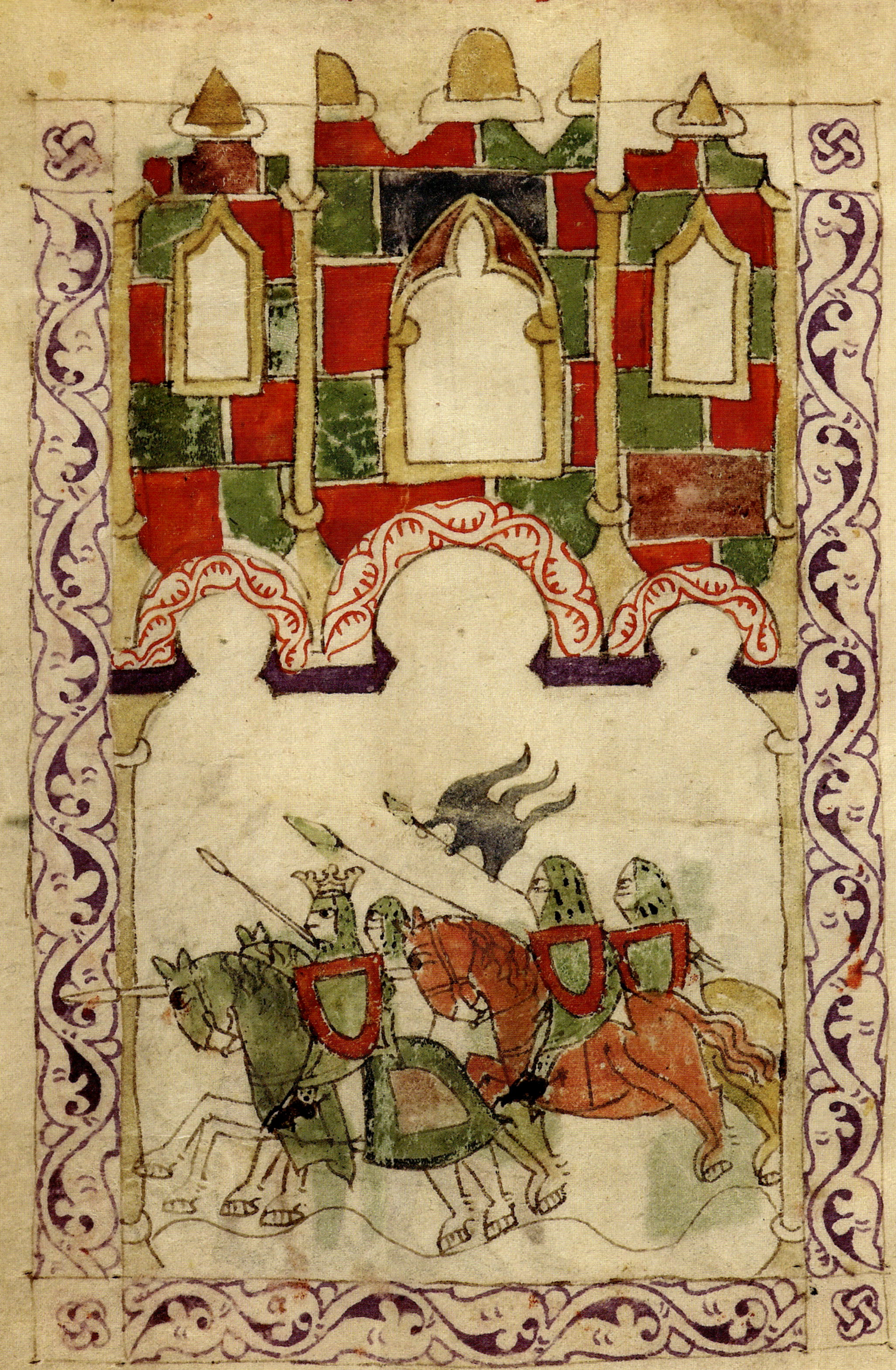

INDEX

67. Hispano-Moresque Haggadah
Egyptians Pursuing the Israelites
Castile, ca. 1300
Ink and gouache on vellum
6 × 5 inches, 97 folios
British Library, London, Ms. 2737

PHOTOGRAPHIC ACKNOWLEDGMENTS

All rights are reserved. Most photographs were provided by the institutions owning the works; their courtesy is gratefully acknowledged. Since certain copyright holders could not be traced, we would appreciate notification of additional credits, which will be included in future editions.

Cover: Courtesy of The Bridgeman Art Library International

Frontispiece: The Metropolitan Museum of Art, The Friedsam Collection, Bequest of Michael Friedsam, 1931. Image © The Metropolitan Museum of Art (32.100.123)

Credits Page: Courtesy of Vivian B. Mann

Allen Cartography, Medford: Courtesy of Allen Cartography, (pages 12-13).

Art Resource: Scala/ Art Resource, NY, (page 69).

Biblioteca de El Escorial, Madrid: Courtesy of Biblioteca de El Escorial, (pages 14, 16).

Det Kongelige Bibliotek, Copenhagen: Courtesy of Det Kongelige Bibliotek, (page 27).

Fundación Tarazona Monumental, Tarazona: Courtesy of Fundación Tarazona Monumental, (pages 90, 150).

Grand Rapids Art Museum: Courtesy of Grand Rapids Art Museum, Gift of Friends and Family of Eugene Masselink, [1965.1.1]; (pages 70-71).

J. Paul Getty Museum, Los Angeles: Courtesy of J. Paul Getty Museum, Los Angeles, California, (pages 22-25).

Musée d'art et d'histoire du Judaïsme, Paris: Courtesy of Musée d'art et d'histoire du Judaïsme, (page 137).

Museo de la Colegiata Borja, Borja: Courtesy of Museo de Borja, (page 54-55).

Museo de Zaragosa, Saragossa: Courtesy of Museo de Zaragosa, (page 60).

Museo Diocesano de Tarragona, Tarragona: Derechos Reservados © Museo Diocesano de Tarragona, (pages 28, 77).

Museo Nacional d'Art de Catalunya, Barcelona: © MNAC-Museo Nacional d'Art de Catalunya, Barcelona. Photographers: Calveras/ Mérida/Sagristá; (pages 49, 66-67,87-88, 120-121)

Museo Nacional del Prado, Madrid: Courtesy of Museo Nacional del Prado, (page 63).

The Art Archive: The Art Archive/Museo de Zaragosa (Saragossa)/ Alfredo Dagli Orti, (pages 45, 73, 104).

The Bridgeman Art Library International: Courtesy of The Bridgeman Art Library International (pages 82-83, 130,138-139, 143, 144-145).

The British Library, London: © The British Library Board [Or. 2737, f.85r; Or. 2884, f.18; Add. 27210. f.2v]; (pages 11, 107, 115, 172).

The Hispanic Society of America, New York: Courtesy of The Hispanic Society of America, New York, (pages 7, 79, 97-98, 128-129, 141-142).

The Library of the Jewish Theological Seminary, New York: Image provided by The Library of The Jewish Theological Seminary, (pages 37, 136).

The Metropolitan Museum of Art, New York:
Images © The Metropolitan Museum of Art
The Friedsam Collection. Bequest of Michael Friedsam, 1931. (32.100.123) / (Pages 102-103)
The Cloisters Collection: 1925 (25.120.929) / (Pages 100-101) & (25.120.257) / (Pages 116-117); 1955 (55.62 a, b) / (Page 113); Bequest of Carl Otto von Keinbusch, 1977. (1977.94) / (Page 113)

The Morgan Library, New York: Courtesy of The Morgan Library, (pages 110-111).

Page 31: After Marisa Melero-Moneo, *La Pintura Sobre Tabla Del Gótico Lineal.* (Barcelona, 2005), 180

Page 35: After Cecil Roth, *The Sarajevo Haggadah.* (Belgrade: Beogradski Izdavač-Grafički Zavod, 1975).

Page 80: After Carmen Lacarra Ducay, et al., *Joyas de un Patrimonio.* (Saragossa, 1990), 103.

Page 84: After Isidro G. Bango Torviso, *Memoria de Sefarad.* (Madrid: Sociedad Estatal para la Acción Culturel Exterior, 2002), 67.

Pages 94,123: After Carmen Lacarra Ducay, et al., *Joyas de un Patrimonio* (Saragossa, 1990), 32.

Pages 18, 20, 38-39, 56, 81, 92-93, 108, 140, 150-151: Courtesy of Vivian B. Mann